Inside Harley-Davidson

An Engineering History of the Motor Company from F-Heads to Knuckleheads 1903-1945

Jerry Hatfield

To Tom Sifton, and in memory of Red Wolverton

First published in 1990 by Motorbooks International Publishers & Wholesalers Inc, P O Box 2, 729 Prospect Avenue, Osceola, WI 54020 USA

© Jerry Hatfield, 1990

All rights reserved. With the exception of quoting brief passages for the purposes of review no part of this publication may be reproduced without prior written permission from the publisher

Motorbooks International is a certified trademark, registered with the United States Patent Office

The information in this book is true and complete to the best of our knowledge. All recommendations are made without any guarantee on the part of the author or publisher, who also disclaim any liability incurred in connection with the use of this data or specific details

We recognize that some words, model names and designations, for example, mentioned herein are the property of the trademark holder. We use them for identification purposes only. This is not an official publication

Motorbooks International books are also available at discounts in bulk quantity for industrial or sales-promotional use. For details write to Special Sales Manager at the Publisher's address

Library of Congress Cataloging-in-Publication Data
Hatfield, Jerry H.
  Inside Harley-Davidson, 1903–1945 / Jerry Hatfield.
  p. cm.
  ISBN 0-87938-388-7 (soft)
  1. Harley-Davidson motorcycle—History. 2. Harley-Davidson Motor Company.   I. Title.
TL448.H3H3753 1990   89-12665
629.227′5′0973—dc20   CIP

On the front cover: A 1937 61 OHV. Affectionately known as the Knucklehead, the 61 OHV was, and is, one of the all-time Harley favorites. *Harley-Davidson*
On the back cover: Circa 1915, this is Harley rider Ray Weishaar on a racing twin. Steel-willed men, iron-clad machines. *Harley-Davidson*

Printed and bound in the United States of America

Contents

	Acknowledgements	5
	Preface	6
1	1903–1915	7
2	1916–1929	29
3	1928–1932	78
4	1933–1935	117
5	1936–1938	138
6	1939–1941	170
7	1942–1945	207
	Index	223

Acknowledgments

I appreciate the help of expert Harley-Davidson enthusiasts in capturing a mountain of facts and interpreting a few matters that have escaped authoritative documentation.

Bob Klein, former Harley-Davidson public relations manager, opened the factory archives to my research.

Bob Mosely of Pohlman Studios gave me unlimited access to the Harley-Davidson archival negatives collection.

Connie Schlemmer, former Harley-Davidson dealer and expert hillclimber, wrote a book on this book, filling the draft with many detailed comments. He also made available dealer files from the 1920s that contained information never previously published.

Chris Haynes amazed me with his knowledge of the 61 OHV Knucklehead and set me straight on many 61 OHV matters. His collection of Harley-Davidson photographs greatly simplified and expedited my efforts.

Carol Moore made editorial contributions.

John Cameron has devoted about fifty years to riding and studying the two-cam twins, and his help made all the difference in telling the two-cam story. John also loaned his collection of *The Harley-Davidson Enthusiast*, spanning the years 1923 through 1945, and *Shop Dope*, spanning the years 1917 through 1945.

Armando Magri, former Harley-Davidson dealer and expert racer, reviewed the entire manuscript and offered suggestions. Armando researched details on paint colors and, as in his racing days, brought home the bacon.

Doug Wilson loaned photos from the collection of his father, who was for many years a Harley-Davidson dealer.

Fran Blake donated material and provided much of the military technical data.

Bruce Palmer edited the military text based on his several years of research. Don Doody offered editorial contributions and placed me in contact with Carman Brown. Carman Brown arranged for photographs taken of his 45 ci overhead valve prototype. Woody Carson contributed photos.

Dick and Rita Sanchez loaned important material.

Joe Herb, former Harley-Davidson dealer and expert hillclimber, provided information—as did Lysle Parker, a restoration expert.

Steve Wright, a fellow motorcycling historian and author, related facts learned in the course of his many thorough and accurate restorations.

Troy Ross loaned parts books and paint chips.

Dr. Earl Chalfant offered suggestions.

Jeff Grigsby, who professionally restores Indian motorcycles, provided Harley-Davidson parts books—quite sporting!

When the going got too tough, several experts referred me to Bud Ekins. "Bud will know," they said. And Bud did.

Charles Cartwright, long-time staffer under Arthur Davidson, related his personal interfaces with Arthur and Walter Davidson.

The late Maldwyn Jones, confidant of the four co-founders, shared his experiences inside the Harley-Davidson engineering department.

The late Charles "Red" Wolverton, Harley-Davidson dealer from 1929 through 1958, stoked the fires of my enthusiasm with facts and stories. Red's first-name friendship with the four cofounders gave him a rare insight into company matters.

The late Tom Sifton, Harley-Davidson dealer from 1929 through 1953, shared many facts and stories drawn from his experience as a dealer and as a builder of some of the fastest Harley-Davidson racing motorcycles. Tom knew the four cofounders on a first-name basis and was thus able to relate inside stories.

Jerry Hatfield
Garden Grove, California

Preface

Harley-Davidson is a tough outfit. Two world wars, the Great Depression, inexpensive American autos, foreign aid, punitive tariffs, a huge patent loss, and tidal waves of British and Japanese motorcycles have failed to kill off the world's oldest motorcycle company. Among the ghosts left behind by the Harley-Davidson Motor Company are three makes of motorcycles that had their turn as the world's most popular mounts: Indian, BSA and NSU. Only two other motorcycles have shared that honor, Honda and Harley-Davidson.

By and large, toughness has not gained sympathy for Harley-Davidson. Survival of the fittest is a phrase not looked upon kindly by many, but in selfishly looking to its own needs, Harley-Davidson has kept its doors open, its workers working and its motorcycles on the market to provide one more choice for motorcyclists.

Welcome to this engineering history of Harley-Davidson's first forty-three years. This is mainly a hardware book that details the evolution of Harley-Davidson motorcycles. But there's more: Much of the material, particularly that covering 1925 and later, is inside information that's never before been published. You will see that there were many obstacles to be overcome in order to keep Harley-Davidson alive. I hope this book gives you a better appreciation of the dealers, the staff, the Harleys and the Davidsons. They were uncommon people.

Chapter 1

1903–1915

The F-head is sorted out

In 1900, 25 million horses and 10 million bicycles handled the personal transportation needs of the American public. To most people, legpower seemed forever the rule. But in 1900, more than 4,000 cars were sold in the United States, making this the first year in which more motor vehicles were sold than horse-drawn car-

First production Harley-Davidsons were built in this configuration in 1903 and 1904. The motor was larger than most rivals, displacing 24.7 ci, 405.4 cc. The oil tank is the thin section strapped on top of the fuel tank. The oil drip feeds through the needle valve under the seat. The cover for the ignition system contact breaker has been left off. Harley-Davidson

riages and wagons. Visionary youngsters like William S. "Bill" Harley and Arthur Davidson were well aware of the transportation revolution that had just begun.

In a later era, Bill and Arthur might have blossomed as computer whizzes, but at the turn of the century young go-getters were caught up in the excitement of motor vehicles. Bill and Arthur didn't set out to establish a business; they just had the motorcycle bug. So, in 1901 they began their motorcycle project. Alas, their work progressed slowly, and after two years Bill and Arthur still didn't have a working motorcycle.

1903
Beginnings

April 28, 1903, may be considered the beginning of the Harley-Davidson Motor Company. Walter Davidson was home from his job in a railroad tool room in Parsons, Kansas, to attend the wedding on that date of his older brother, Bill. This was Walter's first encounter with the experimental motorcycle that his brother Arthur had been developing with Bill Harley. Walter watched a hired hand working, became disgusted with the way a hole was being made in a valve guide, and went to work on the motor himself. With Walter bitten by the motorcycle bug, the Harley-Davidson motorcycle made the leap from hobby to business.

Shortly after, Walter quit his job in Kansas and found a similar job in Milwaukee to fill his daytime hours. He spent his nights and Sundays working with Arthur and Bill in a small machine shop some distance from the Davidson family home. The trio commuted by bicycle. Within a few weeks, their prototype motorcycle was ridden for the first time.

The bore and stroke of the first Harley-Davidson were 2⅛x2⅞ in., yielding a displacement of 10.2 ci, 167 cc. Flywheels measured a mere 5 in. The engine was housed in a beefed-up bicycle frame. Power was inadequate, and on hills the rider was obliged to pedal.

Operations were moved to a better shop belonging to a mutual friend, and a second motor was begun with a bore and stroke of 3x3½ in., yielding a displacement of 24.74 ci, 405.41 cc. The flywheels measured 11½ in., and the frame was designed from the ground up for motorcycle use. The second prototype motorcycle took on a characteristic that was central to Harley-Davidson success: The motor was larger than those used in rival brands, so riders who bought the later production models never complained about power.

We modern riders find it difficult to imagine the thrill pioneer motorcyclists experienced at speeds in the neighborhood of 25 mph. We think of 25 mph as slow because we ride faster most of the time. But 25 mph is thrilling stuff for people whose fastest previous road travel had been by bicycle; thus Bill Harley and Arthur and Walter Davidson were immensely pleased with their progress.

Three Harley-Davidsons were begun in 1903: the second prototype, which was also completed in 1903, and the first two production models, which were completed in 1904. That was the total 1904 production: two motorcycles. The first production Harley-Davidson was sold to a man named Meyer, who put about 6,000 miles on the motorcycle before selling it to George Lyon.

1904
Infant technology

Seeing the enthusiasm and progress of his sons and Bill Harley, William C. Davidson gave them a hand. He constructed a wooden shed behind the family home at 38th Street and Highland Avenue. Measuring 10x15 ft., this was the first Harley-Davidson factory. A lathe and a drill press were obtained along with a gas engine to power them. The night and weekend work had now been going on for a year.

Word-of-mouth advertising began to bring in orders, so serious decisions had to be made. One of these decisions was farsighted: Bill Harley left Milwaukee in 1904 to attend the University of Wisconsin and earn an engineering degree.

Motorcycle designers of 1904 were dealing with the infant technology of internal combustion. Yet some novel ideas were championed vigorously in the printed media by men who were convinced that the period of invention was drawing to a close. Because Bill, Arthur and Walter operated on a shoestring budget, they couldn't get wildly creative with their experiments. So they undoubtedly based their design effort on positions expressed by the leading experimenters. Some of these positions are worth examining.

According to theory, the velocity of the inlet charge wasn't supposed to exceed 100 feet per second, and the velocity of the exhaust gases shouldn't exceed 85 feet per second—about one-tenth of today's maximums. The ideal size of the inlet valve was considered one-twelfth of the piston area, and the exhaust valve ideal was one-tenth of the piston area. Valve overlap was already understood in 1904, but the amount of overlap was minor.

Automatic inlet valves were favored over mechanical inlet valves. The theory went like this: Mechanical inlet valves had fixed opening timing, but combustion chamber pressure in relation to piston position during the exhaust stroke varied with rpm. Accordingly, when a mechanical inlet valve opened, this usually resulted in some exhaust blow-by into the inlet manifold. On the other hand, the automatic inlet valve was self-governing because it would not open until a vacuum was established in the cylinder during the next downward movement of the piston.

A peculiarity of automatic inlet valves was their flat or zero degree valve seat. In other words, the head of each automatic inlet valve was shaped like a little manhole cover. Along with automatic inlet valves, Harley-Davidsons from 1903 through 1914 used exhaust valves with 60 degree seats.

Pistons, scholars said, should be tapered toward the top in order to allow for extra growth of the piston top when hot. The recommended taper was 0.01 in. per inch of piston diameter.

Eccentric piston rings were in favor. In eccentric rings, the horizontal thickness was thinnest at the open end and thickest opposite the open end. The eccentric ring was supposed to exert uniform pressure against the cylinder bore at all points. Thus, eccentric rings were used in Harley-Davidsons from the beginning through to the conversion to tapered cylinder bores in 1914. Piston rings on the early Harley-Davidsons had step-joint ends, so named because of the zigzag cut made through the solid rings to form the open ends. This was supposed to enhance the ability of the rings to hold in compression. Step-joint rings were destined to be a standard Harley-Davidson feature for the next twenty years.

But what about cylinder head theory, and why did Harley and the Davidsons stick with the F-head layout? Some theorists already muttered that all of the valves should be upstairs. The Harley-Davidson was an F-head simply because this concept was successfully used by most of the engine builders of the day. Theory aside, Harley and the Davidsons were practical men. Their practicality would serve them well in an era when radical design departures usually spelled bankruptcy.

To assist in drawing oil into the cylinders, baffle plates were cast into the crankcase. These consisted of a flat surface at the base of the cylinder bore, perpendicular to the bore. One plate was cast into the right side of the crankcase, and the other plate was cast into the left side. When the two crankcase halves were assembled, the plates didn't touch but were separated slightly by a slot through which the connecting rod moved. When the piston began the upstroke, the plates helped form a vacuum beneath the piston, which drew the oil into the cylinder bore. This remained Harley-Davidson practice henceforth, with rare exceptions explained later.

1905
"Fastest single"

Surrounded by the foregoing theories and by the successful examples of other engine builders, the intrepid trio worked at an exhausting pace. In 1905, the backyard factory size was doubled to 10x30 ft. Walter quit his railroad job and became the full-time factory manager and its only full-time worker. The first employee was hired to help Walter run the small shop, and eight Harley-Davidsons left the tiny factory that year.

On December 13, 1905, Sales Manager Arthur Davidson wrote a letter to a prospective customer. He

First production models featured an advanced loop frame, but most competitors used a bicycle-style layout. From 1903 through 1906, color was black with gold striping. In 1906, an optional finish of Renault gray was included. Striping on the early gray models was probably carmine, but there's no documentation to prove this. Harley-Davidson

said, "We claim and have proved that our motorcycles are the fastest single-cylinder machines made, and one of our records, the 15-mile in 19:02 made in Chicago on July 4th shows the reliability and staying cool qualities of our motor."

1906

Arthur also sent to the customer a catalog on the new 1906 Harley-Davidsons, the first published by the company. The catalog stated, "In making our motor cycle we have not endeavored to see how cheap we could make it, but how good, and nothing but the very best materials obtainable are used throughout its construction.

"Our motor with the one-piece cylinder and large diameter of flywheels is of correct design and has ample power to carry the rider up the steepest hills, and it is a source of great satisfaction to the riders of our machine to know that no other motor cycles except special racing machines can pass them either on the hills or on the level."

The 1906 model was an evolution of the first production models and all key design principles were unchanged from 1904. Significant parts changes since 1904 consisted of the new provision for an optional hand-crank, the improved twistgrip control and a slightly larger motor. Other changes were few, if any.

In 1906, the hired crew grew to six. In the autumn, the Davidsons purchased a lot and constructed another shop, this one measuring 80x28 ft. Upon notification by the railroad that the new shop was encroaching on the railroad's right of way, eight or ten friends simply picked up the entire building and moved it back about a foot and a half!

About fifty Harley-Davidsons were produced in 1906. Because of quiet running and the popularity of the new optional gray finish, Harley-Davidsons were soon advertised as the Silent Gray Fellow. Pinstriping on the Silent Gray Fellow consisted of double red lines around the border of the gas tank, toolbox and, later, the battery box.

There was no national road system—that was still fifteen years away in theory and farther away in fact. Instead, riders who dared to take long trips consulted *The Official Automobile Blue Book*, published by the American Automobile Association. In this gem, directions were punctuated by physical features like a big red building, a lake, a railroad crossing, a two-story farmhouse—any landmarks that could be of use. There were road signs, of course, but they were few and far between.

1907
First V-twin

William A. Davidson, the oldest of the three brothers, quit his railroad job in 1907 to join the company. The factory size was doubled by adding a second floor. According to David K. Wright's *The Harley-Davidson Motor Company*, the first Harley-Davidson V-twin was built in 1907. No details of this model have surfaced, suggesting that this was an engineering experiment.

On September 14, 1907, Walter saddled up for his second attempt at an endurance run, a two-day outing from Chicago to Kokomo, Indiana. Of the twenty-seven riders who began the 414 mile run, only three made perfect scores. Walter was one of them.

On September 17, the first stockholders meeting and the first Board of Directors meetings were held; the little partnership had become a corporation. Capital stock totaled $35,000. Eighteen employees were now on the payroll, and production had soared to 154 motorcycles. These were the first Harley-Davidsons equipped with the Sager-Cushion spring fork, a leading-link design concept that would stay with Harley-Davidson until 1949.

1908
Endurance victory

Perhaps the most important competition victory ever earned on a Harley-Davidson was Walter's winning of the Federation of American Motorcyclists national endurance run for 1908. He scored a perfect

---

Specifications

Year and model	1906 (no model designation)
Engine	One cylinder, automatic (suction) inlet valve disposed over two-piece exhaust valve in side pocket (termed pocket valve in United States, inlet-over-exhaust or IOE in Europe*)
Bore and stroke	3⅛x3½ in.
Displacement	26.8 ci, 439.9 cc (estimated)
Bore design	Straight
Piston	Solid skirt, three evenly spaced rings
Connecting rod	Automotive style with detachable big end cap, big end bushing, little end bushing
Lubrication	Oil metered through an oil tank needle valve and consumed in the crankcase (total loss)
Starting	Bicycle pedal action, provision for optional handcrank
Drive	Single-speed belt drive from engine pulley to rear wheel, 1¼ in. endless flat belt, leather-lined front pulley in optional sizes of 4½, 5¼ and 6 in.
Clutch	No separate clutch, gradual power takeup provided by belt tensioning lever
Throttle	Right-hand twistgrip
Brake control	Backward pedaling
Wheelbase	51 in.
Tires	Clincher, 2¼ in. cross section
Weight	185 lb. (estimated)
Suspension	None
Fuel capacity	1½ gal.
Oil capacity	2 qt.
Fuel consumption	67-100 mpg
Speed	5-45 mph
Finish	Black with gold striping, or Renault gray with carmine striping
Price	$200

*Later American verbage referred to both the side-valve and IOE designs as pocket-valve engines, so to avoid confusion, the author has opted for the term F-head, which was later popularized in American automotive circles.

1,000 and was awarded an additional five points for consistency!

The motorcycle press was captivated by Walter, his motorcycle and his company. A writer for *Motorcycle Illustrated* penned, "The Harley-Davidson people have been in business for four years and have made haste wisely and conservatively. Each year they have made improvements, but they have never changed the size of their motor. When they first put their machine on the market most other manufacturers were using very small motors and the Harley-Davidson was regarded as huge and uncouth; but year after year the trend has been in favor of large motors, and today most of the manufacturers are using motors the same size, or nearly so, as the Harley-Davidson started with, and which they have continued to use up to date.

"The Harley-Davidson is built especially for all-around everyday use. It is equipped with 2½ in. tires—¼ in. larger than the usual size; has a spring fork, and many other features which have made it very popular with motorcyclists. In addition to sound construction and good business methods, the machine has been on view at the various meets, and no little of its reputation is due

In 1909, magneto ignition became optional. Sam Hotton

Walter Davidson, shortly after winning the 1908 Federation of American Motorcyclists national endurance run. Walter scored a perfect 1,000 points and was awarded an additional five points for consistency. Good publicity helped sales nearly triple to 1,149 motorcycles in 1909. Harley-Davidson

to the manner in which the president of the concern has exploited it, and that manner is the quiet, effective manner—not the other kind."

To keep up with the demand for their increasingly popular motorcycles, in 1908 another 80x28 ft. section was added to the factory. This increased factory size by fifty percent. The good publicity from Walter's winning of the national endurance run and Arthur's diligent recruiting of dealers paid off with 1908 production tripling that of 1907; 450 Harley-Davidsons were built.

An important improvement was incorporated on the 1908 models. To provide for exhaust valve clearance adjustment, a small steel cap was fitted to the exhaust valve stem. The cap was ground to achieve the proper clearance. Additionally, the cap could be purchased in six graduated oversizes. Incidentally, until 1911 the exhaust valve was of two-piece construction, the cast-iron valve head being riveted to the steel stem.

Model designations during this period were derived by subtracting four from the year, because in retrospect the 1904 model was considered Model 0. Thus, the 1908 one-model range was Model 4.

By now, the first production Harley-Davidson had passed through a series of five owners who had ridden it an estimated 62,000 miles. Word-of-mouth advertising was still a big help to Harley-Davidson.

1909

Wire control was introduced in 1909, with all control wires and sleeves routed through the handlebars. These control wires were commonly referred to as piano wires because they were solid instead of braided. Rear wheel hubs and brakes were purchased from the Thor motorcycle company.

The bore of the single was increased from $3\frac{1}{8}$ to $3\frac{5}{16}$ in., and with the $3\frac{1}{2}$ in. stroke, displacement grew to 30.16 ci, 494.28 cc. This was the first year of optional magneto ignition; the magneto was spun by a train of gears mounted between the magneto drivecase and the drivecase cover.

Styling was changed on the combined fuel and oil tank. The open space immediately behind the steering head was eliminated by elongating the tank. The vertical rear end of the tank was changed to a wedge shape, which fitted flush with the rear frame downtube.

The first Harley-Davidson twin was offered for sale in 1909. This twin proved unsuccessful and was taken off the market the following year, which may account for the 1909 twin's absence from period parts books. The problem with the 1909 twin was the lack of a belt tightening system to take up the slack in the leather drive belt; the belt continually slipped. The 1909 singles also had no belt tightening system, but their lower

From left, William S. Harley, Frank Ollerman and Walter Davidson on 1909 battery ignition singles. Gray finish became mandatory about this time. The original striping is debatable: factory museum models from this era have double striping in red, but the curator says this cannot be documented as correct. Harley-Davidson

power prevented slippage. Either flat belts or V-belts were available.

Bore and stroke of the 1909 twin were 3x3½ in., yielding a displacement of 49.48 ci, 810.83 cc. Cylinders were angled at 45 degrees. Inlet valves were automatic, as in the single. Carburetion was by Harley-Davidson or optional Schebler Model H unit. A rating of 7 hp was claimed, sufficient to produce speeds up to 65 mph. The frame was longer and slightly heavier than that of the single.

1910

In 1910, William S. Harley applied for a patent on a two-speed rear hub. This was a planetary transmission consisting of a center sun gear, a geared outer ring and planet gears between the sun gear and the outer ring. When the planet gears were allowed to turn, this resulted in a drive reduction from the sun gear to the outer ring. When the planet gears were prevented from turning, the sun gear and the outer ring turned at the same rate. This rear hub design never went into production.

Meanwhile, a measure of control was provided on production models by the introduction of a belt idler. For the first time, riders could stop their Harley-Davidsons without killing the motor. Belt size was increased from 1¼ to 1¾ in.

Most motorcycle lighting of the era was provided by acetylene gas generators. A tank dripped water on calcium carbide pellets, which turned the pellets into acetylene gas.

Sometimes things seem much clearer than they are—take the subject of motorcycle lighting. The book *A B C of the Motorcycle* published in 1910 stated, "There is only one lamp to use on a motorcycle and that is the acetylene....Electric lights such as are used on automobiles are out of the question as they require too much extra power over that generated by the magneto." The author didn't foresee the progress of the next five years.

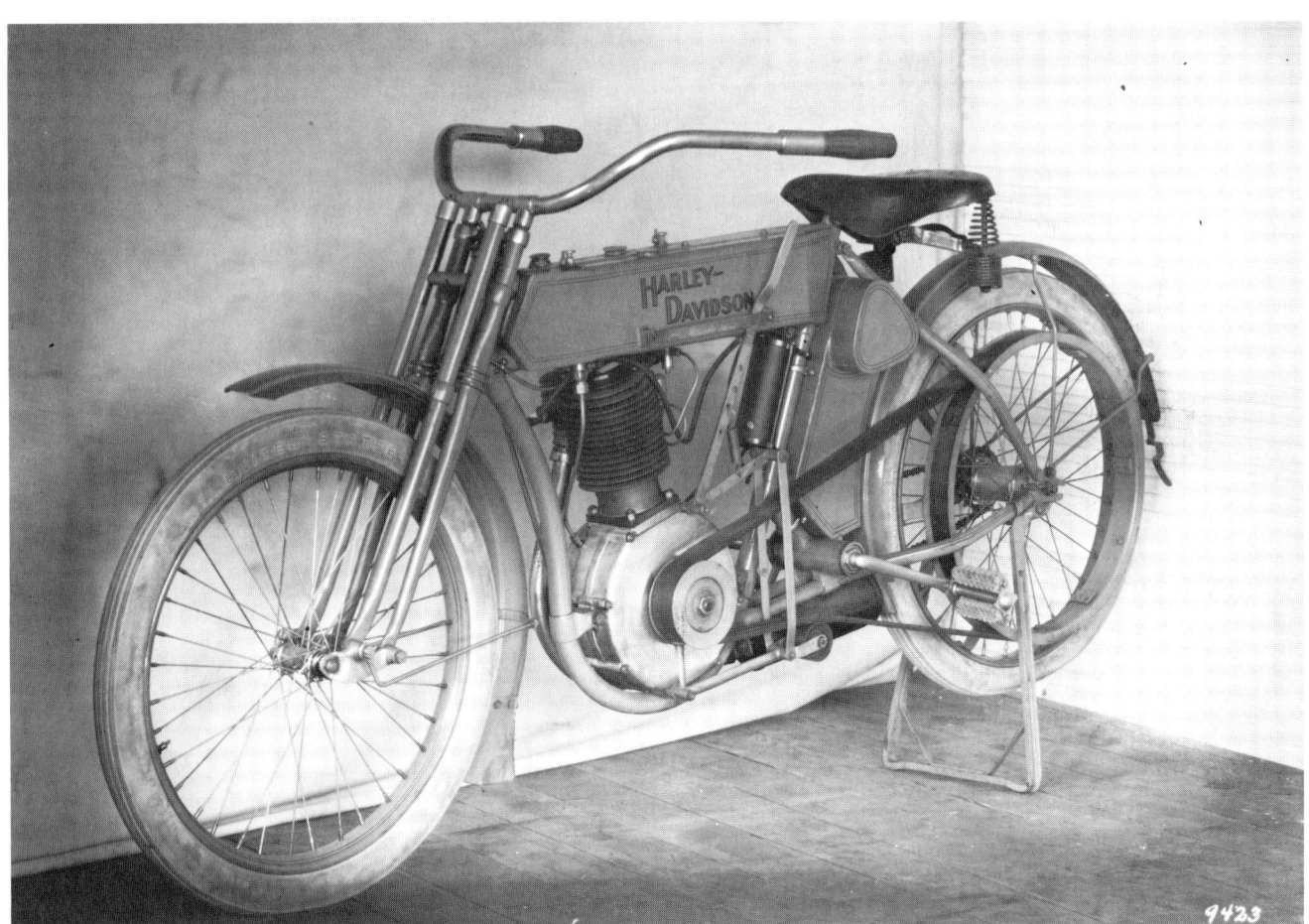

Tank styling and piano wire control were new features in 1909. The left tank was for oil; the right tank was for fuel. Left-oil, right-gas remained the setup through 1915. Sager-Cushion forks were introduced in 1907. The front fender mounted to the spring fork and moved with the fork action; this principle was retained on most models until 1929. Frames from 1903 through 1910 featured a front downtube that curved between the steering head and the forward motor mount. Harley-Davidson

This 1909 twin was Harley-Davidson's first cataloged twin. No belt-tensioning device was provided, so adjustments were frequent. All Harley-Davidsons used automatic inlet valves, which were sucked open by cylinder vacuum. This model was the only F-head with front-mounted magneto. This photo of a museum exhibit was taken about 1924. Tank lettering is correct; the large lettering on some subsequent photos was for publicity photos only or for racing models. Narrow double striping is in red on the Harley-Davidson museum model. No twin was offered in 1910. Harley-Davidson

1911
Mechanical changes

In 1911, vertical cooling fins on the cylinder head replaced the horizontal cooling fins. The cylinder and head remained a one-piece casting; the exhaust valve was a new one-piece all-steel design.

Through 1910, Harley-Davidson frames had a curved front downtube. In 1911, the front downtube was changed to a straight section.

The twin was reintroduced in 1911, this time with a belt tensioning system. The twin featured mechanical inlet valves, but the singles kept automatic inlet valves. Displacement of the twin remained at 49.48 ci, 810.83 cc. Claimed output was 6½ hp. The 1911 frames were the last with the horizontal top rail. This was also the last year in which transmission was limited to single-speed belt drive.

Early Harley-Davidson twins used two kinds of crankcase baffles. Under the front cylinder of the twins was a full baffle, which left only enough room for the rod to pass through and therefore maximized the vacuum under the piston—this was needed to compensate for the lack of natural oil sling from the crankshaft, connecting rods and flywheels. This proved too much of a good thing, so early in the twins' evolution, three holes of about ⅜ in. diameter were drilled in each side of the front baffles, totaling six holes in all. Under the rear cylinder was a half-baffle, so that only about half of the area below the cylinder was closed off—this was needed to reduce the vacuum under the rear piston, since crankshaft and connecting rod oil sling was adequate to supply the necessary oil.

Color confusion

The finish of the 1911 models was given a new touch by replacing the red double pinstripes around the tank edges with a single broad stripe. There's debate among collectors as to the proper striping colors on the 1911–1916 Silent Gray Fellows. One restoration expert says the 1911–1916 striping was dark gray with a hint of blue, centered in gold and edged in red. He furnished an apparently authentic sample chip to a friend, who agreed with the gold center and red edges but decided the original (unfaded) dominant striping color must have been dark blue! And in fact, a color poster has been sold in recent years showing dark blue tank striping. Two students of the Silent Gray Fellows emphatically told the author that the broad stripes were black, however. To add to the confusion, a circa 1920 accessories catalog lists both dark gray and red pinstriping enamels, but no blue or black striping enamel. Incidentally, dark gray was the primary color for the sidecar frames.

The factory began to photograph their collection of Silent Gray Fellows in about 1924, as determined by the photograph negative numbers. These motorcycles may have been rolled aside during original production, or they may have been collected some years later and restored. If roll-asides, they were by definition correctly finished. If restorations, it seems unlikely that the factory staff would have incorrectly repainted the tanks of these Silent Gray Fellows, since some of them were less than ten years old when restored. Such restoration candidates almost certainly would have been collected with enough of their original paint intact to determine the correct colors.

These circa 1924 archive photos were published in several issues of *Motorcyclist* during 1940. In the next-to-last installment on the Silent Gray Fellows, the magazine described the 1914 model and commented, "As formerly the model was enameled in battleship gray color, with red and gold striping."

In conclusion, it appears the Silent Gray Fellows were available with a variety of striping colors. In most of the factory archive photos, the tanks appear to have broad striping of either red or gray. Red striping would have been bordered in black and centered in gold; gray striping would have been bordered in red and centered in gold. Some Silent Gray Fellows probably had dark broad striping—pick your color, dark gray, blue or gray-blue—bordered in red and centered in gold. Too bad the press releases and sales literature weren't specific on these details!

Parts books show two colors of period tank transfers, with either red or gold centers. By inference, the borders were either gold or red, respectively. Both colors of tank transfers are listed with 08 suffix part numbers, which means both colors of transfers were available from 1908 on.

1912
Signal advances

The 1912 models ushered in a new frame that got away from the bicycle look. The top rail now sloped downward at the rear to permit a lower saddle. The saddle was suspended on a spring seat post, a device

This 1911 outfit has a different belt-tensioning setup from the earlier models. This was also the first year of vertical cooling fins on the cylinder head. The striping pattern changed to a broad stripe; while stripe colors are debatable. The 1911 frames were the first with a front downtube, that was straight from the steering head to the front motor mounts. Harley-Davidson

Another look at the tandem seating. Harley-Davidson always emphasized taking a friend along on rides. This photo is the second oldest in the Harley-Davidson collection, number 149 out of more than 30,000. Harley-Davidson

that provided a remarkable degree of comfort because of the long soft spring action. The rear section of the front fender was given a slender valance.

On earlier Harley-Davidsons, pedal crank chain adjustment was accomplished bicycle-style by relocating the rear wheel in the frame. This led to complications because the drive belt was consequently readjusted—like it or not. For 1912, the pedal cranks were mounted on a hub that had eccentric end pieces holding the hub in the frame. Thus, the pedal crank chain could be adjusted by loosening, rotating and retightening the pedal crank hub—all without disturbing the rear wheel or the drive belt.

The 1912 twins were offered with a 3½ in. stroke and either a 3 or 3 5/16 in. bore, displacements being 49.48 or 60.32 ci, 810.83 or 988.55 cc. These twins were the first models to feature a hand oil pump to supplement the drip feed through the needle valve. The larger twin, Model 8E, was the first Harley-Davidson equipped with chain drive. The Model 8E twin also introduced a timed breather system. A breather gear was installed so that the ports of the gear and its crankcase bushing registered at just the right time in relation to the locations of the pistons. The downstrokes of pistons forced crankcase air and oil mist through the breather gear into the timing case, and from there through a vent tube which dumped the air and oil mist on the front chain. In principle, the slotted breather gear remained a Harley-Davidson feature henceforth.

The 8E twin scored two other Harley-Davidson firsts: It was the first with connecting rods having

The 1912 models featured new styling and a lower seating position. The first seat post debuted and placed 9 in. of springs under the rider. A lower handlever controlled the rear hub clutch, called a "free wheel" in factory literature. Pedals are eccentrically mounted to accommodate pedal chain adjustment; earlier models required the rear wheel to be moved to tighten the pedal chain. Harley-Davidson

This view of the 1912 single shows the pinstriping detail. This photograph of a museum exhibit was taken about 1924, when Harley-Davidson began this practice. Museum samples of this era have a broad red stripe centered in gold and edged in black. Tank lettering was available from 1908 in either gold with a red outline or red with a gold outline. Tank lettering is correct style. Harley-Davidson

The Deep South, 1912. This was the last year of automatic inlet valves on singles. The small bicycle-style rear hub brake last appeared in 1913. From 1910 to 1913, the Thor rear hub and brake were built by the Aurora company, also makers of the Thor motorcycle. The large tank lettering is nonstandard. Harley-Davidson

17

roller-bearing big ends, and the first with a ball-bearing mainshaft. The self-aligning ball bearings were on the sprocket side only.

Another signal advance was the 1912 clutch, Harley-Davidson's first. The clutch mechanism was mounted in the rear hub. The leather drive belt turned a separate spoked belt rim, which transmitted power through the clutch hub to the rear wheel. Control was by a handlever on the left side of the tank. With this clutch, riders could easily accomplish a smooth start from a dead stop, a feat that had been challenging with the old system of drive belt tensioning. The bicycle pedals were still there for starting the motor, but no longer would Harley-Davidson riders be seen pedaling off before easing motor power into operation. The motorbike days were drawing to a close.

Harley-Davidson production growth 1904-1912

Year	Total production	Growth, over past year	Cumulative growth, from 1907 incorporation
1904	2	100%	
1905	8	300%	
1906	50	525%	
1907	154	208%	
1908	450	192%	192%
1909	1,149	155%	646%
1910	3,168	176%	1,957%
1911	5,625	78%	3,552%
1912	9,571	70%	6,115%

Note: As a point of comparison, consider the following: If the population of Nevada were to grow over a five-year period at the Harley-Davidson cumulative rate for 1907 through 1912, Nevada would be the nation's most populous state.

1913
Phenomenal growth

For 1913, belt drive was limited to the Model 9A single. Other models were the 9B single with chain drive, the 9C twin and the 9G forecar. The latter was Harley-Davidson's first model designed specifically for commercial use. All twins now had roller-bearing connecting rods and ball-bearing (sprocket side) mainshafts, but singles still had plain-bearing big ends and mainshafts.

The singles' bore remained at 3 5/16 in., but the stroke was increased from 3½ to 4 in., so displacement grew to 34.47 ci, 564.89 cc. The singles were dubbed the 5-35, denoting 5 hp from 35 ci. On these 5-35 singles, the intake and exhaust chambers were enlarged as an experiment to be carried out by the riders. The experiment proved successful, and the lessons learned were

In 1913, mechanical inlet valves were first offered on the singles. Note that the inlet pushrod exits from the timing case instead of the crankcase. Win a trivia bet: technically, these early singles were the first two-cams. The strange device next to the exhaust pipe is an exhaust whistle. The inlet valve spring was still small and weak, like the earlier suction-operated automatic valve springs. In fact, this single runs perfectly fine with the pushrod removed! Woody Carson

Chain drive arrived on the 1912 Model BE twin. Twins had longer frames than singles in order to fit the magneto behind the crankcase. Therefore, singles and twins used different tanks. The large tank lettering is nonstandard. Harley-Davidson

later built into the twin-cylinder range. All 1913 singles featured mechanical inlet valves, a feature introduced on 1911 twins.

Pistons, rods and flywheels were now balanced as an individual unit. Pistons were made of a lighter iron alloy to improve engine rpm acceleration. A new design of carburetor hot-air intake eliminated whistling and breathing noise that had been objectionable on earlier models.

Remember that first production Harley-Davidson? The company ran an advertisement in 1913 that said Harley-Davidson Number One was still running and had accumulated 100,000 miles.

Gasoline in those days was sold by general stores, hardware stores and blacksmiths. An event of note was the December opening of the first drive-in gasoline station in Pittsburgh. In the next seven years, the number of drive-in stations would grow to 15,000.

While Harley-Davidson was enjoying phenomenal growth, the American motorcycle industry as a whole was beginning to level off. In 1913, Henry Ford established his first moving assembly line, and the installment plan was used for the first time in automobile sales. Passenger car sales for 1913 were up nearly thirty percent over 1912 sales. Harley-Davidson, Indian and Excelsior were still growing, but only at the expense of the also-rans. From the turn of the century through 1913, eighty-three American motorcycle companies had come and gone.

1914
A year of change

A number of changes were introduced on the 1914 models. These were the first with the so-called step

This unrestored single is finished with broad dark-gray striping. The red outside borders have almost faded away. The center stripe is gold. Period photos in the Harley-Davidson archives appear to capture the same dark-gray striping. Woody Carson

starter, featuring an arrangement of pawls and cams to prevent the motor from backfiring through the bicycle-style pedals. Riders could stand on one foot while using the other to start up, and it wasn't necessary to place the motorcycle on the center stand in order to start the motor. The step starter was forward acting through the bicycle-style pedals. The engaging pawls and ratchets were in the left side of the pedal crank mechanism.

With the 1913 simple inlet valve mechanism, the timing case cover was altered instead of the crankcase. However, racing singles of this era were built up by blanking off one cylinder of a V-twin, so racing singles had only one cam gear. Perhaps the reason for working the road model's inlet pushrod from the timing case instead of the crankcase was to use up stocks of existing single-cylinder crankcases, built in the days of automatic inlet valves. Woody Carson

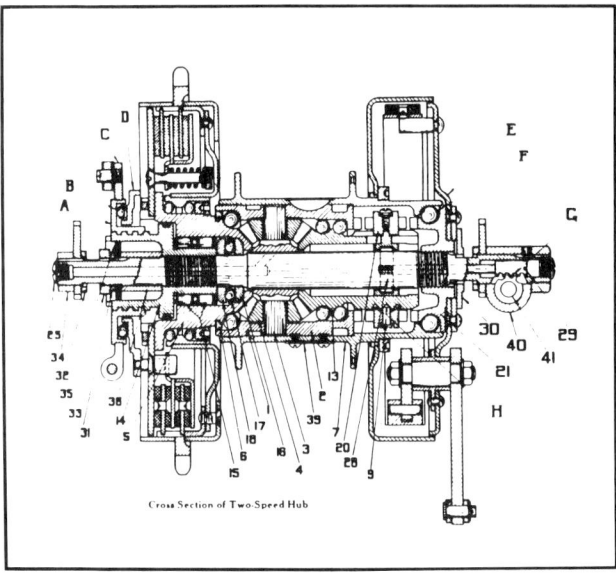

The two-speed rear hub debuted in 1914.

The first footboards made the scene. They were attached to heavy metal straps or sidebars, affixed to the frame with studs. This would be Harley-Davidson practice henceforth.

The first clutch pedal and first brake pedal completed the rider's new facilities. The rider's feet could rest on the boards or the pedals; the clutch could be controlled by the pedal or the handlever, and the brake could be actuated by the brake pedal or by pedaling backward on the bicycle-style pedals. The new brake featured internal expanding-band operation.

The two-speed rear hub transmission was another big improvement, and three sets of bevel gears were employed. A bevel gear integral with the driving hub and a second bevel gear integral with the driven cone faced each other as they rotated around the rear axle. These driving and driven bevels were part of the inner hub shell.

Between the driving hub and the driven cone was a four-legged crosslike piece that also rotated around the rear axle. The outer ends of the cross were fixed to the outer hub shell. On the end of each of the four cross legs was a small bevel gear, so these four small bevel gears were always in mesh with the driving hub bevel gears to the left and the driven cone bevel gears to the right.

When in low gear, the four small bevel gears were free to rotate around their cross legs. These four gears of the cross fixture therefore accomplished a drive reduction from the driving hub bevel gear to the driven cone bevel gear. Consequently, the driving inner hub shell moved faster than the driven outer shell through which power was transmitted to the wheel.

The rider shifted gears with a lever on the left side of the tank, which in turn caused a shifting rod on the right end of the axle to move inward or outward through a hollow section of the rear axle. The outward (right) position was for low gear. When moved inward (to the left), the shifting rod engaged dogs that locked the driven cone to the four small bevel gears. As a result, the three sets of bevel gears—driving hub, crosspiece and driven cone—were locked together. Therefore, the outer hub shell—the driven part—rotated at the same speed as the driving inner hub shell. The two-speed hub was lubricated with a grease gun at 1,500 mile intervals.

Prior to 1914, exhaust valve springs had been exposed. The new models featured a two-piece telescoping enclosure over each exhaust valve spring.

On all models, the chainguard was padded and had a larger opening for the countershaft. The 1914 guard was furnished by the factory on orders for 1913 models. Mudguards or fenders were widened from 3¾ to 4½ in.

Prior to 1914, the company had bought most of its wheel hubs from Eclipse, Thor or Corbin and most of its brakes from Thor. Now Harley-Davidson used their

This 1914 outfit shows off several accessories, including a couple of firsts and a last. The front speedometer gearing drives through a metal tube instead of a flexible housing. The large canister by the rear wheel supplies gas for the lights. Footboards and the two-speed rear hub were introduced in 1914. The shift lever sits atop the tank. This was the last year of the under-the-seat oil tank, introduced on the 1911 Model 7D twin. The broad medium-hue stripe is typical of period photos; it appears lighter than museum examples and lighter than the red tank lettering. There are no pinstripes on the chainguards. The large tank lettering is nonstandard. Harley-Davidson

own front wheel hubs, rear hubs and brakes on all models except the Model 10A belt-drive single. The Model 10A continued with the Eclipse front hub, Thor rear hub and Thor brake in order to use up these parts.

In 1914, the connecting rod big ends on all singles were fitted with roller bearings as used a year earlier on the twins. Since the first Harley-Davidson, all singles had featured automotive-style two-piece connecting rods with bolted-on lower ends. With the exception of the Model 10A, all 1914 singles were fitted with one-piece connecting rods like the male rod of the twin-cylinder set. The 1914 single was fitted with a hand oil pump to supplement the oil tank needle valve, a feature begun two years earlier on the twins.

To use up old parts, the Model 10A single was offered in 1914 as the last belt-drive Harley-Davidson. An external contracting-band brake was unique to this model.

Twins through the early 1914 models featured crankcases with eight lugs; late 1914 twins received nine-lug crankcases. In addition to the standard F Series motors with a ¾ in. inlet manifold, the company offered faster A motors with 1 in. inlet manifolds. A and F motors had motor numbers prefixed by an A or F. All twins except the Model EH were fitted with a mechani-

The 1914 tank assembly. This job remained a handcrafted process for the next fifty-plus years. Many handcrafting tasks like this prevented American motorcycle factories from implementing the dramatic cost-cutting measures achieved by automobile factories. Harley-Davidson

cally operated rotary relief valve. This feature continued throughout Harley-Davidson history.

The company started a unique engineering tradition in 1914 that would endure for the next twenty

The two-speed shift lever is a little more obvious in this case, with the rider's right knee as background. This machine is a 1914 Model 10G Forecar. The tank lettering is the correct size and appears to be gold. Gold with red borders and red with gold borders were the optional lettering schemes on the Silent Gray Fellows. Broad stripes in period archive photos are of medium hue and are definitely not black or dark blue, as was sometimes used in restoration work. However, Harley-Davidson apparently offered optional striping colors, and the predominance of medium-hue striping doesn't rule out other striping schemes. One unrestored example has been found with broad stripes of dark gray, centered in gold and bordered in red. Two other owners report unrestored Silent Gray Fellows with broad stripes of black, centered in gold and edged in red. Harley-Davidson

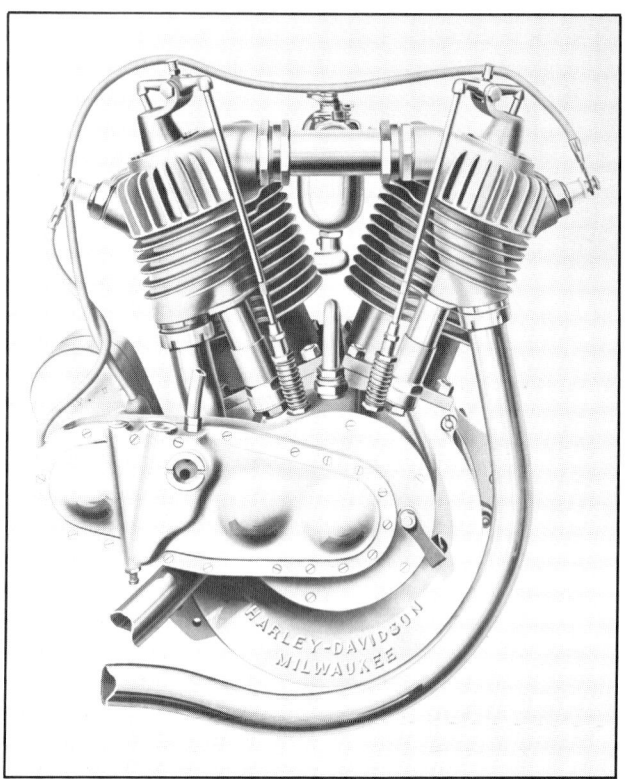

Stock 1915 motor. Enclosed exhaust valve springs arrived on 1914 models, and the new motor-driven oil pump arrived in 1915. Exposed inlet rocker arms and pushrods required frequent checking and adjustment—at 800 mile intervals instead of 1,500 mile intervals as on the exhaust valve tappets. The inlet valve mechanism remained worrisome throughout F-head production. Note the location of spark plugs—in the valve chambers or "pockets." Harley-Davidson

years. Instead of using tapered pistons and straight, uniform diameter cylinder bores, Harley-Davidson switched to straight pistons and tapered cylinder bores. The top of each cylinder bore was 0.003 in. smaller than the bottom. To properly fit new piston rings, the rings were measured for clearance about ½ in. from the bottom of the cylinder—they couldn't be measured from the top of the cylinder bore because the cylinders and heads were one-piece castings. Rings that had less than the recommended clearance were simply hand-filed to size.

The following hasn't been verified due to the sketchy nature of parts books. Sometimes old parts aren't shown in later parts book revisions because newer parts will work in their place, and sometimes parts are changed without changing part numbers. Anyway, it seems likely that Harley-Davidson switched from the old eccentric piston rings to concentric rings at this juncture, concurrent with the switch to tapered cylinder bores. The popular period automobile and motorcycle engineering books of Victor Pagé stressed the obsolescence of eccentric rings.

Harley racers

Much has been written about the glories of Harley-Davidson racing, record setting and other forms of competition so these areas will only be highlighted here. Harley-Davidson had a policy of not racing—until 1914.

For the July 4, 1914, Dodge City 300, several racing stars entered on Harley-Davidsons with under-the-

Despite the parts bin tag, this rear cylinder is from the 1911-1919 era. This is a pre 1920 cylinder because the vertical fins around the spark plug do not have the characteristic taper of the 1920 style. Troy Ross

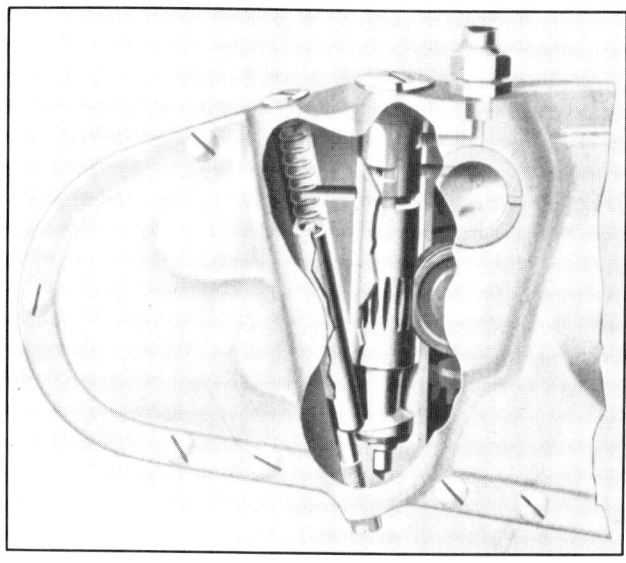

This 1915 oil pump took most of the guesswork out of riding and eliminated the common problem of over-oiling. Over-oiling caused overheating by filling the engine with oil and forcing the engine to act as an air compressor. This pump design was used from 1915 through mid 1922. By the way, we don't call them "engine-cycles," and factory literature always favored the term "motor," so "motor" will be the preferred term henceforth. Harley-Davidson

table factory support. The Milwaukee motorcycles showed good speed, but their reliability wasn't up to the long haul. All pretense at non-involvement was abandoned in November when an officially sponsored Harley-Davidson team appeared at the Savannah 300. The company was making a racing investment that, in relative terms, was as strong as any before or since.

Incidentally, on 1914, 1915 and 1916 racing motors, the motor number was preceded by an M.

An event of note occurred in Cleveland, Ohio, in 1914. At the intersection of Euclid Avenue and 105th Street, the city installed an electric traffic signal, complete with red and green lights as well as buzzers. Two long buzzes permitted Euclid Avenue traffic to proceed, and one long buzz allowed 105th Street traffic to move. This was the first traffic light in the United States. The growing traffic congestion which the new light symbolized, and the ever higher speeds of motor vehicles, were further removing the motorcycle from its origin as an adjunct to pedal bicycling.

1915
Further improvement

Four important improvements graced the 1915 lineup. A three-speed transmission was introduced, a two-unit electrical system offered an alternative to gas lighting, motor power was increased and oiling was improved. With these changes, the concept of the Harley-Davidson F-head motorcycle was essentially complete. The remainder of F-head history would be a process of refinement.

The three-speed transmission was a sliding-gear countershaft layout with the primary and final drive chains on the same side. This produced lower twisting loads than crossover transmissions with the primary and final drive chains on opposite sides. Loads in low and second gear were carried on ball bearings and phosphor-bronze bushings; high gear was free-running. An interlock was incorporated to prevent shifting gears without clutching.

Two models were offered with a gear-driven Model 15 magneto-generator developed by the Remy

```
Specifications
Year and model ..................... 1915 Model 11J
Engine ..................... Two cylinder, F-head
Bore and stroke ............ 3 5/16x3 1/2 in. (8.41x8.89 cm)
Displacement ................... 60.33 ci, 987.67 cc
Bore design ................................. Tapered
Connecting rods ......... Male and female (knife and fork),
  big end roller bearing, little end bushing
Lubrication ............ Total loss, oil pumped by integral
  drivecase cover and oiler, supplemental handpump
Starting .......................... Bicycle pedal action
Drive ..................... Chain primary, chain final
Clutch ................................. Dry, multiplate
Throttle ...................... Right-hand twistgrip
Brake control .......................... Right pedal
Wheelbase ................................. 59 1/2 in.
Tires ............ 28x3 in. (diameter includes tire) in 1915
  terminology, or 22x3 in. in current terminology (diameter
  includes wheel only)
Weight ................................... 325 lb.
Suspension .............. Front: leading link; rear: none
Fuel capacity .......... 11 1/2 pt. (1 7/16 gal.) in main section,
  3 1/2 pt. (7/16 gal.) in reverse section
Oil capacity ............................. 5 pt. (5/8 gal.)
Fuel consumption .................. 50 mpg (estimated)
Speed ........................... 60 mph (estimated)
```

The 1915 primary drive, clutch and gearshift controls. The cam on the horizontal clutchshaft engaged a segment on the vertical gearshift shaft to prevent shifting without declutching. Harley-Davidson

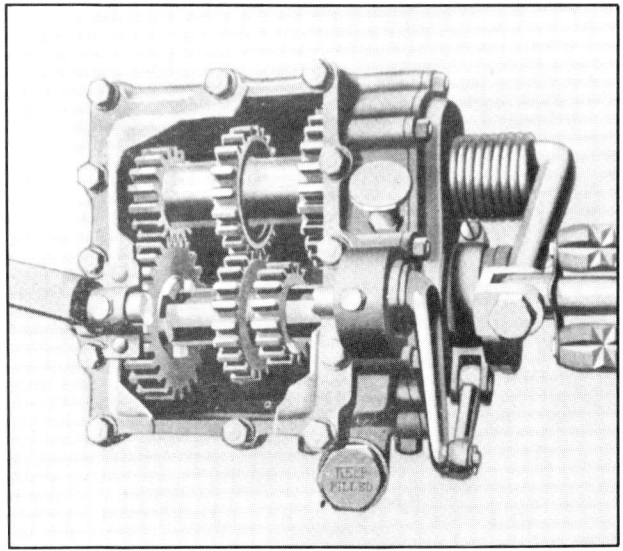

Introduction of the three-speed countershaft transmission came in 1915. Ball bearings and phosphor-bronze bushings were featured. This photo is actually from a 1916 catalog. The 1915 models still featured starting by dual bicycle pedals. Harley-Davidson

Electric Corporation. Remy had an established service network to handle warranty or routine repairs. The Model 15 magneto-generator featured a vacuum-controlled battery cutout. A small air line connected to the inlet manifold supplied the vacuum, which closed a contact switch and permitted the battery to supply current for lighting. Thus, forgetful riders could leave the light switch on after a ride with no effect on the battery—you have to wonder why they didn't use a multiposition switch for both the ignition and lights. Another nicety was the removable taillight, which could be used as an inspection light.

Numerous motor changes were introduced to increase power. Harley-Davidson boasted they were the only motorcycle manufacturer to guarantee a horsepower rating. They guaranteed 11 hp on the twins, but also mentioned that dynamometer tests measured up to 16.7 hp. The company claimed a thirty-one-percent increase at 2500 rpm and a forty-seven-percent increase at 3000 rpm. The extra power came from new cylinders with larger inlet ports, the cylinders mating with a larger Y-shaped inlet manifold and carburetor.

Inlet and exhaust valves had 45 degree seats instead of the 60 degree seats used since the introduction of mechanical inlet valves. Inlet valves were larger—at least that's what the advertisements said. The 1915 inlet valves were larger than those in the 1914 standard motors, but they may not have been larger than the inlet valves of special 1914 A motors. In any case, the 1915 valves, cylinders, manifold and carburetor were descendants of the 1914 A motor.

Other 1915 motor changes were completely new, straight from the drafting table. The connecting rod big ends rode on a new four-row roller bearing, two rows for each rod. The bearing width was 1¾ in. wide compared to the previous 1⅜ in. wide roller bearings. The new roller bearings were the first of Harley-Davidson manufacture, and the bearing surface area was up by forty-six percent. Heavier flywheels sported a crankpin with a 1 in. diameter instead of a ⅞ in. diameter.

Prior to 1915, motor lubrication was accomplished by drip feeding through a needle valve or by using a handpump. There was always the threat of under-oiling and motor seizure, but, although this occasionally hap-

The 1915 models like this one were the first with electric lighting. Sidecars were popular with rural mail carriers. Careful study of the original photo shows that the sidecar frame and springs were a darker color than the sidecar body and motorcycle. Period accessories catalogs listed gray and dark gray, the latter mentioned as the color for sidecar frames. Harley-Davidson

pened, the fear of under-oiling meant that most riders kept their motors over-oiled. Over-oiling was also a serious problem. Overuse of the handpump resulted in excessive oil blow-by past the piston rings and an oil-diluted intake charge. To compensate, riders enriched the fuel-air mixture, which worked but with a noticeable loss in power. Excessive oiling also increased carbon buildup and accelerated wear.

To cure both the under- and over-oiling as well as to simplify operation, an automatic oiler was provided on the 1915 models. This oiler was integral with the cast-aluminum drivecase cover and was driven by a worm gear made integral with one of the magneto drive gears. The worm gear mated with notches in a vertical shaft, turning the shaft. The turning vertical shaft was ported to alternately align with supply and discharge passages for the pump. At the base of the vertical shaft was an integral face cam, or circular ramp, which raised an angled cylindrical pumping plunger against spring pressure. The face cam ramped up over about half the circumference of the vertical shaft before ending abruptly. As the shaft and integral face cam turned past this point, the spring-loaded plunger then dropped from the top of the cam ramp onto the low end of the cam profile, ready for another cycle.

The pump fed through a sight glass so riders could be assured of its proper operation. The maximum demonstrated pressure requirement was 4 psi, but the company claimed the new pump would feed against a resistance of up to 70 psi. The tank-side handpump was retained for emergency use and for crankcase replenishment after periodic drainage and flushing.

Due to the precision tolerances on the new automatic oil pump, dealers were advised to return any unserviceable automatic oil pumps to the factory for maintenance. Dealers were also advised to return the drivecase along with the integral pump and case cover so the factory could lap in the operating shaft with the oiler assembled to its drivecase. This procedure compensated for the slight warping of the cover when mated to the drivecase.

Other motor changes were aimed at improving reliability and serviceability. Exhaust valves were now adjustable with an exhaust lifter pin screw. Previously, exhaust valve clearance was adjusted by fitting a small steel cap to the exhaust valve stem and then grinding the cap to the proper thickness.

On twins, a 1915 change in exhaust valve clearance instructions highlights a commonly misunderstood point. The factory continued to specify a 0.004 in. clearance for the rear cylinder exhaust valve, but changed to a 0.006 in. clearance for the front exhaust valve. The reason for providing additional clearance for the front exhaust valve was that, contrary to popular opinion, the front cylinder of V-twin motors typically runs hotter than the rear cylinder. This is because the front cylinder gets less oil sling from the crankshaft, connecting rods and flywheels.

As before, on each cylinder there was a conical tower providing the fulcrum for the intake rocker arm. This fulcrum, termed either a cap or a cage, was redesigned to work with a larger and newly shaped intake valve cap nut in order to improve gas sealing. In the motor base, larger studs supported the valve lifters, or roller arms in factory terminology.

Forked connecting rods had a tie boss added to join the right and left sides for added strength, a feature that continued henceforth. The connecting rod wrist pin bushings were given a spiral groove for oil distribution and were slotted at the top to act as an oil trough. The crankcase breather pipe now exited the crankcase at the top of the valve action housing.

A new all-steel muffler with a larger expansion chamber and tailpipe reduced back pressure. The muffler had a new type of foot-controlled cutout.

The oil tank on the Models 11E, 11H and 11J twins was moved from its former seat post location to become part of the gas tank assembly between the steering head and the seat. Oil tank capacity was increased and oil supply pipes were enlarged. The handpump was made an integral part of the oil tank. The pump was provided with a lockdown device to prevent bystanders from operating it and filling the crankcase with oil during the owner's absence. On all twins, the left fuel-oil and the right fuel tank were available in extra-large size. The extra-large right tank introduced notched-out sections to make room for the inlet rocker arms.

For a 1915 100 mile board track race in Chicago, Harley-Davidson produced these Chicago motors. Their distinctive feature is the placing of the spark plug in the cylinder proper instead of in the valve pocket. The spark plug hole is near the man's little finger. The hole in the middle of the cylinder is used to measure piston location in order to set timing. John Cameron

Detail refinements were made to the internal expanding-band rear brake. The brake was made double-acting by applying leverage on both ends of the band. This improved hill holding, especially on sidecar models. With the exception of the three-wheeled forecar, the brake arm connection on the frame was strengthened and the round rear frame members reinforced so that brake loads wouldn't twist the frame.

Cylinder primers for cold-weather starting were redesigned to minimize compression leakage. Grease cups replaced oilers on the fork rocker plates. The front seat post bearing was widened. The handlebar manufacturing process was changed with a claimed 100 percent increase in strength and no weight increase.

On the three-speed transmission, an oil deflector was fitted to the left (drive) side of the gearbox. The deflector consisted of a slightly dished brass washer that was fitted tightly on the mainshaft, with the concave side toward the steel bushing in the transmission case. This helped, but did not eliminate oil escaping through the mainshaft bearing. This setup was used through and including the 1936 side-valve big twins.

The two-speed rear hub transmission was still offered. Ball bearings were added to the left side to take up the thrust of the bevel gears.

Chicago racers

In September 1915, at the Maywood board speedway in Chicago, the Harley-Davidson factory team fielded a batch of special F-head twins. Although Excelsior won the 300 mile feature event, Otto Walker rode his Harley-Davidson to a new 100 mile record of 89.11 mph. These racing models had the spark plug located in the main combustion chamber rather than in the valve pocket, and they became known as the Chicago Harleys. While the Chicago models were fast, no spark plugs of the era could withstand the extra heat absorbed by being set in the main combustion chamber. Consequently, this was a short-lived experiment.

Ensuring survival

The F-head concept was now through the initial sorting out process shaped by rider demands and a fiercely competitive American motorcycle industry. Henry Ford's unpredictable success with his Model T Ford was killing the American motorcycle industry and forcing the American motorcycle into a subordinate

All F-head cylinders were complicated castings. Cylinders and heads were one piece. The Chicago motor has seven cooling fins on the exhaust manifold instead of five as on other racers and stock motors. The valves are housed one above the other in a separate chamber, or valve pocket in period terminology. Until 1928, the F-head valve pocket was completely separated from the cylinder proper to provide ample space for cooling air. John Cameron

Circa 1915. The rider is Ray Weishaar (pronounced Wisher). The engine is not a Chicago motor, as these were abandoned due to melting spark plugs. Harley-Davidson

role as a pleasure vehicle. As a result, Harley-Davidson sales from 1913 through 1915 tapered off. Annual sales and percentage growths for 1913 and 1914 were $12,904 and thirty-four percent, and $16,284 and twenty-six percent, respectively. These annual growth rates still compared favorably with the automobile industry gains of twenty-eight percent and eighteen percent for those years.

But 1915 was a new ballgame. In that year, Harley-Davidson sales growth of $16,645 represented a two percent annual growth, while the American automobile industry skyrocketed with a one-year growth rate of sixty-nine percent. Clearly, a new era was at hand.

In a weakening industry, unable to outvalue the Ford, Harley-Davidson set itself to the task of ensuring its survival by gaining a bigger share of the shrunken market. The all-out racing program launched in 1914 was continuing with win after win in the most prestigious races, such as the Dodge City 300. This racing success was paralleled by ever increasing success in the show rooms.

Uppity Harley-Davidson had started a dozen years ago as a backyard project; by 1915, the giant Indian motorcycle company of Springfield, Massachusetts, had taken painful notice of their Milwaukee rival. Springfield and Milwaukee had become synonymous terms for the two companies. The only other healthy motorcycle company was the Excelsior firm of Chicago, but Springfield and Milwaukee were leaving Chicago behind.

The F-head had been sorted out. Meanwhile, the cruelly efficient economy had sorted out the motorcycle companies into three groups: the big three, the strugglers and the has-beens.

Board track racing was close, even in long races. Teamwork was required to set up drafting schedules. Prior to 1914, Harley-Davidson had a no-racing policy. Factory racing support started under the table for the July 4, 1914, Dodge City 300 mile road race and went public in November for the Savannah 300 mile road race. From 1915 through 1921,

Harley-Davidson dominated the prestigious long races, and the factory team captured every national championship in 1921. Beginning in 1922, the company de-emphasized racing by choosing only a few events for sponsorship. Harley-Davidson

Another view of a 1915 outfit. Sidecars enjoyed a brief period of competitiveness with inexpensive cars prior to the success of the Model T Ford. In 1913, Ford established their first moving assembly line, and the installment plan was used for the first time in the automobile industry. New Fords were priced about the same as sidecar outfits, so the sidecar concept lost out in the battle for mass appeal. Nationwide in 1915, motorcycle sales rose two percent while cars gained sixty-nine percent! Harley-Davidson

Chapter 2

1916–1929

F-heads, Sports and Peashooters

1916

The 1916 model was the first year in which the model number was prefixed by the last two digits of the year instead of the old subtract-four system. The 1916 two- and three-speed models featured a new rear-stroke starter. Single-speed models still used the old bicycle-style forward-stroke starter with both right and left pedals.

The appearance of the 1916 models was improved by newly styled tanks with rounded edges. Total capacity of the tanks increased from twenty to twenty-two pints. Filler caps were larger, now with a 1½ in. diameter instead of 1⅜ in. The new tanks could not be fitted to earlier models.

A standardization policy resulted in the same basic frame being used for both the twins and the singles, although there were slight differences in the single-speed and three-speed fittings. Frame standardization also standardized footboards and brake rods. The 1916 frame was more heavily reinforced below the steering head to withstand sidecar stress. The steering head bearing was improved by changing to the two-point

Rounded tanks appeared in 1916. This is a single-speed model. Fenders were wider and had more space between them and the tires. The forward front fender brace was new for 1916. Harley-Davidson

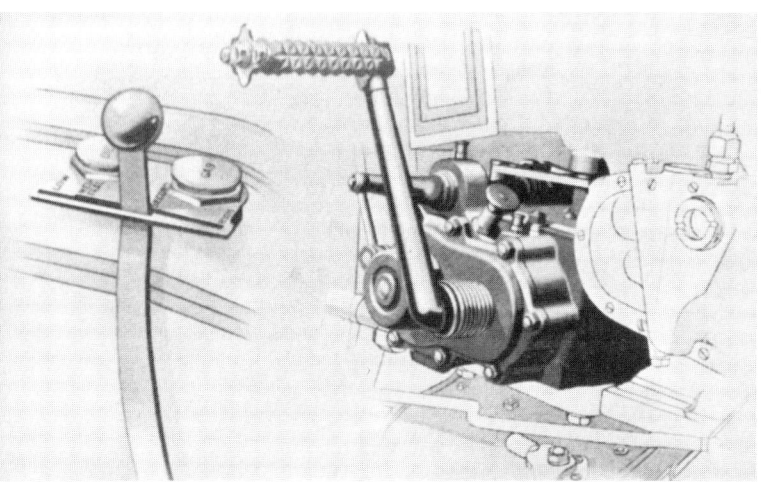

The shift gate came out on 1915 three-speeds. The rear stroke starter was new for 1916 and was called a step starter. Some riders of pre 1916 models sawed off the left bicycle pedal in order to achieve the look of the single-pedal 1916 models! Harley-Davidson

concept with larger head cones and by adding two more balls to the arrangement.

The front fork was wider, and there was more space between tires and fenders, or mudguards in factory parlance. Fenders were wider, now measuring 5¼ in. from edge to edge instead of the former 4½ in. An optional flat front mudguard was available (and continued to be through 1921). Wheel rims were claimed to be fifty percent stronger. Detail improvements were made to the front hub, which could be fitted to earlier models.

Advertising mentioned that both the inlet and exhaust valves had 45 degree seats. A year earlier, only the inlet valves had been advertised as having the 45 degree seats.

In the transmission, the countershaft (also called the layshaft) was supported by roller bearings instead of bronze bushings. The countershaft was heavier and made of chrome-nickel steel.

The clutch thrust bearing was improved by incorporating a new outer ball race and housing, so the bearing became self-aligning. Oil retainers were improved.

A new heat-treating method was applied to most working parts. Details of this process weren't disclosed in sales media, but the claim was that scaling (also called flaking) was eliminated because oxidation wasn't possible with the new method. This eliminated the need to sandblast new parts, which in turn eliminated long run-in periods to achieve smooth bearing surfaces.

The clutch handlever was shortened. For sidecar use, an optional ratchet brake lock could be fitted to the right footboard. An auxiliary handbrake was also available for sidecar use. The auxiliary brake was an external contracting-band unit. A new drive gear for the magneto or generator was fitted. The generator was changed

New for 1916 was the dual-function left tank with separate fuel and oil compartments. Earlier left tanks were for oil only. The lever on the left handlebar is for an auxiliary external contracting-band brake. The magneto was probably located in the rear to avoid water splash. Unfortunately, magneto adjustment required removal of the chainguard. Harley-Davidson

from Model 15 to Model 250, and featured a mechanical switch instead of the vacuum-controlled battery cutout used in 1915 only.

Overhead-valve racers

Three racing models were advertised in the company media: the 16-R twin-cylinder speed roadster, the 16-S single-cylinder stripped stock and the 16-T twin-cylinder stripped stock. Most key features, such as forks, handlebars, clutch and brake, were optional.

The biggest racing news was too late for the new-model press releases: new racing singles with four overhead valves and twins with eight overhead valves. Design was under the direction of William S. Harley, but according to the recollections of old-timers, William Ottaway did most of the in-house work. Ottaway first came to prominence as head of the Thor motorcycle racing team, later running the Harley-Davidson racing team.

Theorists had long proclaimed the superiority of overhead-valve engines, and since 1911, the Indian four-valve racing singles and eight-valve racing twins had hammered the point home. The Indian overheads had parallel inlet and exhaust valves. But meanwhile, intensive engineering efforts were ongoing in the aviation field in response to the demands of World War I. The standard aviation engine combustion chamber had inlet and exhaust valves disposed at an included angle of 90 degrees, thus forming the classic hemispherical combustion chamber. Clearly, Harley and Ottaway concluded, the answer to Harley-Davidson racing problems was to capture the best of both worlds. They wanted racing engines with four-valve hemispherical combustion chambers.

To get the best possible results from the proposed new racers, which were referred to as Four-valve and Eight-valve models, Harley-Davidson hired England's Harry Ricardo. Ricardo was the leading freelance theorist and practitioner in the young science of cylinder head flow physics. His engineering effort concentrated on cylinders and heads, which were actually cast as one unit as in F-head practice. The standard F-head bore and stroke of $3^{5}/_{16} \times 3^{1}/_{2}$ in. was retained. Exhaust pipes were only about 18 in. long.

The F-head valve mechanism was modified so that the eight-valve action was generated by a four-lobe cam instead of a two-lobe cam. A discussion of the F-head valve mechanism follows in order to understand the reason for the new racing valve action.

On the F-head twins, each of the two cam lobes was the basis of both inlet and exhaust valve action for the dedicated cylinder of that lobe. F-head independent valve timing could be accomplished only by changing the geometry of the roller arms—we call these cam followers or valve lifters today. Reshaping a cam lobe would affect the action of both valves of the dedicated cylinder, so that was too tricky. For each cylinder, the pair of roller arms hung from a common pivot and followed along on opposite sides of the lobe. The roller arm rollers tracked down the middle of the lobe.

On the 1916 Eight-valves with four cam lobes, valve action could be tailored by regrinding the cam as well as by reshaping the roller arms. This was important because the cam contours could be more easily studied and duplicated, and the consequences of changes could be more easily predicted than trying to achieve these ends through changes in the valve lifters. On the Eight-valves, each valve lifter roller was offset, one on the back side of its support arm and the other on the front side, so that each roller followed its separate lobe.

About six Eight-valves were built, and they were immediately successful. In America's most prestigious race, the 1916 Dodge City 300, Irving Janke rode an Eight-valve to victory and Floyd Clymer set the 100 mile record on another Eight-valve. Over the next several years, Harley-Davidson's team strategy in the long races consisted of setting a blistering pace with the Eight-valves, then moving in for the kill with F-head racers, which were considered more reliable. As for the Four-valves, a handful of these were mainly used in the less prominent Midwestern dirt track events. Nevertheless, these dirt track races were important engineering laboratories, since the Four-valve and Eight-valve cylinder heads were identical.

Big racing news was created by the 1916 Eight-valves, the first of several types. Two later versions were distinguished by open exhausts, and varying combinations of timing covers and valve actuation were used. The 1916 Eight-valves had a single cam gear as on the road models, but used a four-lobe cam instead of the standard two-lobe cam. The timing cover was the same as on the road models. Restoration by John Cameron. Sam Hotton

1917

Mechanical changes

For 1917, the standard F-head road models received the four-lobe cam setup introduced on the eight-valves. Incidentally, this modification could be made to the 1913 through 1916 F-head models.

A change to the valve roller arms was made on February 8 and was effective with motor number 17T-8927. Later roller arms could be rebushed at dealerships, but earlier roller arms had to be entirely replaced and the old roller arms returned to the factory for exchange credit.

The clearance between the exhaust valves and lifter pins was increased to between 0.008 and 0.010 in. for both cylinders, whereas earlier motors had a 0.004 in. clearance for the rear cylinder and a 0.006 in. clearance for the front. This change was in response to ever-increasing speeds and corresponding engine temperature gradients that put parts under more stress. Also new for 1917 were the pushrod spring covers, provided for the twins only.

Standard motor valve timing was radically changed to provide the same valve overlap as on the special motors. Inlet valve opening was advanced from 0.79 mm before top dead center to 3.9 mm BTDC. Inlet valve closing was delayed from 3.1 mm after bottom dead center to 19.0 mm ABDC. Exhaust valve timing was changed only slightly.

By 1917, pistons had lightening holes drilled around the skirt and a groove above the lower edge of the skirt. Pistons of this style may have been available before 1917; the parts books aren't clear on this point.

Due to the war in Europe, the German Bosch magnetos were no longer available. Instead, spark was provided by Dixie magnetos.

Fast motors

Harley-Davidson launched a series of "fast" motors, beginning with motor number 500. These motors were assembled with greater precision than stock motors and with looser clearances throughout and were block tested to ensure ideal setup. These special fast motors were continued in 1918 and 1919, and all motor numbers were assigned from the 500 to 999 range. Despite the range of 500 available motor numbers, actual production was probably considerably less.

The following new parts were introduced on the 500 motors: front and rear cylinders, front and rear inlet valve housings, inlet valve caps, inlet housing cap (cage) clamp nuts, inlet valves, inlet valve springs, inlet pushrods, pushrod springs, exhaust valves with a key for each, and right and left crankcases. As Harley-Davidson hated to throw anything away, the 500 motors used two other parts that were carryovers from previous standard models: the sprocket shaft ball race, which had been used on 1912-1916 standard motors, and 2 in. casing studs, which had been used on 1912-1914 standard motors.

Other changes in the 1917 lineup included the inlet (front and rear) housing and inlet housing cap on standard motors, inlet manifold, inlet valves, inlet valve springs, pushrod springs, pushrod spring covers, right and left crankcases with bushings on 61 ci motors, gearbox, transmission mainshaft roller bearing instead of bushing, clutch hub shell ring, clutch key ring, rear mudguard, rear wheel (less tire) and brake, toolbox and cover, front and rear inlet lifter arms and exhaust roller arms.

Olive standard

The styling of the 1917 models introduced a change that would apply to fourteen of the next sixteen years: olive paint became standard. This color has often been

The 1917-1919 motor. Exhaust valve springs were enclosed beginning in 1914, and inlet valve pushrod springs were enclosed beginning in 1917. This photo appeared in the 1920 catalog, but the 1920 motors actually appeared slightly different. The 1915-1922 oil pump was integral with the magneto drive cover. Harley-Davidson

Color was olive for 1917 to 1921, as shown on this single-speed 1917 model. V-twin and single-cylinder crankcases were also painted olive for 1917 to 1921. Striping for 1917 to 1921 was in Pullman Coach, a deep green bordered and centered with metallic paint, probably gold. The last year of the single-speed option was 1918. Harley-Davidson

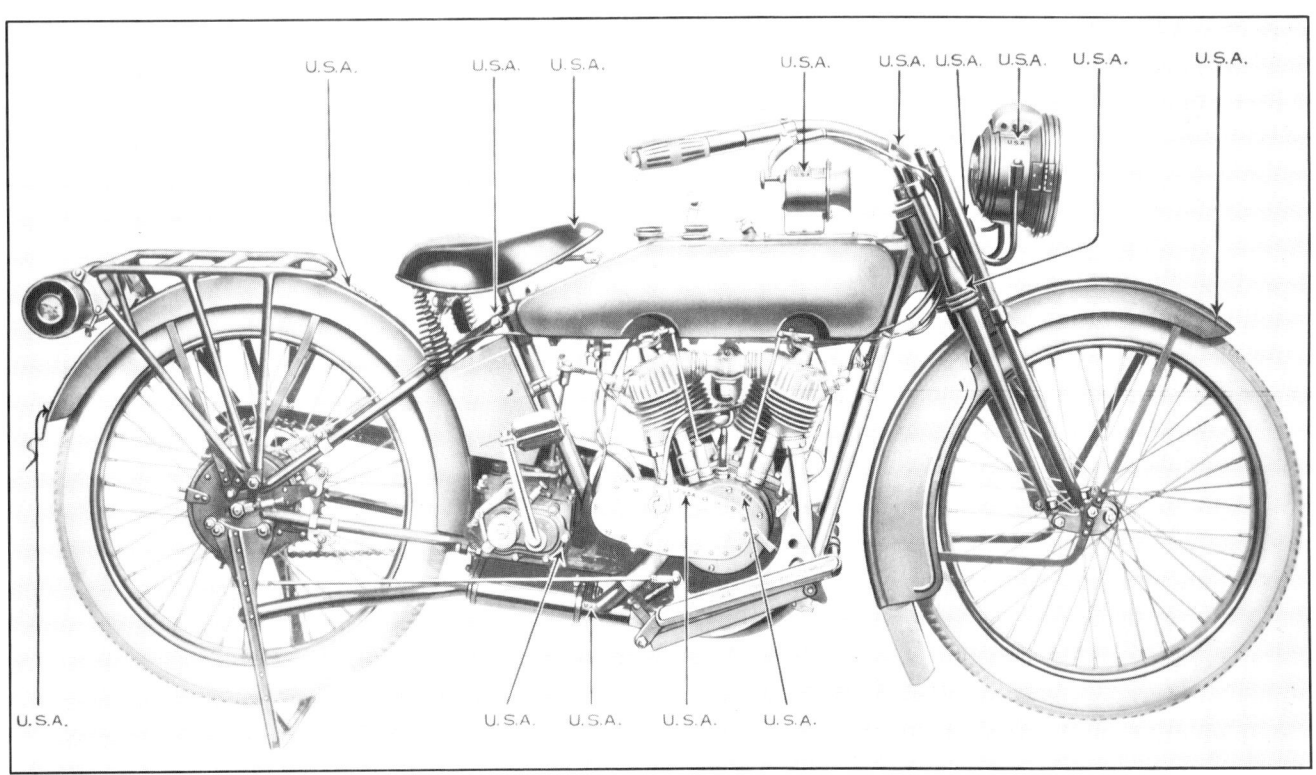

Uncle Sam liked his initials all over the place. Most of the US Army's World War I motorcycles were Indians, but Harley-Davidson supplied more than 15,000 of the 70,000 total. Post-armistice deliveries swelled the company's total to more than 20,000. In World War I, the Army considered the motorcycle a combat vehicle, although most were used for messenger service and traffic control. Harley-Davidson

Action shots made great publicity, but most World War I use was for courier and traffic patrol duties. Harley-Davidson

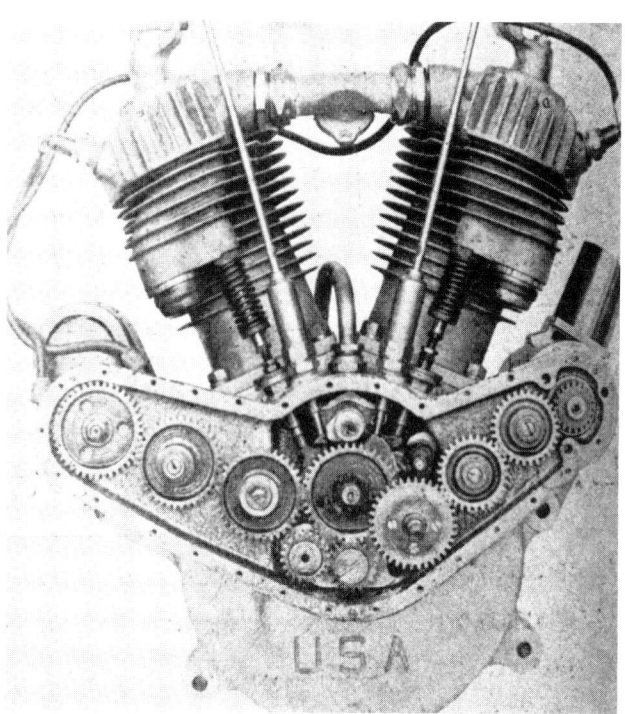

In 1918, the motorcycle industry collaborated on a composite design of the Liberty motor for the USA motorcycle. Harley-Davidson's good war record was rewarded by their motor being selected as the basis of the Liberty motor. The USA motorcycle project was canceled at war's end. Motorcycle Illustrated

referred to as olive drab, and even the factory used this term, but the finish was high gloss, not drab as in military use.

Striping was coach green, a dark hue that was also termed Pullman Coach after the Pullman company, which built and rented sleeper railroad cars. A broad coach green striping outlined the tanks, and a single center stripe of coach green ran down the middle of each fender rib. The broad stripes were edged and centered with metallic pinstripes, probably gold. Harley-Davidson began supplying military motorcycles in 1917, and the new olive color was fashionable during World War I.

1918
World War I

About 70,000 motorcycles were used by the American forces during World War I. Indian supplied the great majority, and in fact, its contract prevented deliveries of civilian models for several months. Harley-Davidson supplied about 15,500 motorcycles prior to the war's end and another 4,500 shortly later, for a total of 20,000 military Harley-Davidsons in the era. Indian's inability to supply dealers was an important turning point in the battle for number one in American sales, a battle that Harley-Davidson had entered back in 1914 when it went racing.

At the direction of the US War Department, motorcycle manufacturers collaborated on a composite design intended to be the future standard military motorcycle for the United States. Called the USA, the standardized motorcycle was claimed to share the best features of the leading makes. The Excelsior contribution was the so-called Keystone frame, which used the motor as a stress-bearing member. With the USA motor removed from the frame, there was a gap between the front and rear frame sections. Indian's share of the glory was minor—unless it had a hand in the front forks, which were not photographed or described in archival records.

The heart of the USA motorcycle, the Liberty engine, was a Milwaukee product. The government's selection of the Harley-Davidson motor was a testimony to the reliability of Harley-Davidsons under military conditions. This was quite a compliment to the company, since arch-rival Indian had built the bulk of World War I motorcycles. Nothing more was heard from the USA motorcycle project after the fanfare in August motorcycle magazines, as the war was shortly to end.

Production modifications

The first few Harley-Davidson 1918 twins were fitted with the Model 250 Remy generator as in 1916 and 1917, but most 1918 twins were equipped with the Model 235 Remy generator. A new circuit breaker was mechanically operated by a centrifugal switch. Other new parts for 1918 twins included the oil hole cover, upper exhaust valve cover, lower exhaust valve cover, relief pipe clamp and screw, generator drivecase, magneto gear, generator intermediate gear, generator drive gear, generator gear stud, generator stud collar, foot clutch lever rod, clutch hub shell and sprocket, clutch driving hubs and nuts, miscellaneous small clutch parts, generator control rod, handbrake handle and front chainguard.

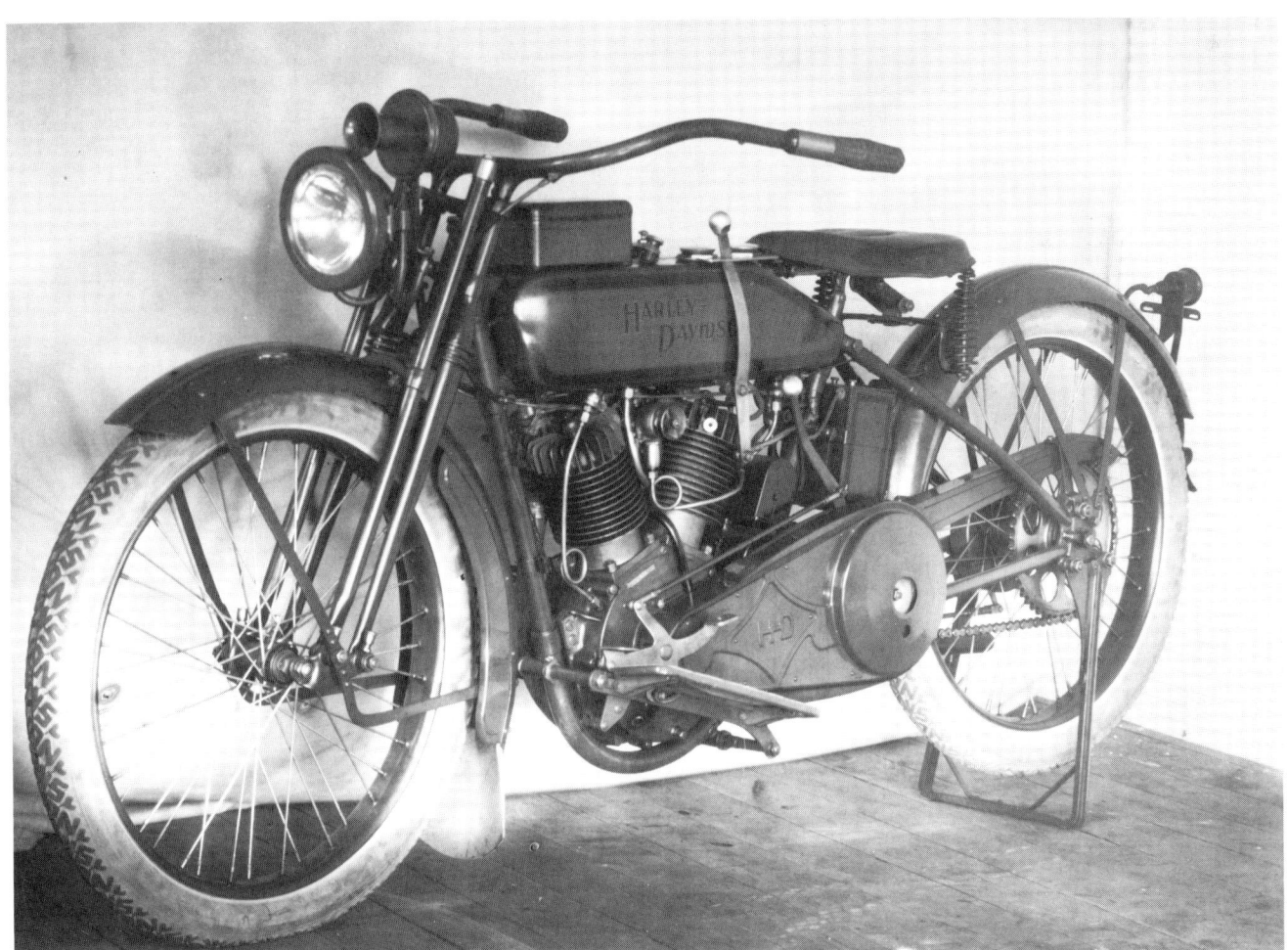

The 1918 model. The 1918 clutch could be lubricated by the rider with an oilcan. Earlier clutches required dealer disassembly, grease packing and reassembly. The broad coach green striping border was changed from metallic to pea green, and the center stripe was changed from metallic to black. This finish was used from 1918 through 1921. Harley-Davidson

Unpeeling a circa 1919 Two Cam Eight-valve twin. The first Two Cam twins were distinguished by this "banjo" timing case cover. Some say the first Two Cam models came out in 1917, but the earliest photos to surface date from 1919. The motor number is 238V1, but owner John Cameron believes this is a dummy number, because the Two Cam base was redesigned in 1922. The huge oil pump was never used on road models. This particular racing engine is believed to have been used by famous British racer Freddy Dixon. John Cameron

New parts for singles included the oil hole cover, relief pipe clamp and screw, front chainguard and the Berling magneto.

To bridge the gap between the timing case and the rear-mounted magneto, only a single large gear was used. Since the large gear drove the oil pump, the pump had to be big to offset its slow movement. The two equal-sized gears each spun two cam lobes. John Cameron

Prior to 1918, lubrication of clutch bearings was by periodic disassembly and repacking with grease. Harley-Davidson recommended this be done by dealers because of the special wrenches required. For 1918, a design change enabled the rider to provide lubrication by adding a few drops of oil through the actuating plate. The recommended interval between lubrications was 1,000 miles.

Tanks and fenders continued to have coach green striping. However, the edging was changed to pea green and the center pinstripe was changed to black. Incidentally, Harley-Davidson never used the term pinstriping, but called the paintwork hair line striping.

1919
Variety eliminated

Supposedly at the suggestion of the War Industries Board, unnecessary variety was to be eliminated, so only the three-speed twin was offered at the beginning of the 1919 season. Also, any standard make of tire might be provided.

Miscellaneous new V-twin parts for 1919 included a set of engine casting clamp plates (usable on older models) and handlebars that were 2½ in. wider and enameled in olive drab.

On late 1919 models, the old worm-actuated clutch gave way to a new cam-actuated clutch. Other new late 1919 clutch features included the clutch-actuating cam guard, clutch pullrod, and clutch connecting link and pin.

First Two Cams

For official factory riders, a handful of Eight-valve motors were assembled with a new valve-lifting mechanism that became known as the two-cam principle. This change caused the motorcycles to take on the name Two Cam. The idea was to reduce the reciprocating weight by installing two cam gears instead of one, thus reducing the length of the cam followers, or lifter arms in factory terminology.

There were already four cam lobes, of course, so the intended meaning of the term Two Cam was different. Instead of one cam gear with four lobes there were two cam gears, each with two lobes. In the slang of the era the aggregate of each gear and its lobes was termed simply a cam. The two-cam principle was also applied to the several F-head racers built in 1919. Because of this change the F-head racers took on the name Two Cam.

A new larger oil pump was fitted to both the F-head and Eight-valve racers, as well as a combined magneto-drivecase cover and timing case cover. This new so-called banjo timing case cover on the Eight-valves did the double duty of covering both the magneto timing gears and the valve mechanism. Earlier Eight-valves and the F-heads used a separate cover for each of these components, so to gain full access to the valve-lifting mechanism on earlier Eight-valves and on the F-heads, it was necessary to first remove the magneto drivecase and then remove the timing case proper.

Two Cam twins used shorter valve lifters than road models, which increased maximum rpm. The factory referred to these lifters as roller arms. John Cameron

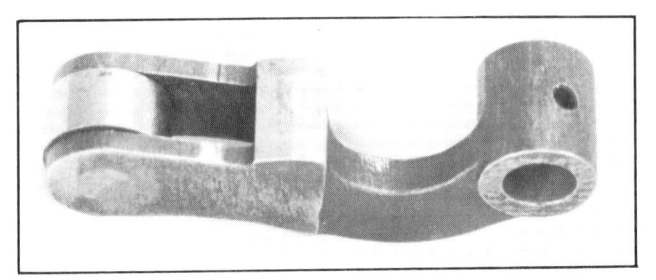

This is the rear exhaust roller arm. The pad in the middle shows wear from the exhaust valve stem. John Cameron

The 1919 Two Cam with timing gears removed. John Cameron

The two-cam principle eventually resulted in the public's naming of these racers; hence the name Two Cam, which came from the two cam gears. John Cameron

Drilled connecting rods from the Eight-valve motor were a racing staple. Harley-Davidson used the forked (female) rod for the front cylinder and the simple (male) rod for the rear cylinder until the late 1930s. John Cameron

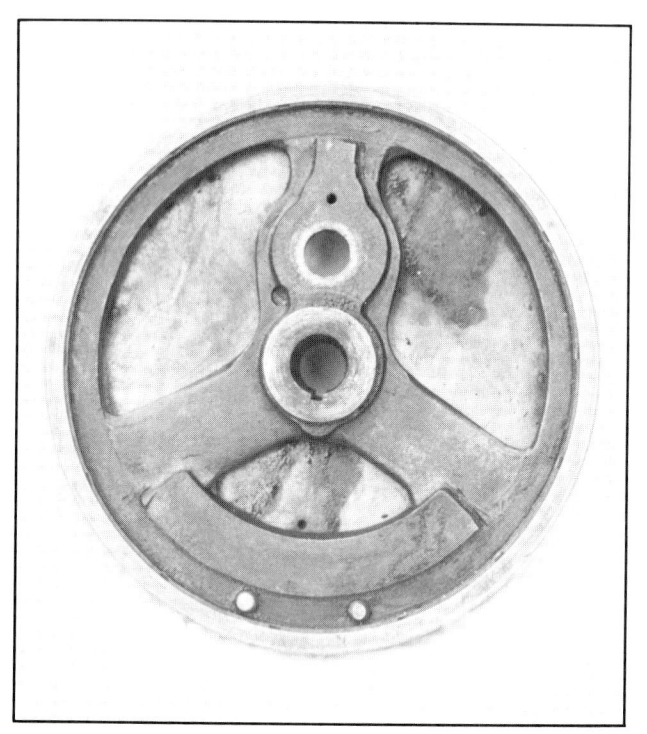

Webbed or spoked flywheels on this racing engine were the rule on road models as well, until the 1921 Seventy-four F-head debuted. This racing flywheel was modified by some period tuner, as a sheet-metal cover has been riveted to the back side. Presumably, this reduced crankcase drag. John Cameron

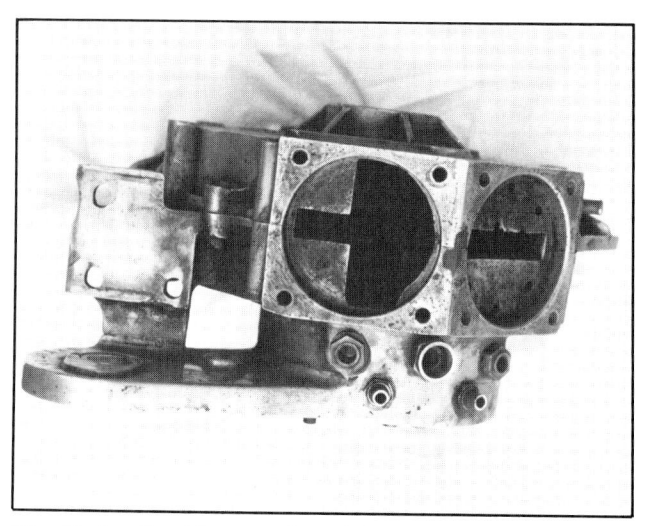

The Harley-Davidson road model big twin from circa 1911 through 1929 used the full baffle under the front cylinder and the half-baffle under the rear cylinder, as shown here. John Cameron

The new combination cover on the Eight-valves simplified matters by providing direct access to all ignition and valve timing parts.

The 35.6 ci, 584 cc Sport arrived as a mid 1919 model. Although electric lights became available in 1920, some riders still preferred acetylene lighting. Sport crankcases were unpainted throughout production. Harley-Davidson

Sport model

In midyear, the middleweight Sport model was introduced as a 1919 model. The motor was a horizontally opposed side-valve twin with a bore and stroke of 2¾x3 in., yielding a displacement of 35.64 ci, 584.03 cc. An unusual feature was a single casting that combined the intake and exhaust manifolds; the popular theory of the time was that heating the intake charge was beneficial to combustion. The cylinder heads were not detachable. The outside flywheel was built up from a steel hub riveted to pressed steel discs, and a pressed steel cover ensured that the rider's legs wouldn't get caught in the flywheel.

A single camshaft transmitted cam motion directly to the intake and exhaust valves, a trick that was possible by angling the intake valves. This probably was detrimental to performance due to the unusual combustion chamber shape. The advertised rating was 6 hp.

The Sport motor featured true unit construction of the motor and gearbox; both sections were housed in a common pair of right and left castings. The crankshaft and connecting rod big ends turned on roller bearings. Power was transmitted through a primary drive of three helical gears to a wet clutch, two features that would later be popularized by the rival Indian Scout. Ports were drilled in the intermediate (middle) gear, which was in effect a rotary crankcase breather valve.

The three-speed transmission featured sliding-gear operation. A plunger pump supplied oil through a rotary valve that, unlike the V-twin pump, didn't require any spring action. Crankshaft oil sling ensured adequate lubrication of the transmission because the motor and transmission were in a common cavity. Rear drive was by a totally enclosed chain.

Accessibility was stressed. Valve guides were screwed into place and could be easily replaced. Valves in both cylinders could be ground without removing the motor from the frame. When decarbonization of the

Specifications

Year and model	1919–1923 Sport
Engine	Side-valve, horizontally opposed twin
Bore and stroke	2¾x3 in.
Displacement	35.64 ci, 584.03 cc
Compression ratio	3.75:1 (estimated)
Horsepower	6 bhp
Gearbox	Three speed, sliding gear, housing cast integrally with motor
Shift	Left hand
Clutch	Wet, multiplate disk, actuated by left foot
Wheelbase	57 in.
Wheels and tires	26x3 in. (26 in. outside tire diameter, 20 in. diameter wheels from rim to rim), clincher tires
Suspension	Front: trailing link with compression spring; rear: rigid
Weight, fully serviced	250 lb.
Seat height	29½ in. without load, 28½ in. with 140 lb. rider
Fuel consumption	70 mpg (claimed)
Top speed	50 mph (estimated)

A circular pressed steel cover fit over the outside flywheel of the Sport. All Harley-Davidsons could be purchased without lights. Unlike the other models, the front fender was fully sprung—it didn't move up and down with the fork action, in other words. Harley-Davidson

39

cylinders was necessary, they could be removed and replaced without removing the motor from the frame.

The frame was of the Keystone type, in which the engine acted as a stress-bearing member of the motorcycle. The forks were unusual. Trailing-link suspension was provided, as with the Indian, but the bottom trailing links acted through pullrods to pivot another central link near the steering head. On this second link, the side opposite the pullrod acted to keep a central spring in compression. The springing mechanism had twice as many wear points as the Indian leaf-spring layout, although the Harley-Davidson setup did have a more compact and neat look.

The 1919 (and early 1920) Sport models were not available with electric lights. However, acetylene lighting could be fitted.

1920
Expansion

New 1920 road model V-twin parts included the front and rear cylinders, inlet pushrods previously used only on the 500 motors, pushrod spring covers, right and left flywheels on E motors only (through 1923), clutch dust ring, rear brake band, brake lever (on drum), headlight body (earlier 1920s), headlight body (later 1920s), headlight reflector and miscellaneous small headlight parts.

Some 1920 V-twins were delivered with no compression plates, while others were delivered with a plate under either the front or rear cylinder. These variances were due to the factory objective of equalizing the compression ratio in both cylinders in order to improve engine dynamic balance. Foundry operations were unable to control combustion chamber volume to the desired accuracy, so combustion chamber volume was measured and compression plates were installed as required in order to equalize the compression ratios of both cylinders.

The special fast motors were now termed E motors instead of 500 motors. The E motors were equipped with aluminum pistons and drilled connecting rods. Factory instructions for E motor tuning stressed the need to vary the compression ratio according to the length of the race, with shorter races calling for higher compression and longer races calling for lower compression. The compression ratio was changed by inserting or removing cylinder base compression plates. Other racing tips included larger sprockets for long races and low-grade fuel to reduce overheating. Teardown and inspection were recommended at 100 mile intervals.

As with the 500 motors, fittings were looser throughout than on standard models; for example, the gear shaft was fitted 0.0005 in. looser than standard. Piston

One camshaft actuated all valves of the Sport. There were two cams: an inlet cam and an exhaust cam. Unusual tilting of the inlet valves probably robbed power. Cylinder heads were not removable. Although the Sport introduced the gear-driven primary and wet clutch to America, the Indian Scout made these features famous after the Sport died out. Harley-Davidson

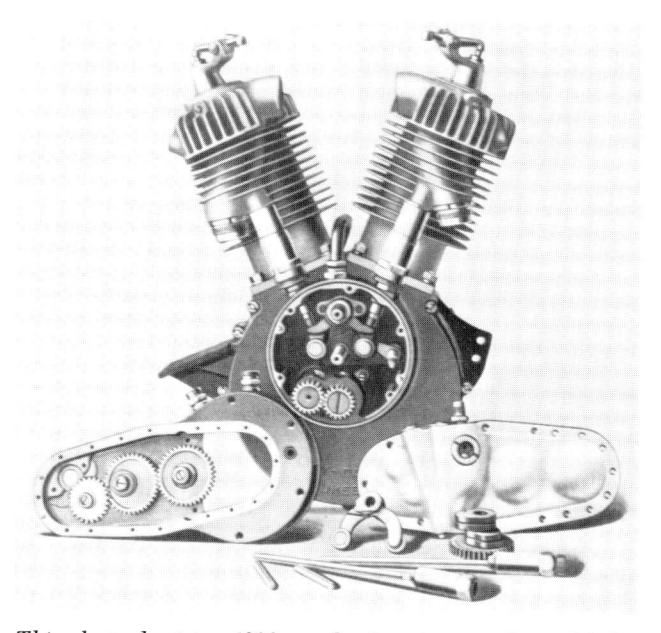

This photo depicts a 1920 standard engine—or does it? Sales catalogs were prepared each summer, so the lead-time for catalog preparation can trick restorers. This photo appeared in the 1920 catalog, but the engine is a 1917-1919 style. The four separate cams were introduced in 1917. Harley-Davidson

40

This motorcycle was probably photographed in the summer of 1919 in preparation for the 1920 catalogs. Meanwhile, engineering changes were being finalized. Production 1920 models had later-style inlet pushrod spring covers and later-style cylinders. Harley-Davidson

This photo shows the 1920 motor actually used on production models. Cylinder head fins are more tapered near the spark plugs than on earlier motors, and inlet valve spring covers are new. Harley-Davidson

Cylinder head finning of the 1920 motors was along the same lines as in the 1911–1919 models. Vertical fins on the valve pockets were more rounded than on the earlier models, however. Unlike the earlier engines, the horizontal fin immediately below the spark plug opening is now completely separate from its counterpart on the cylinder proper. Troy Ross

41

The 1903-1921 flywheels (except 74 ci) were webbed style, sometimes referred to as spoked style. The motor number is L20T14758, the L signifying a generator-equipped motor. The first "solid" flywheels appeared on the 1921 Seventy-fours. Note the little knurled screws on the side of each cylinder head: these were primers. The rider backed each screw off a few turns, which opened up the port in the middle of the screw, then inserted a primer gun lifted from the fuel tank and pumped in fuel. There were two reasons for the primers. Priming provided the rich mixture needed in super cold weather. Additionally, priming loosened gummy oil deposits in cold weather, which otherwise would make starting difficult. Primer cups were used from 1914 through 1937. Harley-Davidson

and cylinder clearance at top dead center was 0.004 to 0.005 in. instead of 0.003 in. In addition, all E motors were block tested. Motor numbers were L20E1000 and up; cylinders had the letter E stamped on the left side of each cylinder base flange.

A "dealers" racing frame was introduced. This frame was open at the bottom, which permitted the installation of either the earlier 500 motor or the later E motor by using different side plates. In the dealers frame, cylinders could be removed with the motor installed in the frame.

In midseason, electric lighting became available on the Sport. This brought with it the first battery case, a new toolbox cover and locks.

Other new 1920 Sport model parts included some 3 3/8 in. long front motor clamp plate studs (instead of 2 5/8 in. long studs), front motor clamp spacer (used when necessary), front footboard support, foot clutch lever, foot clutch lever friction spring, clutch-operating rod end, starter crank bracket bolt (instead of cap screw) and luggage carrier brace for magneto models.

The managers decided the company could save money and produce better motorcycles by building its own generators and coils. Thus, all late 1920 electric models were fitted with Harley-Davidson generators and coils.

When the final factory addition was completed in April 1920, its usable floor space of 542,258 sq. ft. made it the world's largest motorcycle factory. By comparison, the Indian factory had 520,000 usable sq. ft. Harley-Davidson employed 2,400 workers; Indian em-

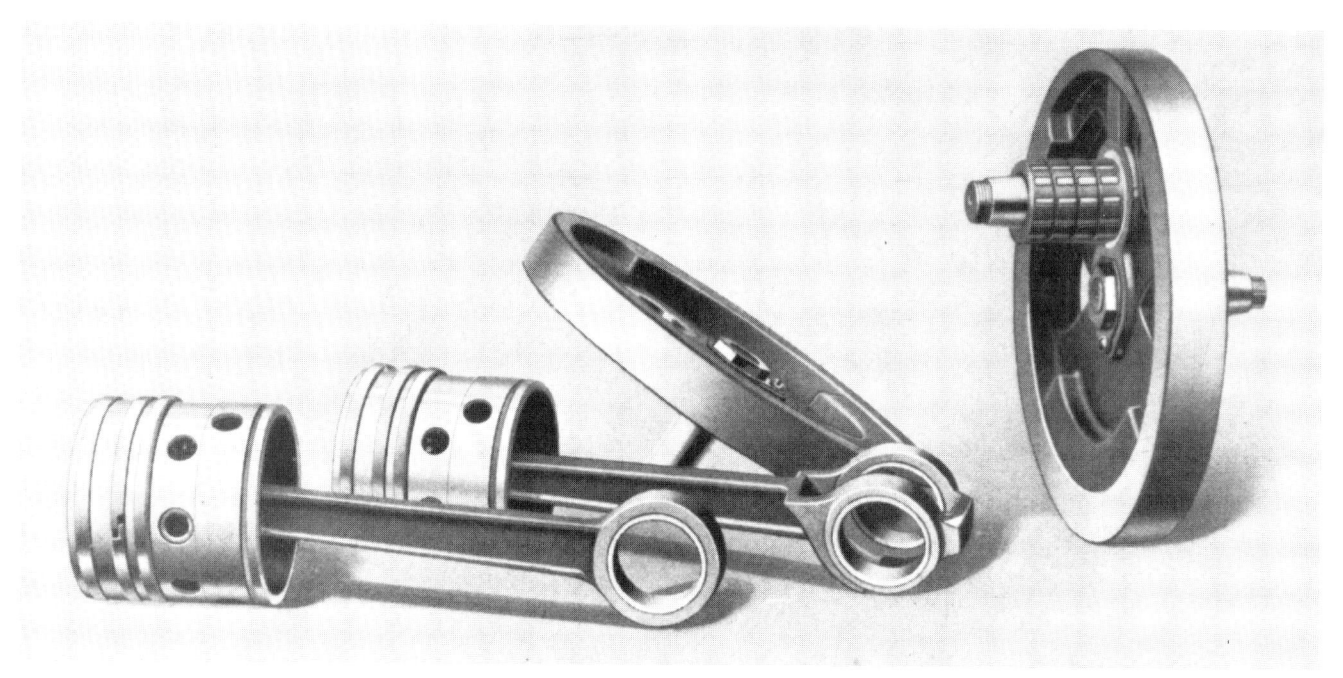

Pistons, connecting rods and flywheels of a 1920 V-twin. Holed pistons were introduced in 1917 or earlier. The groove near the bottom was for picking up oil. The so-called step-joint ring is shown. The two pairs of crankpin double-row roller bearings were introduced in 1917. Harley-Davidson

ployed 2,200 workers. The Harley-Davidson plant capacity was 35,000 motorcycles per year; the Indian plant capacity was 30,000 motorcycles per year, and the Excelsior plant capacity was 20,000 to 25,000 motorcycles per year. Ironically, Harley-Davidson became committed to plant expansion just as the era of explosive growth ended. Between 1918 and 1920, while final expansion proceeded, it probably became clear to the founders that they had been overly optimistic. In any case, the full measure of Harley-Davidson factory capacity would not be required until World War II.

1921
Debut of the Seventy-four

History was made with the introduction of the new 74 ci, 1200 cc F-head V-twin for 1921. This model was referred to as the 74 in factory literature but was commonly known as the Seventy-four. A Seventy-four would remain in the Harley-Davidson inventory through 1980. Its increased capacity was obtained by increasing the bore from $3^{5}/_{16}$ to 3.424 in. (advertised as $3^{7}/_{16}$ in.) and increasing the stroke from $3^{1}/_{2}$ to 4 in. The total capacity of the nominally 74 ci model was 74.66 ci, 1207.11 cc. To handle the fueling of the new Seventy-four, the Schebler carburetor throat diameter was increased from 1 to $1^{1}/_{4}$ in.

Exhaust valves had been previously made of chrome-nickel steel, and chrome-nickel exhaust valves were continued on the 61 ci twin, now termed the Sixty-one to distinguish it from the new Seventy-four. However, on the Seventy-four, the exhaust valves were made of a new alloy called silchrome, also referred to as silichrome or sil-chrome. The chromium content in steel, whether chrome-nickel or silchrome, provided hardness. In the new silchrome, however, silicon

A 1920 storeroom full of V-twin and Sport motors. Carts were rolled over to the assembly area. Harley-Davidson

attracted oxygen while the steel was molten, and the oxygen was then driven to the surface before the steel cooled and hardened. The result was a more uniform texture to the steel—no Swiss cheese effect, you might say—which increased the reliability of the end product.

The Seventy-four featured solid flywheels instead of a webbed or spoked construction. Other necessarily new parts on the Seventy-four F-heads were right and left crankcases, and front and rear exhaust pipes.

Because of the longer stroke on the Seventy-four, the factory was concerned about overheating. Riders were advised to use the auxiliary handpump at higher speeds, bringing the handpump into use between 35 and 40 mph. An injection of one-third of a full pump

The 1920 F-heads in assembly. Each motorcycle was built up by one man, with occasional help from another. There was no moving assembly line. These are apparently among the last 1920 models assembled, which would mean this photo was taken around March 1920. Harley-Davidson

Another 1920 assembly shot, taken only a moment apart from the F-head scene. These Sport models, however, show the 1921 tank trim. Production proceeded in batches, and these are the first of the 1921 models to be assembled. Harley-Davidson

Frame shop in 1920. Sidecar frames are being prepared by the workers at the bench. Frames for V-twins and singles hang from the rafters and are also in the foreground. Sport model frames are on the floor in the right midrange. Machinery is belt-driven from a system of overhead belts and pulleys. Harley-Davidson

This rural scene typifies most of the roads of 1920. Motorcycle engineers were later to be challenged by smoother and straighter roads that permitted ever higher speeds for ever longer stretches. Note the single, broad coach green stripe in the middle of the fender; this was the pattern for 1917 through 1921 models. Harley-Davidson

was recommended every few miles. The recommended running-in procedure stipulated no speeds in excess of 30 mph for the first 200 miles.

Front and rear fenders were new and featured a center rib, which was not pronounced. Side panels were added to the front fender. New Sixty-one and Seventy-four parts for 1921 included the exhaust lifter pin bushing on Seventy-four models, front and rear connecting rods, pistons, piston rings, piston pins, front stand, front footboard support rod (heel brake), right and left gasoline and oil tanks, toolbox cover (electric models), right and left upper mudguard sides, and rear hub shell. Late 1921 Sixty-one models were fitted with new solid flywheels.

Factory literature refers to A and B motors, implying that these came into use during the late teens. The A designation had been used in 1914 for special high-speed motors, but was now used to denote motors built for police use. These police A motors were identical to standard motors in every respect except that looser fits were incorporated throughout the reciprocating action. The B motor was a special high-compression model designed for use in high-altitude areas. The A motor was still being built in 1921, but the B motor was no longer in production. A, B and E (racing) motors were identified by their letter stamped on the left side of the cylinder base flange.

A 1920 winter-equipped sidecar rig. The headlight was moved above the horn on the 1920 models. Harley-Davidson

New-style cylinders and pushrod spring covers are also shown on this 1920 racer. This motorcycle has the dealer's racing frame. Unlike factory-team frames, its cylinders could be removed from the crankcase without first dropping the entire motor. The motor was 61 ci to comply with American rules for long tracks and road racing. Harley-Davidson

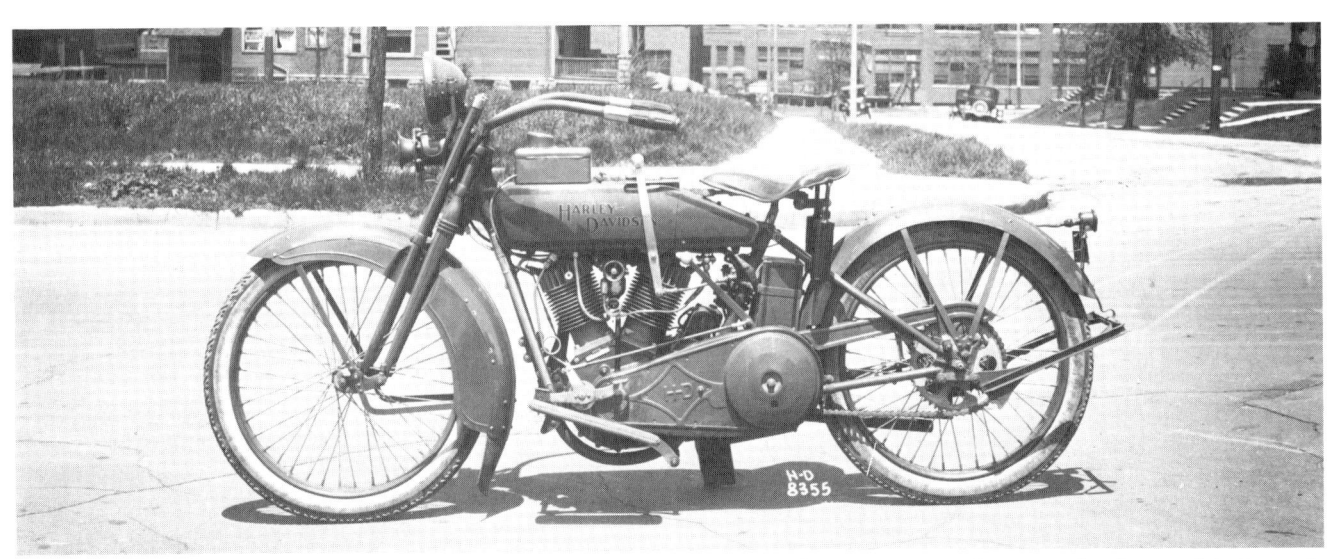

This could be the first Harley-Davidson Seventy-four. For 1921, the V-twin front fender valance was extended along the front section. Narrow forks required a concave section on the front fender from 1921 through 1923. Fenders had a slight center rib or crown. In the center background is the main factory building; in the left background is the final factory addition nearing completion. This photo of a preproduction model was taken in early 1920. Harley-Davidson

The Sport tank trim was simplified for 1921. Inlet and exhaust manifolds were cast together throughout Sport production. Harley-Davidson

New Sport model changes for 1921 included the brake lever guide, headlight body and new tank decor. The Sport model tank trim was now like the big twin, with the Harley-Davidson name but without the decorative shield previously used.

The company managers decided to include a big single-cylinder model in the lineup as a commercial model. This was the 37 ci Model CD, which was described as "simply a twin 74" motor with one cylinder removed."

An unusual problem was the necessity of closing the factory from mid-March through mid-April due to oversupply and reduced sales. Because of this downturn, the management lowered the salaries of all officers by fifteen percent. The company suffered its first loss during the 1921 business year. On a brighter note, Harley-Davidson was able to pay off all loans used to finance the expanded facility, which would be used by the company for the next fifty years. Even with the cutback, Harley-Davidson now boasted in advertisements that it was the world's largest producer of motorcycles and sidecars.

After its initial rush of enthusiasm back in 1914, company interest in racing gradually diminished. On the one hand, racing had improved the Harley-Davidson image, but on the other hand, as the years passed there seemed to be less direct relationship between victories and sales. Walter Davidson was impressed by the fact that Dodge City, Kansas, continued to order Indian police motorcycles despite four consecutive Harley-Davidson wins in the Dodge City 300, the era's most prestigious race. A few more Eight-valve and Four-valve racers were built in 1921, to the 1919 configuration, and again in 1922. The latter were for overseas

For half-mile dirt track events, 30.50 ci singles were built throughout the 1920s. These were based on V-twin parts. This is a 1921 example. Harley-Davidson

customers, as the company withdrew all racing support at the beginning of the 1922 season.

On the touring scene, a landmark event occurred. A system of state roads planned in 1916 was joined together and given the first national highway numbers.

1922
Minor advances

The most obvious change to all 1922 models was the switch from olive finish with broad coach green striping to brewster green with fine-lined gold striping. The gold striping outlined the tanks and fender side panels and also appeared on each fender on each side of the center ribs.

Compression on the 1922 solo V-twins was lowered by inserting cylinder base compression plates of $1/16$ in. thickness (1921 solo motors had no compression plates). On Seventy-four motors above 22JD6649, cylinders were $1/16$ in. longer, which eliminated the requirement to insert compression plates on solo models. These longer cylinders were designated by an arrow on the right side of each base flange. Early sidecar motors for 1922 used both $1/8$ in. and $1/16$ in. compression plates instead of just the $1/8$ in. plates used on 1921 sidecar motors. The 1922 sidecar motors above 22JD6649 reverted to the $1/8$ in. compression plates only. The 37 ci Model CD single was again offered, but this would be its second and final year of production.

New 1922 V-twin parts included right and left crankcases, gearbox and cover, and front forks. On the forks, both the rigid and spring forks were new as well as the cushion springs and buffer springs. All 1922 Sixty-ones had solid flywheels (which were phased in with late 1921 models). Late 1922 V-twins were fitted with longer roller bearings for the male connecting rod. The same retainers were used, but they were installed with the open ends facing each other, so twelve long rollers replaced twenty-four short rollers.

In the middle of the 1922 V-twin production run, the centrifugal battery cutout switch was replaced by a manual switch with a buzzer. As soon as the switch was

In 1922, V-twin color changed from olive to Brewster green, which continued in 1923. The new dark hue was used on the V-twin crankcases. Striping was double-lined gold. This preproduction example is basically an early 1922 model; late 1922 models had a new oil pump and integral drivecase cover. The motor is a 61 ci version because there are five cooling fins carried over the exhaust ports—74 ci models had six such fins. The auxiliary heel brake on this motorcycle was delayed until 1923 models debuted. The foot pedal worked both the main internal expanding-band and the auxiliary external contracting-band rakes. The heel pedal worked only the external brake. Harley-Davidson

Internals of the double-acting oil pump, introduced in late 1922, effective with motor number 8001. The sight glass was continued to assure riders of proper operation. Harley-Davidson

turned on, the buzzer was activated. After the motor started, generator current deactivated the buzzer.

Late 1922 V-twins above motor 8000 were fitted with a new double-plunger oil pump. The pump consisted of a horizontal cylinder with notches that mated with the worm gear drive from the engine. The cylinder was drilled and ported and contained two small spring-loaded plungers, one on each side of the cylinder and near the periphery. A ramp cam on the left end of the cylinder kept the two plungers reciprocating. The rider could adjust the pump by turning a screw on the left end of the cylinder, which moved the cylinder toward or away from the ramp and, in combination with the cylinder porting, had the effect of increasing or decreasing the effective stroke of the two plungers. The rider selected a washer or combination of washers to install under the screw head, to hold the screw in proper position. The cylinder was ported so that while one plunger was drawing in oil, the other was pushing oil into the motor.

The 1923 hinged rear fender eased tire changes a bit, as shown with this Sixty-one. The rider still had to remove the chain and disconnect the brake. New for 1923 was the standard foot-operated external contracting-band brake. Harley-Davidson

New inlet and exhaust valve springs were claimed to have longer life. The sidecar wheel design was changed to keep dirt out of hubs. Wider and stronger mudguard braces were provided.

The Sixty-one E motors were equipped with aluminum pistons and drilled connecting rods. In midseason, Seventy-four road models were available with DCA motors, which also featured aluminum pistons and drilled connecting rods.

Both the E and DCA pistons had four unevenly spaced rings. All piston rings were bevel-jointed, meaning that the joint of each ring was formed by an angular cut through the ring. The factory cautioned that the use of step-joint rings with aluminum pistons could cause seizure.

The two top rings were compression rings. These had plain or flat faces; that is, they were not beveled on the edges. The third ring was a combination compres-

This 1928–1929 Sixty-one cylinder points out details of the 1923–1929 cylinders. This style of head finning debuted on the 1923 74 ci DCA and DCB models. Application was broadened in 1924 to include the Sixty-ones and was used on all twins from 1925 to 1927, and on some Sixty-ones in 1928 and 1929. Adjacent to the valve pocket are fore-and-aft head fins extending over half the head—the other half of the head used radial fins. This rear cylinder is actually a 1928 or 1929 example because the primer plug has been moved rearward in order to clear the air cleaner first installed on the 1928 models. Troy Ross

Late 1923 and 1924 top-of-the-line Seventy-four motors were termed DCA or DCB models and were equipped with new cylinders featuring less rounded cylinder head fins and seven cooling fins on the exhaust manifolds. Sixty-ones kept the old-style rounded cylinder head fins and five fins on the exhaust manifolds. DCA engines had aluminum pistons; DCB engines had iron-alloy pistons. After stocks of older-style Seventy-four cylinders were used up, all Seventy-fours from 1925 through 1927 used these cylinders. Incidentally, the period parts books can lead you astray. The parts books state these cylinders were also used in 1928 and 1929, but there were differences in the latter two years, explained later. Since the 1928–1929 cylinders were interchangeable with the 1923–1927 cylinders, the parts department thought there was no point in assigning a new part number. Harley-Davidson

In 1923, the Two Cam timing case was redesigned. These Two Cams still used the indirect-action valve mechanism with pivoted roller arms or lifters actuating each valve. The 1923 configuration can be distinguished from later versions by the fact that there are no removable lifter blocks on top of the crankcase. John Cameron

sion and bearing ring and was located just above the piston pin. The fourth ring was a combination bearing, oil and tension ring and was located near the bottom of the piston skirt. Both the third and fourth rings had one beveled edge and were installed with the beveled edge down.

After the E and DCA motors wore enough to become noisy, quietness and efficiency were usually restored by replacing only the lower two rings. The replacement rings were called "oversize thickness" rings, which meant the outside diameter was still standard but the inside diameter was slightly smaller. The replacement third ring was 0.001 in. thicker, and the replacement fourth ring was 0.0025 in. thicker because of greater wear on the bottom ring. For older motors that were bored out, assorted sizes of oversize thickness third and fourth rings were available to match the larger-than-standard first and second rings. Oversize thickness rings were only used on aluminum pistons. Incidentally, the pins of aluminum pistons were larger than those of iron alloy pistons.

The most significant new 1922 Sport model parts, all on late 1922s, were $^{31}/_{64}$ in. rollers for the big end instead of ⅜ in., crankshaft and crankshaft counterweight. Many minor changes were also incorporated.

Detail Sport model changes were made in the front fork, frame, toolbox door and lock on magneto models, and in the toolbox cover and lock on electric models. Also, the front mudguards (sides), rear mudguard (rear end) and luggage carrier, chainguard, battery case, and magneto gear and key were changed in detail.

1923

Eleven improvements were advertised for the standard 1923 V-twin lineup. A roller-bearing rear hub replaced the earlier ball-bearing hub, and the brake pedal control was improved. The manual ignition switch with automatic warning alarm made its official debut, although this item came out on mid 1922 models. An improved double-plunger oiler, introduced on late 1922 models, likewise became an official 1923

The last year of the Sport was 1923, which was badly outsold by the V-twin Indian Scout. Harley-Davidson

improvement. In the electrical system were a new Staylit shock absorbing taillamp and a larger generator that charged from 12 mph and up. The rear mudguard was hinged to simplify tire changes. Silchrome exhaust valves were new on the Sixty-one and improved on the Seventy-four. New cylinder barrels on the Seventy-four featured more squarish cylinder head cooling fins, and seven fins on the exhaust manifold instead of five fins.

No changes were introduced on the Sport model. Apparently the company already realized that the days were numbered for the Sport, which was being badly outsold by the V-twin Indian Scout of similar capacity and weight.

Although Harley-Davidson was taking a low-key approach to racing, continuing development gave birth to a new variant of the Two Cam valve-lifting mechanism. The new 1923 Two Cams featured a new timing case cover that might loosely be described as bean-shaped instead of banjo-shaped. Valve action was still indirect, meaning that pivoted cam followers were still used. The crankcase casting included the lifter blocks through which passed the inlet pushrods and exhaust valve stems. The new Two Cam racer layout was also applied to the Four-valve and Eight-valve racers.

Aluminum pistons and drilled connecting rods were new road model features for 1924. The aluminum pistons proved unreliable, so they were not offered in 1925. The ideal operating range for motors with aluminum pistons was 3400 to 4000 rpm. Motors with cast-iron pistons worked best between 3200 and 3500 rpm. Although the 1924 sales catalog represents this as a 1924 motor, the finning near the front spark plug is of the pre 1924 variety. The engine is a Seventy-four because there are seven cooling fins wrapped around the rear exhaust port. Harley-Davidson

1924
Bigger and better

The Sport model was missing from the 1924 lineup as it was outgunned in the marketplace by the V-twin Indian Scout. The Sport didn't have the power of the Scout, nor the V-twin sound, look and feel that were so popular. Dying with it were its hallmark features of side valves, helical-gear primary drive, wet clutch, unit construction and trailing-link front forks. Side valves would return soon to Harley-Davidson, but unit construction and a wet clutch were twenty-four years away (in the 1948 125 cc model). The helical-gear primary drive has yet to reappear in American-built HarleyDavidsons.

For 1924, the 61 ci models were available only with the aluminum pistons featuring four unevenly spaced bevel-jointed rings, slot-cut rings in factory lingo. However, the 74 ci twins could be provided with two other piston and ring combinations. One option was the old-style cast-iron piston with three unevenly spaced step-joint rings. The other option was a new style of iron alloy piston with three narrower and deeper rings to reduce ring friction. On the iron alloy pistons, the bevel-jointed rings were evenly spaced near the top of the piston. Front and rear cylinders were new on the Sixty-ones.

Buyers of 1924 models could choose the standard Schebler Model H carburetor, or they could specify either of two optional carburetors. One choice was the Schebler De Luxe, which had been optional since 1917. The new optional carburetor was the Zenith. Harley-Davidson wanted two suppliers in order to obtain lower bids for future orders.

For 1924 only, a box-shaped muffler was fitted. Olive color reappeared as the mandatory finish and remained so until a few (unadvertised!) options began to appear around 1926. Striping from 1924 through 1929 was maroon, centered in gold and edged in black. V-twin crankcases were painted olive from 1924 through 1927. Harley-Davidson

A new larger battery had four plates instead of three plates, with a resulting forty-percent increase in capacity. The battery was secured by two large wing nuts, the plates were anchored with heavier straps and the terminals were moved to the outside of the box. On the generator, the three brushes were increased to $5/16$ inch square and their angle of contact with the commutator was changed to reduce sparking and heat buildup. The generator body was larger to accommodate these changes.

A larger muffler, now box-shaped, was fitted to the V-twins. Later in the year, brackets were designed and built so that riders of 1915 and later models could fit the new box-shaped muffler to their models. Running gear lubrication was now handled by an Alemite gun, so it wasn't necessary to disassemble anything in order to pack grease. Minor changes were made in the transmission.

Other new V-twin parts included new flywheels with different balance factors for the drilled rods and aluminum pistons, front exhaust pipe on the Sixty-one, and front and rear exhaust pipes on the Seventy-four. The 1924 V-twins were the last to have the horizontal top frame rail; they weighed 380 lb. without gasoline and oil.

Color was changed back to olive green, but the old broad coach green striping wasn't used. The new narrower striping was maroon edged in black and centered in gold. On the fenders, striping outlined the side panels and one stripe appeared on each side of the center rib.

William S. Harley in the sidecar and Walter Davidson in the saddle show off a 1924 combination. The experimental motor features the spark plug in the combustion chamber proper instead of in the valve pocket, like the 1915 Chicago motors.

This motor never went into production. The last full year of the clear headlight lens was 1924. This was also the last year the front fender braces mounted directly to the spring fork. Harley-Davidson

The fender center rib was now higher, or more pronounced, and the front fender main section extended farther ahead of the side panels than previously.

In April 1924, four company executives departed for tours of overseas markets to assess the advisability of a new line of lightweights. William S. Harley and Walter Davidson visited western Europe, Sales Manager Gumpert visited southern Europe, and Authur Davidson visited Australia and New Zealand. Harley and Walter Davidson spent three months on their tour. The group concluded that a lightweight single should be launched to satisfy these overseas markets.

Upon his return from Europe, Harley began to devote increasing time to a lawsuit threatened by the Eclipse company. During the teens, Eclipse had manufactured a motorcycle clutch that they sold to several motorcycle companies. Eclipse (later Bendix) accused Harley-Davidson of infringing various patented clutch features, beginning with the worm-actuated clutch introduced on the 1914 Harley-Davidson two-speed models and continuing through the present cam-actuated clutch.

The dialogue between the two companies became more intense. It became clear that Eclipse was interested in winning a judgment so large that Harley-Davidson wouldn't be able to pay. This would enable Eclipse to take control of the Harley-Davidson factory.

Side-valve strategy

In the next several weeks, meanwhile, the singles design strategy was established. There would be two types: overhead-valve sports models and side-valve economy models. The touring executives were impressed with the worldwide popularity of side-valve motorcycles and of course were painfully aware of Indian's success with side-valve motorcycles in America.

Side-valve evolution was a surprising success story. The side-valve concept had already lived beyond the expectations of many engineers, and yet side-valve progress hadn't leveled off.

A side-valve engine is a minor miracle. Think of it: The fuel-air charge comes through the inlet manifold, turns up through the inlet port into the combustion chamber, is ignited in an area off to the side of the cylinder bore, moves sideways and then down against the piston top, expends its energy and then moves up, sideways and down through the exhaust port. To make matters worse, if the compression ratio exceeds about 6.5:1, then the engine power falls off because of insufficient breathing.

Side-valve engines remained competitive because of constant experiments and small increments of progress in the shaping of combustion chambers. In the motorcycle field, some of the earliest successful experiments with combustion chamber contours occurred in the Indian and Norton organizations. Indian's work originated in the F-head days, as far back as 1911, according to British motorcycle historian Peter Hartley. Hartley credits Irish rider Charles B. Franklin with independently discovering the squish principle during a meet at the Brooklands track. Franklin migrated to the Indian engineering staff and became the dominant force, ultimately designing side-valve racers that were faster than the Harley-Davidson and Indian eight-valve overheads.

England's Norton marque had a reputation for building side-valve motors with above-average power.

Standard spark plug location is shown on this 1924 Sixty-one ridden by William Ottaway, racing boss during the glory years of Dodge City and the long board tracks. The 1924 Sixty-one cylinders were a new design. Note the new fore-and-aft head fins just inboard of the valve pocket. Wider 1924 forks didn't require a dished out section in the front fender. Fender ribs or crowns were deeper than before. Coach green striping was changed from a single center stripe to a double stripe on either side of the rib. Harley-Davidson

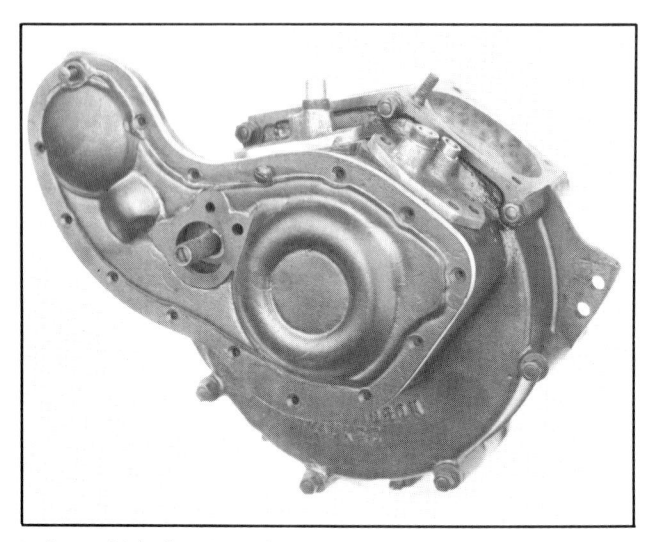

In late 1924, the Two Cam timing case was redesigned to provide removable lifter blocks that accommodated the new roller tappets. Valve action was directly from the cam lobes through the tappets. Because the pivoted lifter arms were eliminated, maximum rpm was increased. The motor number of this example is 27FHAD515. The black finish is nonstandard to suit owner John Cameron, who specializes in custom Two Cams. John Cameron

One of its rider-engineers, D. R. O'Donovan, tested single-speed side-valve Norton motors on the Brooklands course during the teens. Test results caused motors to be sorted into two groups, the Brooklands Specials (BSs), guaranteed to run 75 mph, and the Brooklands Road Specials (BRSs), guaranteed to run 70 mph. The intriguing thing here is that there was no way of predicting whether any particular motor would wind up as a BS or a BRS. The faster motors were just those that benefited in some yet-to-be-understood manner from the random results of the Norton foundry. In other words, the faster motors had the better cylinder heads, but whatever made them better was either unmeasurable or uncontrollable—or both. A subtle thing, this cylinder head shaping.

The best known of the side-valve experimenters was England's Harry Ricardo. In 1919, Ricardo patented what he called the squish principle, in which the combustion chamber was shaped so as to introduce turbulence during the compression stroke. The turbulence in turn produced more thorough combustion and increased power by keeping the fuel-air charge circulating around the spark plug area. British side-valve motorcycles of Ricardo heritage began to appear as 1921 models, with the motorcycle manufacturers' ad-

The old loop frame gave way to this lower and more graceful frame on the 1925 models. Front and rear downtubes terminate at their lower ends and are joined by an engine plate.

Acetylene lighting, front stand and luggage rack were common on export models. Note the auxiliary handclutch lever near the rear cylinder. Harley-Davidson

vertising hype implying that all of the invention was internal to their companies.

The surprising worldwide success of side-valve motors pushed Harley-Davidson toward the new side-valve singles. Indian's continuing side-valve excellence in America and Harley-Davidson's satisfaction with its side-valve singles would later steer Milwaukee to side-valve V-twins.

In mid 1924, New England sales representative Charles Cartwright paved the way for an unusual sale. The young communist government of the Soviet Union inquired about the purchase of 1,200 sidecar rigs on credit, and Cartwright traveled to New York City to listen to their proposal. Cartwright then arranged to have President Walter Davidson meet with the Soviets, and Walter agreed to the sale. Signing for the Soviets was a Mr. Karsov.

Two Cam racer update

The following hasn't been verified by factory records or photographs, but two long-time Two Cam enthusiasts assert that the next update to the Two Cam racers occurred in late 1924. The geometry of standard motors and earlier Two Cam motors required four pivoted cam followers, sometimes called roller arms or lifter arms. These roller arms on standard F-heads and earlier Two Cams transmitted the centralized lobe motion to the valves. The latest Two Cam setup did away with the roller arms—valves were operated almost directly from the lobes instead of indirectly through the rev-limiting roller arms.

The Two Cam lobe action passed through roller tappets on the way to the valves, but the tappets were relatively light and acted directly in line with the inlet pushrods and the exhaust valve stems. Two Cam enthusiasts refer to these last-generation examples as direct-action Two Cams. To further reduce reciprocating weight, the pushrods were hollow. The end result was extra rpm for the latest Two Cams. The outward appearance was different because the lifter blocks (through which passed the inlet pushrods and the exhaust valve stems) were bolted to the crankcase instead of cast in, as on earlier Two Cams.

One other 1924 happening is worth telling. Ethyl (leaded) gasoline was introduced, paving the way for high-performance overhead-valve engines that would later supplant the F-head and side-valve designs.

1925
New frame

The biggest change for 1925 was a new frame that lowered the saddle position 3 in. and permitted the use of more streamlined tanks. The front downtube terminated at its lower end instead of wrapping underneath the motor. Under the motor was a new steel channel. The battery was lowered and stood upright instead of slightly tilted. The new look added 25 lb., raising the unserviced weight to 405 lb.

The wider 1925 frame allowed wider 27x3½ in. tires in place of the former 28x3 in. tires. Both wheel and tire combinations listed were based on the outside diameter of the tires; wheel sizes from rim to rim were 22 in. through 1924 and 20 in. from 1925. New tubes used automobile-size valves instead of the smaller type, which made servicing easier. With the wider frame and an offset rear sprocket, tire chains could be used in snow or mud. The rear chainguard was wider, longer and more sturdily attached. The rear fender was also longer.

Up front, the forks had softer cushion and recoil springs. Handlebars were newly shaped, and the gearshift lever was moved forward. Tank filler caps were larger. Sixteen Alemite fittings were provided instead of twelve.

A new saddle was called the bucket type, meaning there was a concave shape instead of the old flat-topped bicycle saddle. A new saddle bracket enabled the rider to adjust the saddle to any of six positions. The seat post cushion spring was lengthened from 9 to 14 in.

The muffler was changed to a long one-piece tubular-shaped speedster type with internal baffles for quieter operation. A muffler cutout was maintained and was foot-operated. Sales literature claimed a "fine

Some 1925 models used the old-style clear headlight lens, as in this example. The fork-mounted cylindrical toolbox debuted. Front fender braces attach through the fork rockers instead of directly to the spring fork. The rider is factory representative E. C. Smith, later executive secretary of the American Motorcycle Association and de facto boss of American racing for many years. Harley-Davidson

Beginning with the 1925 models, the front downtube was "double butted," or "triple diameter." Harley-Davidson

The long, soft action of the seat post gave almost as much comfort as rear suspension. The clutch had six main springs. The primary drive was a single chain on all F-heads. Harley-Davidson

tone" for the muffler, although not clarifying if that was with the muffler in the muffled or cutout mode!

Several motor changes were made. The left crankcase was made thicker at the driveshaft hole to accommodate a longer sprocket shaft bearing. Accordingly, the primary chain was moved outward ⅝ in. The crankcase studs for the chainguard were improved.

Aluminum pistons had proven unreliable on the 1924 models, so for 1925, iron alloy pistons were fitted to 61 and 74 ci motors. The new pistons were claimed to be only slightly heavier than aluminum and included narrower and deeper piston rings to reduce ring friction. The piston and bevel-jointed rings were the same design and material as had been optional on the 1924 74 ci motors of Models FDCA, FDCB, JDCA and JDCB. For the first time in Harley-Davidson history, cast-iron pistons and step-joint rings were no longer available.

A new foot-operated compression release replaced the former twistgrip technique, which had combined with spark timing. Now riders could retard the spark timing to the maximum for slow running without bringing the compression release into effect. The Schebler Model H carburetor was standard, but the Schebler De Luxe and Zenith units remained optional. The De Luxe carburetor featured a new low-speed button that could be raised to either of two positions, one for cold starts and the other for an intermediate warmup position.

To mate with the wider motor, the transmission was widened by ⅝ in. The transmission case was reinforced on the drive side, and an oil drain plug was added so riders no longer had to remove the transmission in order to flush the case. A longer roller bearing was fitted to the main gear, and the mainshaft roller bearing was now Alemite-lubricated. To facilitate the use of the Alemite grease gun, an extended gearbox tube was provided on the left side. The transmission mainshaft was lengthened from 10 to 10⅜ in.

A new lower transmission bracket resulted in a lower kickstarter position, which was easier for short riders to use. The transmission's left main bronze bushing was improved, according to sales literature. This turned out to be a questionable improvement.

The new transmission bushing setup featured a double-diameter mainshaft that stepped down to the smaller diameter where the mainshaft passed through the main drive gear (or clutch gear). The bushing was made in two halves, then mounted on the mainshaft and

In August 1925, 21.35 ci, 350 cc racing began. The rider is Jim Davis, winner of many championship events. Harley-Davidson

Overhead-valve, electrically equipped BA models for export looked like this from 1926 through 1928, except that 1928 models had a front brake. Export equipment included front license plate, front stand and luggage rack. Harley-Davidson

keyed to the shaft. The bushing was turned down to fit into the main drive gear, then the crack where the two halves joined was filled with solder. From 1925 through 1930, there were numerous instances of the mainshaft breaking at the stepdown. Also, there was a number of cases where the bushing key sheared so that the bushing turned on the mainshaft. These problems eventually led to a redesign on the 1931 models.

Some 1925 models used the traditional clear headlight lens, but most were fitted with the new diffusing lens, as shown in factory literature. The diffusing lens had vertical ribs in the glass and remained a flat lens as opposed to convex. Other changes included adjustable headlight bracket supports, a longer and more reliable headlight switch, a clip on the rear fender to secure the taillight cable and a new brighter taillamp. A stronger and shorter rear stand was easier to use, and a new waterproof metal cover was put on the generator-mounted spark coil.

After unsuccessful attempts to resolve the Eclipse company's allegations of patent infringements, the affair progressed to a formal suit in the federal district court in Philadelphia. Hearings began in January.

Meanwhile, development of the 1926 model 350 cc, 21 ci (nominal figures) singles was nearly complete. Harley-Davidson was still pitting the Zenith and Schebler carburetor companies against each other. Accordingly, when the moment came to install a Schebler carburetor on a prototype single, William S. Harley was upset to learn that a boss on the crankcase prevented the fitting of any Schebler carburetors. Harley had already ordered the permanent metal patterns for the crankcase and cylinder, so engine redesign was out of the question.

Schebler carburetor engineer Maldwyn Jones, a former member of the Harley-Davidson racing team, was rushed to Milwaukee to investigate. Upon arrival, Jones noted a Zenith technician fitting a Zenith carburetor to a prototype. Jones did some rapid measurements of the prototype single and then abruptly left for Schebler, back in Indianapolis. Night and weekend work at Schebler enabled them to design and build a carburetor that would fit, and within less than a week Jones was back in Milwaukee showing Harley the new aluminum Schebler carburetor expressly built for the singles. Harley was impressed with that kind of know-how and determination, and that, plus competitive pricing, won Schebler the production contract for all future carburetors—twins as well as singles.

Production of the new line of 1926 model side-valve and overhead-valve road-going singles began on June 1. The 1926 side-valve and overhead-valve singles were aimed largely for Europe, Australia and New Zealand.

A big Milwaukee race meet on August 9 introduced the American public to the 21.35 ci, 350 cc racing class.

The overhead-valve, single-cylinder Harley-Davidson entrants were racing versions of the new line of 1926 model road-going singles currently being publicized. These racers specifically and to a certain extent all of the new-generation Harley-Davidson singles would become known as the Peashooters. The overhead-valve versions would make the most history, but the side-valve roadsters would far outsell them in the years ahead.

1926
Side-valve single introduction

Mindful of the Eclipse patent suit, Harley-Davidson took no chances with their new side-valve singles, introduced late in the summer of 1925. Design of the new side-valve cylinder heads was licensed by Harry Ricardo. Royalties paid to Ricardo insured Harley-Davidson against potential patent suits. Unlike the British companies that used Ricardo heads, Harley-Davidson went public with its heritage and boasted genuine Ricardo heads.

The 1926 singles had a nominal displacement of 21.35 ci, 350 cc—factory literature referred to them as either 21 ci or 350 cc machines. The bore and stroke of 2⅞x3¼ in. yielded an actual displacement of 21.10 ci, 345.74 cc. Models listed were the Model A side-valve with magneto and no lighting, Model B side-valve with battery ignition and lighting, Model AA overhead-valve with magneto ignition and no lighting, and Model BA overhead-valve with battery ignition and lighting. The frame, front forks and seat post of the new singles were along the lines of the big twins. Unlike the twins, how-

Specifications	
Year and models	1926 Models A, B, AA and BA
Engine	AA and BA: overhead-valve single; A and B: side-valve single
Bore and stroke	2⅞x3¼ in.
Displacement	21.10 ci, 345.73 cc
Horsepower	AA and BA: 12 bhp at 4000 rpm; A and B: 8 bhp at 4000 rpm
Gearbox	Three speed, sliding gear
Shift	Left hand
Clutch	Dry multidisk
Clutch operation	Left foot
Ignition	A and AA: magneto; B and BA: battery and coil
Electric lighting	A and AA: none; B and BA: yes
Wheelbase	56½ in.
Wheels	Clincher
Tires	26x3.30 in. (3.30x20 in. in modern usage)
Suspension	Front: leading link; rear: rigid
Weight	AA: 245 lb.; A: 251 lb.; BA: 263 lb.; B: 269 lb.
Seat height	28½ in.
Fuel consumption	50 mpg (estimated for all-around use), 80 mpg (advertised)
Top speed	AA and BA: 60 mph (estimated); A and B: 55 mph (estimated)

The side-valve Twenty-ones were better sellers than the overhead-valve models. The Twenty-ones had unpainted crankcases throughout production. The front fender is fully sprung—V-twins still had an unsprung front fender. The small lever on the front of the crankcase is the compression release. Harley-Davidson

61

This is the lowest priced version of the Twenty-one, the Model A without the generator. This example is equipped with acetylene lighting. "Accessory package" probably means this example was bound for a foreign market. Forty percent of Harley-Davidson production was exported during this era. Harley-Davidson

ever, the new singles had a fully sprung front fender, which was accomplished by mounting the fender braces to the rigid fork instead of the spring fork. Standard or shorter speedster handlebars were optional.

Rider's view of a 1926 single. The twins looked about the same from the cockpit. Harley-Davidson

Simplicity and strength of the singles were touted. Company advertising claimed only twenty minutes were required to remove the cylinder head, decarbonize and reinstall the head. The gear side featured a ⅞ in. phosphor-bronze bushing, and the sprocket side had a ⅞ in. roller bearing. The upper connecting rod bearing was $^{39}/_{64}$ in. in diameter, and the piston pin was of finely ground case-hardened steel.

Two cam gears with ¾ in. wide lobes acted directly on mushroom tappets. Each cam was integral with its cam gear. A port was provided in each cam gear that aligned with a companion port in the timing case cover at the proper time, allowing the crankcase pressure to be vented outside.

The singles had a cushion sprocket that used four rubber blocks between the sprocket hub and sprocket. Power was transmitted through a single-row primary chain covered by a sheet-metal guard. The clutch had a single centrally mounted large coil spring. The transmission was a three-speed sliding-gear type.

On electric Models B and BA, the single-unit electrical system was patterned after the big twin layout. The battery-equipped singles had a switch panel with a key lock and control levers, a feature that was also introduced on the big twins. Another feature common to both the singles and the twins was the use of balloon tires, the industry's term for the new fatter profile, lower pressure tires. Singles had 26x3.30 in. tires

(3.30x20 in. in modern usage), and twins had 27x3.85 in. tires (3.85x20 in.).

On the big twins, generator output was increased by a new armature with larger wires and larger brushes. A new automatic relay cutout provided generator control. The big twin battery had twice the capacity of previous batteries. These were the last twins available with an optional Zenith carburetor.

Harley-Davidson was arguing in court that their actuating cam introduced in late 1919 was fundamentally different from the earlier actuating worm. Eclipse was arguing that the actuating cam had a helical face and hence was fundamentally the same as the earlier actuating worm. To get away from Eclipse patent infringement claims, detail changes were incorporated in the 1926 big twin clutch. The actuating cam was discarded in favor of an actuating fork. The fork got its input from a pushing motion instead of a turning motion, as in the actuating cam layout.

The clutch arm motion was changed from vertical to horizontal. With the new clutch arm layout, there was no provision for a transmission lockout to prevent gear shifting without declutching. A new gearbox filler plug was mounted on the front right side of the gearbox for easier access.

Other changes to the 1926 V-twins included wider fenders, a new rustproofing process for wheel spokes and nipples, and a new muffler cutout that deflected gases away from both the rider and sidecar passenger.

Optional light color finishes were first offered on 1926 big twins. The light color was used throughout, except for pinstriping. Photos of these light-color motorcycles began to appear with increasing frequency in *The Harley-Davidson Enthusiast*. Occasionally the photo captions would mention white as the color, leaving up to conjecture the finish on machines with undescriptive captions. This is more than a little strange, since neither the sales catalogs nor the new-model editions of *The Harley-Davidson Enthusiast* mentioned the availability of optional finishes.

At about this time, Harley-Davidson became committed to a side-valve strategy for the next generation of twins. First priority was given to a middleweight model in order to compete with the highly popular 37 ci Indian Scout. In view of subsequent developments, it

Optional colors began to appear in 1926. Some were white, as noted by captions in The Harley-Davidson Enthusiast; *others were probably cream. Neither of these paint options were mentioned in sales catalogs, press releases or* The Enthusiast. Doug Wilson

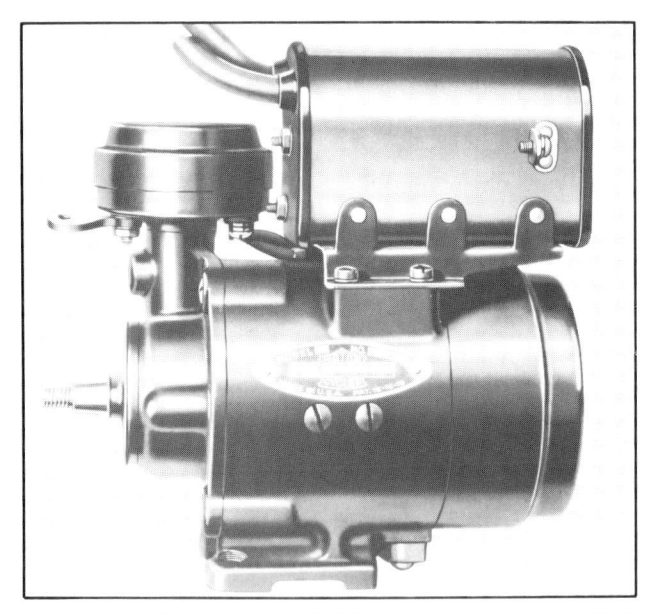

Harley-Davidson began to build its own generators in 1920. This is a 1927 example without the distributor. Harley-Davidson

seems probable that the original Harley-Davidson sidevalve middleweight was also a 37 ci model.

1927
Year of minimal changes

This was another year of minimal changes in the Harley-Davidson line. The most important change was the elimination of the distributor on the big twins. Sparks were now provided through a circuit breaker alone, which caused a waste spark to occur on the exhaust stroke of one cylinder while the working spark occurred on the compression stroke of the other cylinder. Harley-Davidson made much of its new distributorless ignition system because distributors and magnetos (which Indian used) had a reputation for giving trouble in wet weather. A catalog photo showed a man spraying water on the ignition system, and the caption claimed the elimination of the distributor had caused this happy waterproof state. Also, with the aim of improving reliability, the factory eliminated ten electrical connections.

An unexpected problem appeared on the prototype 1927 model twins with the new ignition system.

The distributor was eliminated on the 1927 models so that both spark plugs fired on every revolution. The system was claimed to be waterproof. This 1927 setup required new ignition-control adjustment—the old adjustment permitted the ignition to be retarded so much that the waste spark backfired through the carburetor. The lever in the arcuate slot, forward of oil pump, is the compression release. Harley-Davidson

Classic F-head lines are epitomized in this 1927 model. The year 1927 was the last year of olive-painted crankcases on V-twins. Harley-Davidson

Many kinds of commercial sidecars were tried in the 1920s, such as this 1927 bread outfit. Harley-Davidson

65

Backfiring was rampant when the motor was operated with fully retarded ignition. The preliminary diagnosis was that Schebler had built a bad batch of carburetors. Maldwyn Jones was called to Milwaukee and concluded the new ignition layout was the culprit. Because William S. Harley was skeptical, Jones made a special testing rig that enabled the rider to use or turn off the waste spark while riding. The waste spark was positively confirmed as the cause of the backfiring. The waste spark had been occurring so late on fully retarded ignition that combustion was occurring on the inlet stroke. To cure the problem, new factory adjustments prevented the rider from retarding the spark timing as much as had been possible on the earlier models.

The overhead-valve Models AA and BA singles received new Ricardo cylinder heads. A number of running changes were made to all singles without changing the part numbers. The muffler was changed to reduce back pressure. The frame was reinforced at several points. The gearbox bracket was changed to a drop-forged design. Saddles got a more pronounced bucket shape. Brake design was changed to incorporate a hinged band like the twins. The clutch spring was heavier. Fuel tanks were reinforced at several points. Crankcase lugs (mounting tabs) were larger. The foot-clutch-operating pedal was made adjustable. Relocation of the transmission oil drain plug made servicing easier. Additional standard equipment was provided with each new single: an Alemite grease gun, tire pump and adjustable wrench.

In October, a running change was made to 1928 Seventy-fours and singles. Pistons were changed from a three-ring to a two-ring design. The Sixty-ones continued to use three rings.

First public mention of the future 45 ci side-valve twin was by President Walter Davidson in his annual address to the stockholders in October. Davidson omitted any descriptive language other than to refer to the plans for a "small twin." Although targeted for an appearance at the forthcoming February 1928 show, development was behind schedule and the model wasn't expected to debut until later in the 1928 season. The sales forecast was 5,000 small twins per year.

The racing department built F-heads and Eight-valves throughout the 1920s. This 1927 Eight-valve racer has the direct-action Two Cam valve gear and unusual open-port cylinder heads, a style introduced in 1923. Three other styles of Eight-valves were built. These were the 1916 style with a four-lobe, single-camshaft base, a standard timing cover and conventional dual exhaust ports; the 1919 style with a Two Cam base, banjo cover and conventional dual exhaust ports; and the 1921 style with a Two Cam base, banjo cover and moderately elongated and somewhat triangular open exhaust ports. Harley-Davidson

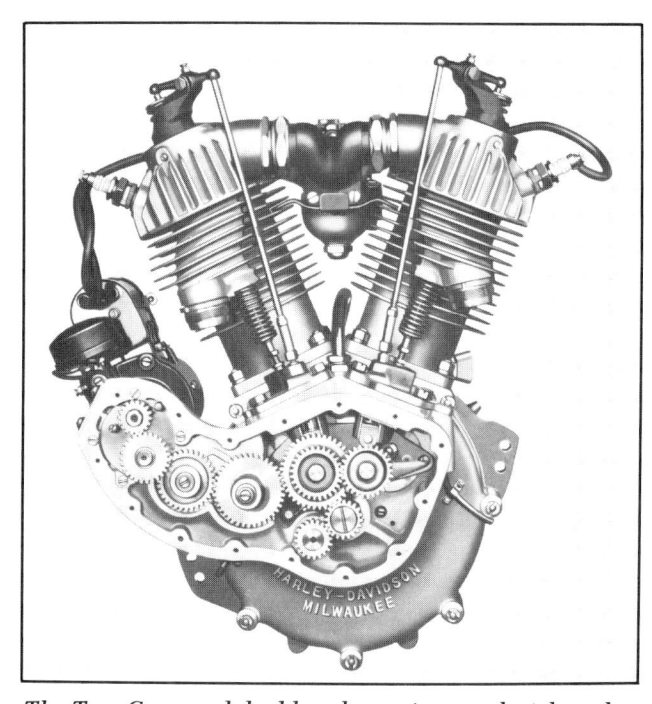

The Two Cam used double valve springs on the inlet valves and had no inlet pushrod springs. Two Cam exhaust valve springs were uncovered. Note that the eleven cylinder cooling fins are of uniform diameter from top to bottom, which means this is a 74 ci motor. The 61 ci Two Cam motors had the six top fins of uniform diameter and the five bottom fins gradually tapering in diameter. Harley-Davidson

In November, another running change was made, this time to both the Sixty-ones and Seventy-fours. A bracket was eliminated on the oil pump control to minimize the likelihood of riders catching their pants leg on the pump during kickover.

At least one Eight-valve was built in 1927, to the 1923 configuration. A photo of this motorcycle is in the Harley-Davidson archives.

1928
Production Two Cams

The highlights of the 1928 line were the new 61 ci and 74 ci Models JH and JDH, known as the Two Cam Sixty-one and the Two Cam Seventy-four. The Two Cam models were announced in November 1927, too late to appear in the 1928 model catalog. Although a new public offering, the two-cam principle had been used in racing and hillclimbing motors since 1919, but two-cammers had only been available to the factory team and to a few favored dealers.

The new road-going Two Cams used a direct-action valve gear, with cam lobes acting through tappets instead of roller arms. This was the current racing configuration, introduced in late 1924. The Two Cam jobs used narrower tanks than standard twins and 18 in. wheels instead of 20 in.

The 1928–1929 Two Cam models had removable lifter blocks that had a raised section that routed oil back to the crankcase. Oil return from the front lifter block was routed through a channel in the lower part of the block to the flat surface on the front of the timing case, from which the oil fell back into the timing case. Rear lifter block return was the same setup. This motor number is 29JDH12528H. John Cameron

The 1928 Two Cam JDH Seventy-four. Two Cam models featured smaller tanks with a 4.75 gal. capacity instead of 5.3 gal. Special Sport Solos (with one cam gear) also used the smaller tanks. In all of its glory, the JDH was one of the world's fastest standard motorcycles in 1928, capable of an honest 85 mph in standard trim and 100 mph with tender loving care. Harley-Davidson

No, cylinder heads weren't removable on the Two Cams—or any F-heads. Owner John Cameron sawed this one off as part of an experiment. The timing plug can be seen in the middle of the combustion chamber roof. John Cameron

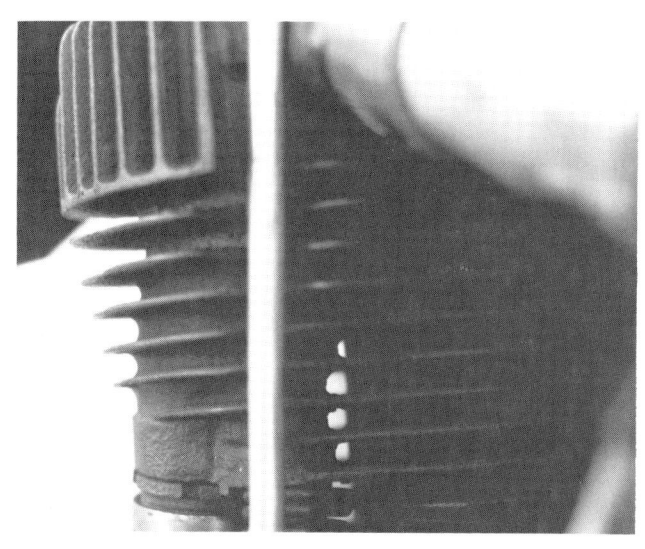

This closeup of a cylinder shows the cooling fins wrapped around both the valve pocket and the cylinder proper, and air channels. These features made their debut in 1928. John Cameron

For sporting riders not willing to go the Two Cam route, there were the new Special Sport Solo models, the 61 ci JL and 74 ci JDL. The L motors were high-performance versions of the standard (one-cam) motors that featured larger inlet valves and valve cages. Like the Two Cam models, the Special Sport Solo models had narrower tanks that gave an impression of nimbleness and 18 in. wheels that lowered the saddle height about 1 in. Shorter roadster handlebars were standard on both the Two Cams and the Special Sport Solos.

The Riccy, or Riccy chip, a bronze plug threaded through the timing plug hole of the F-heads. Lots of compression and lots of power! John Cameron

Graduated sizes of cylinder barrel cooling fins were a feature of the racing 61 ci Two Cams. The road model 61 ci JL, not a Two Cam, mimicked the racing look with the same style of barrels. Oddly, no other road-model twins featured the racing-style barrels. The black engine finish on John Cameron's motorcycle is non-standard. John Cameron

The 74 ci JDL used standard cylinder barrels, but the 61 ci JL had cylinder barrels that mimicked the appearance of the 61 ci racing Two Cams by having tapered cylinder cooling fins. On the JL, the cooling fins were larger at the top of the cylinder and progressively smaller toward the bottom of the cylinder.

For those with good factory connections, there was still another high-performance variant, available only in the 61 ci displacement. Designer Harry Ricardo had a hand in the development of Harley-Davidson team racers. Among Ricardo's legacies was a special F-head cylinder design that not only enhanced combustion turbulence but raised the compression ratio to the then spectacular level of 10:1! Operation required special fuels such as benzol. These Ricardo head cylinders were sold in limited numbers to favored dealers for use in local races, speed runs and hillclimbs. The Ricardo Sixty-ones had tapered cooling fins, as on the 61 ci F-head JL.

The Two Cam Sixty-one and Seventy-four and the Special Sport Solos were fitted with Dow metal (magnesium alloy) pistons. These Dow metal pistons were domed, which raised the compression ratio. The Dow metal piston twins were fitted with two kinds of new and unique piston rings as well as with the standard narrow compression rings found on other motorcycles. Two pairs of thick guide rings were fitted to each Dow metal piston on the twins, one pair near the bottom of

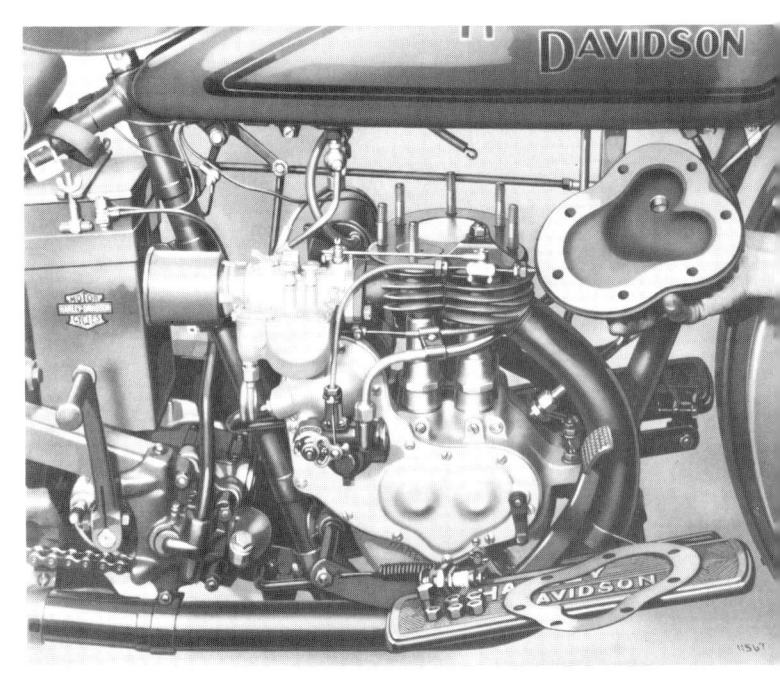

The message here is that the singles were easy to maintain. Harley-Davidson claimed that only twenty minutes was required to remove the cylinder head, scrape out the carbon, reassemble and ride away. Harley-Davidson

the skirt and the other pair below the compression rings.

The guide rings weren't rings in the ordinary sense of the term. This takes a little explaining. A better name

A throttle-controlled oil pump was introduced on the 1928 models. The factory sometimes called this the all-speed oiler. Harley-Davidson

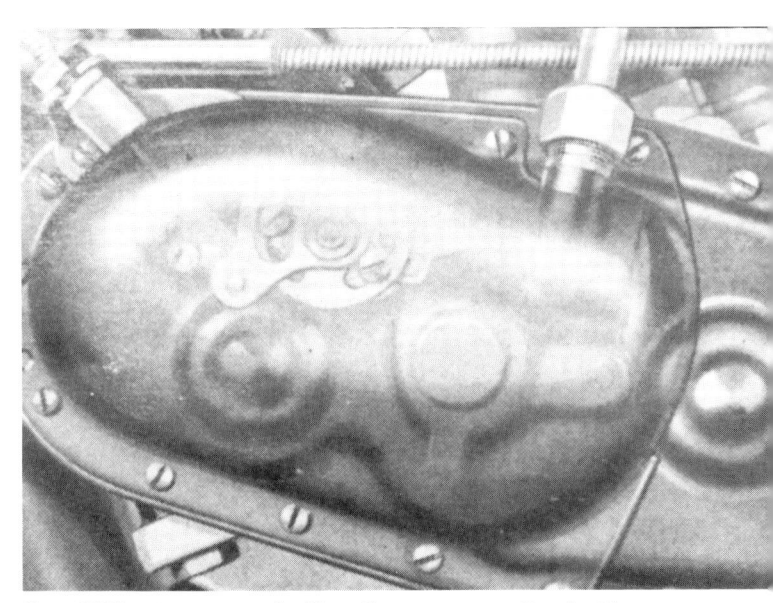

Late 1928 twins, except the Two Cams, were outfitted with a cover over the oil control to prevent damage during falls. Harley-Davidson advertised this as a new feature in the 1929 model sales literature. Harley-Davidson

The 1928 and 1929 Seventy-fours had new-style cylinder head finning. The fore-and-aft fins adjacent to the valve pocket were extended completely over the head. Also new to both the Seventy-fours and the Sixty-ones was the carryover of horizontal valve pocket fins to the cylinder proper. Between each horizontal fin, air channels separated the valve pocket and the cylinder. Troy Ross

for these guide rings would be guide half-rings. Each pair of guide rings looked like a regular piston ring that had been cut in two equal halves. Thus, each guide ring wrapped around slightly less than half the piston circumference, and a pair of these rings went into each piston ring groove. The guide rings measured 7/32 in. from top to bottom and 1/8 in. from outside circumference to inside circumference.

Behind each guide ring (or pair of half-rings) was a cushion ring, sometimes referred to as an expander ring. The cushion ring was no more a ring than the guide ring. Each cushion ring was like a hexagon opened on one corner. When a cushion ring was placed behind a guide ring, the cushion ring was compressed into shape—the open hexagon became a true hexagon. When thus installed, each closed cushion ring tried to open up, which resulted in a continuous load being placed against each guide ring. In effect, the two pairs of guide rings assumed most of the bearing load of each piston.

This principle proved quite satisfactory and was continued until the advent of the T-slot pistons in late 1934 models. Dealers liked the setup because a motor could be restored to new clearances simply by replacing worn guide rings and tired cushion rings. This was particularly important because reboring of tapered Harley-Davidson cylinders was an expensive process,

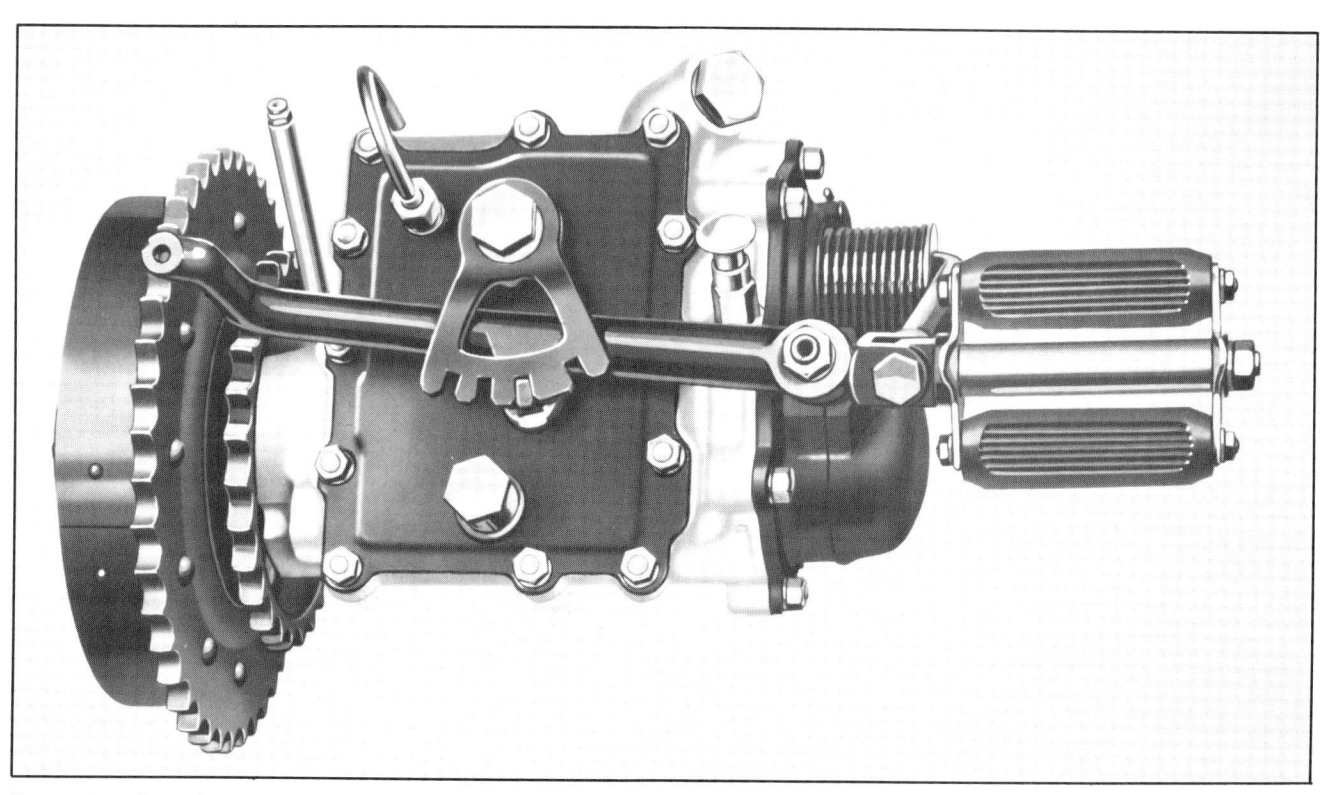

From 1915 through 1925, three-speed models had a vertical clutch arm and a gear-clutch interlock. The long horizontal clutch arm debuted on the 1926 transmission, but without the gear-clutch interlock. The interlock returned on the 1928 transmission, as shown here. Harley-Davidson

done either at the factory or at independent shops with this unusual capability. The only drawback to the guide rings and cushion rings arrangement was additional running noise. The overhead-valve singles also used guide rings and cushion rings. Less sporting 1928 twins and singles continued to use ordinary iron alloy pistons.

American riders believed front wheel brakes were unnecessary and even dangerous on the predominantly unpaved roads of the United States. But paved mileage was increasing rapidly, so Harley-Davidson introduced its first front wheel brake on the big twins in 1928. Even so, American design philosophy continued to consider the front wheel brake an auxiliary device, and one that should be used sparingly. Accordingly, neither Harley-Davidson nor its domestic rivals gave much attention to making front wheel brakes really strong. Incidentally, Indian also brought out its first front wheel brake in 1928. Midway through 1928 model production, an additional front wheel brake return spring was added to make the brake action more positive.

Speaking of wheels, Harley-Davidson introduced larger rear wheel spokes as a running change on 1928 models. The larger rear wheel spokes were fitted to all machines shipped after January 1, 1928.

An important 1928 big twin motor change was the introduction of a throttle-controlled oil pump. Oil mileage varied widely depending on speed, so a throttle control took some of the guesswork out of keeping the motor properly oiled. The throttle control mechanism was exposed to the elements and potential fall damage on the early 1928 models; late 1928 models featured an oil control cover. Another first was the new air cleaner.

A gearshift lock gate on the big twins precluded the gears from being shifted without clutching. This feature originally appeared on the 1915 models, but had been absent on the 1926 and 1927 models due to the redesigned clutch arm.

Harley-Davidson began flirting this year with the idea of building the four-cylinder Cleveland motorcycle. Cleveland was discouraged and late in the year offered to sell out to Harley-Davidson. This was an interesting proposition, for in 1927 Indian had done that trick with the Ace Four, now called the Indian Four. However, the founders decided to pursue their own plans for four-cylinder production, so in December Harley-Davidson notified Cleveland that it was not interested in purchasing the Cleveland plant.

The 1928 singles shared the new big twin features of a front wheel brake, throttle-controlled oil pump and air cleaner. Singles fenders were wider, and the rear fender was hinged. New front and rear chains were wider, 5/16 in. instead of 1/4 in., but had shorter pitch, 1/2 in. instead of 5/8 in. On the side-valve singles, Dow metal pistons were introduced as standard equipment.

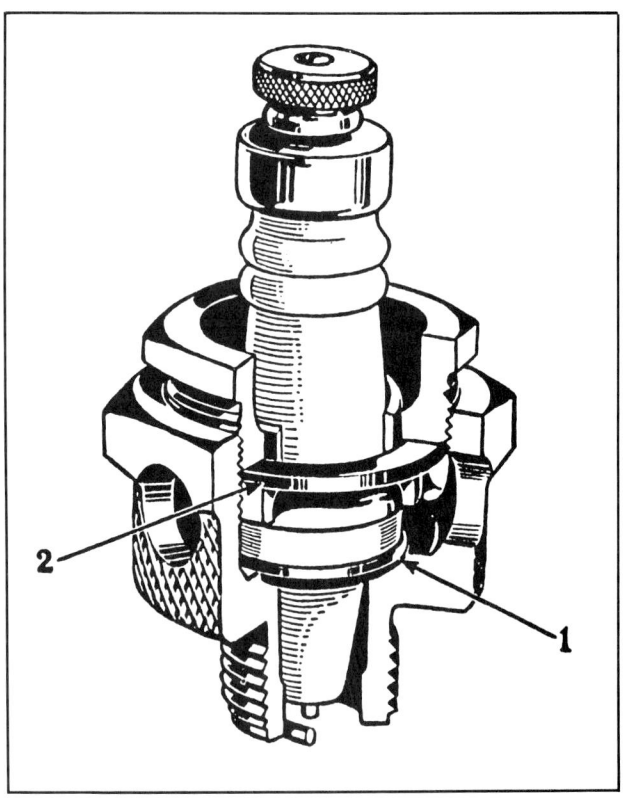

Spark plugs were three-piece, consisting of the body, the porcelain and the locknut. Heat flowed from the porcelain through the copper gasket (1) to the plug body. Although three-piece plugs worked well in water-cooled engines, the higher heat of air-cooled motors caused the body to expand, which loosened the locknut and broke the path of heat transfer to the body and the cylinder head. Harley-Davidson solved this problem with the new 1928 air-cooled spark plug shown here. Besides enlarging the body and providing holes for airflow, the new air-cooled spark plug had a large spring steel washer (2), which kept fairly constant pressure on the copper gasket even when the body expanded from heat. These plugs were made in 18 mm and the older 7/8 in. sizes, and in three heat ranges. Porcelains were made by Champion. Information from Connie Schlemmer. Harley-Davidson

The air cleaner was new for 1928. The rear cylinder primer cup had to be relocated rearward to gain access around the air cleaner. Harley-Davidson

Meanwhile, the overhead-valve singles continued with aluminum pistons.

A nineteen-tooth cushion motor sprocket replaced the earlier thirteen-tooth version. A new cushioning mechanism consisted of eight rubber blocks installed between the inner hub and the outer sprocket—the earlier layout used only four rubber blocks. A forty-six-tooth clutch sprocket replaced the earlier thirty-six-tooth clutch sprocket. The transmission sprocket was changed from fifteen teeth to nineteen teeth, and the rear sprocket changed from thirty-four teeth to forty-seven teeth. Sprocket sizes hardly changed because sprocket teeth were smaller to work with the new shorter pitch chains. The new sprocket combinations resulted in slightly taller gearing, a 5.99:1 ratio instead of a 6.28:1 ratio.

Two sequences of running changes were made on the inlet valve mechanism of all big twins. In mid 1928, the inlet rocker arms were changed to incorporate a larger diameter bushing (fulcrum). Later 1928 two-cam motors were given rocker arms with a still larger bushing.

Optional colors

Here's a curious piece of Harley-Davidson history. As earlier noted, beginning in 1926, new Harley-Davidson big twins could be special-ordered with white finish and possibly with other light color finishes such as cream. Although not mentioned in sales catalogs or in the new-model editions of *The Harley-Davidson Enthusiast*, many additional extra-cost special-order finishes were available beginning in 1928. The factory service bulletin, *Shop Dope*, number 423, dated April 9, 1928, lists the following "standard optional colors" for a $3 surcharge on twins: coach green, azure blue, police blue and maroon. Cream or white could be obtained on twins for a $27 surcharge. "All other colors" bore a $24 surcharge on twins. Surcharges for singles were slightly less for each category.

Many Harley-Davidsons were finished in two main colors, some with contrasting tank panels and fender

During 1928, Harley-Davidson considered buying out the Cleveland Motorcycle Manufacturing Company, builders of this in-line four. Indian did such a maneuver in 1927, when they bought out the Ace Four and reintroduced it as the Indian Ace, which later became the Indian Four. Cleveland Motorcycle Company

centers, others with only the contrasting tank panels. There is no mention of two-color finishes in the sales catalogs or in the new-model editions of *The Harley-Davidson Enthusiast*, but two-color V-twins and singles are featured throughout the pages of the magazine from 1928 on. The standard olive green finish is easy to spot in black-and-white photos, so it's obvious that many of the two-color jobs were olive green with contrasting tank panels—probably cream or white—or with both contrasting tank panels and fender centers. Some two-color models appear to be white with darker panels and fender centers; others appear to be black or dark blue with light-color panels and fender centers.

Here's the biggest scoop of all: The 1928 (and probably later) Harley-Davidsons could be special-ordered with any—repeat, any—color or colors. Several "standard optional colors" were stocked, including black as well as the previously mentioned colors. Moreover, arrangements could also be made through the local dealer to special order any color of finish. Remember the phrase "all other colors" in the *Shop Dope*? To underscore the any-color(s) option, the Harley-Davidson exhibit at the 1928 New York City motorcycle show featured motorcycles in the following colors: peach-and-rose combination, robin's egg blue, red and purple—yes, purple. This information comes from *The Harley-Davidson Enthusiast* for March 1928.

1929
Two Cam tuning and Eclipse settlement

For 1929, changes to the 61 and 74 ci F-head twins were minimal. All big twins got the inlet rocker arms with larger bushings, which had been phased in on late 1928 Two Cam models. Inlet housing caps—the fulcrum for the rockers—were beefed up on the standard twins. To combat oil leakage, inlet pushrod assemblies of the standard twins were revised to include a felt washer and retainer cap on the lower end. Front and rear cam gears and bushings were new for the two-cam motors. A four-tube muffler was introduced. An oiler cover (phased in on late 1928s) and oiler cover cap were added to the standard and L models. In midyear, com-

Another of the almost endless variety of commercial rigs, this one is a 1928 version. The front brake was a new feature on all twins and singles. Harley-Davidson

73

mercial models were fitted with larger front wheel spokes.

Dow metal pistons became standard in the overhead-valve singles, (side-valve singles got this feature in 1928). On all singles, the clutch spring layout was changed. The single centrally mounted large coil spring was replaced by twelve small coil springs dispersed around the clutch circumference. During the 1929 model production run, these twelve springs were replaced by fourteen smaller but longer springs.

Styling highlights for all models included the new twin bullet headlights and the four-tube muffler. The four-tube muffler was quieter than earlier mufflers, yet the large muffler volume meant that power didn't suffer. In fact, riders were cautioned not to open up the tailpipes because this would only increase noise without increasing power, and power could even be reduced by the extra decibels. Motorcycle riders at England's big concrete racetrack, Brooklands, had learned the same lesson when forced to adopt large mufflers on their racing mounts. Harley-Davidson anticipated a demand for the four-tube muffler on earlier models, and therefore brackets were designed to enable riders to fit the four-tube muffler to 1925–1928 twins and singles. However, riders of these earlier models probably weren't eager to give up their noise.

The standard color remained the familiar olive green with maroon striping centered in gold and edged in black. "Standard optional colors" for 1929 were azure blue, police blue, coach green, maroon, fawn grey, cream and orange. The availability of optional paint schemes continued to be undiscussed in sales catalogs and in *The Harley-Davidson Enthusiast*, although the latter included many photos of motorcycles with special one- and two-color finishes. Many of the two-color jobs had olive green as the primary color. Based on resurrected unrestored motorcycles of the era, one of

These lovelies were shown at the 1928 New York Motorcycle Show. Note the special paint job of the motorcycle on the left. Although not mentioned in sales catalogs or in the new-model editions of The Harley-Davidson Enthusiast, *extra-cost, special-order finishes were available beginning in 1926. Harley-Davidson*

This phantom view of the parallelogram forks on this 1929 model shows the long springs that were the secret of the soft ride. England's Brough-Superior used practically identical forks under the Castle trade name. Steering was light and positive. Rigid fork members were beefed up in 1928 to withstand brake loads. Pre 1928 forks could not be satisfactorily modified to add a front brake. Harley-Davidson

the more popular combinations was olive green with orange tank panels and fender centers. Presumably, any combination of the "standard optional colors" could be used in the two-color finishes—maroon and cream, for example. Information on optional colors was confined to a periodic assessories bulletin mailed to dealers.

New standard or solo handlebars were optional on F-heads. Singles had standard or speedster bars.

Sporting road riders had gradually raised the Two Cam model's power to levels well beyond that of stock Two Cams and road model Indians. Two approaches were used. Some obtained genuine Ricardo 61 ci cylinders and combined them with a Seventy-four crankshaft to obtain 68.9 ci. Compression plates, shorter pistons or both were necessary to keep the piston from topping out against the combustion chamber roof and also to lower the compression ratio from the racing level of 10:1 to something more manageable on the road.

There weren't many of the genuine Ricardo racing cylinders available, so an ingenious substitute was

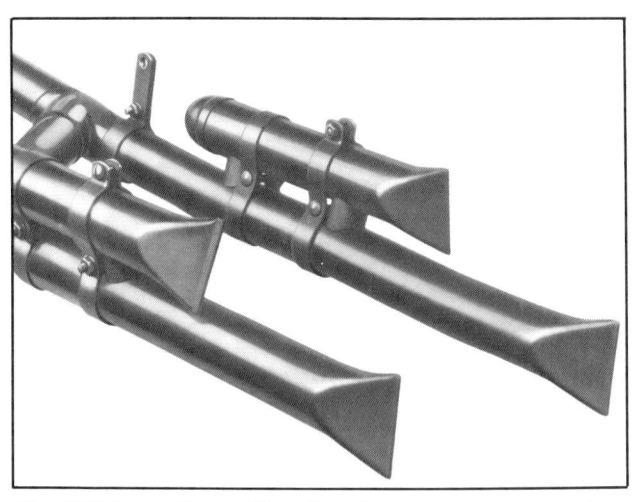

The 1929 four-tube muffler offered quieter operation without a performance penalty. A retrofit kit was available to fit the four-tube mufflers to earlier models, but demand was slight because the four-tube mufflers were too quiet. The four-tube muffler was dropped from 1930 production. Harley-Davidson

The 1929 JD assembly line. The assembly line process was installed sometime after 1920. This photo was taken in late 1928. Harley-Davidson

devised by Two Cam fans looking for extra power. To get maximum power from the regular 74 ci cylinders, a bronze insert called a Riccy chip or simply a Riccy was placed in the combustion chamber. The Riccy name was in honor of Ricardo, who had developed the insert technique for experimentation prior to settling on the final configuration of the 61 ci Ricardo cylinders.

The Riccy was a precisely shaped mass of bronze about the size of the palm of your hand. The combustion chamber casting of all F-heads had a hole directly over the center of the cylinder bore. A threaded plug was screwed into this hole for operation. The plug was removed to set the timing of the motor by measuring the distance of the piston from top dead center. The Riccy was molded around a stud that was bolted to the roof of the combustion chamber through the timing hole. The beauty of the Riccy was the ability of the tuner to vary the size and shape of the insert to achieve the desired result, which made casting and recasting of cylinders unnecessary. For the factory and for Ricardo, the Riccy had been a convenience. For home-grown tuning, the Riccy was more than a convenience—it gave tuners the ability to achieve high performance without the prohibitive expense of doing their own trial-and-error casting and recasting. With the Riccy modification and 6.5:1 compression ratio, the Two Cam Seventy-fours produced 50 hp at 5000 rpm.

On February 11, Harley-Davidson settled its long-running battle with Eclipse: Harley-Davidson paid Eclipse $1,100,000—in cash. This was a staggering sum in those days and no doubt was a bitter experience for the four founders, who in effect paid the settlement from their hard-earned personal stakes. Characteristically, the founders had planned ahead, so the prompt payment ended Eclipse's hope of taking over Harley-Davidson.

In September, Sales Manager Arthur Davidson recommended purchasing the Cleveland Four, patterns and all. A Cleveland Four was already in the factory for study. Engineering Chief William S. Harley favored hiring Cleveland's former designer, Everett DeLong, and giving DeLong a free hand in either updating the Cleveland Four or creating an entirely new Harley-Davidson four-cylinder model. Harley won the point, and DeLong was subsequently hired by Harley-Davidson.

Swan song for the Two Cam. Half of the unusual four-tube muffler is seen in this view of a fully equipped model. Harley-Davidson

During 1928 and 1929, the engineering and production staffs were extremely busy planning and implementing the new 45 and 74 ci side-valve twins that would last for a generation. The 21 ci singles enjoyed their last boom year in 1929 due to tariff walls being erected. As for the F-heads, 1929 was their swan song.

Dog eat dog

The F-heads had proven good enough to survive twenty-seven years—no small feat in those dog-eat-dog days. Many other companies had built motorcycles that were better on paper—Feilbach, Merkel, Pope, and Cyclone, for example. The Feilbach Limited, another Milwaukee product, was available with shaft drive in 1914, but the company went broke in 1915. The Flying Merkel used a telescopic front fork and a swinging-arm rear suspension from 1909 until production ceased in 1915. Pope used overhead-valve engines from 1913 until it folded in 1918. From 1913 through 1915, Cyclone reaped considerable publicity from its racing exploits with overhead-cam motorcycles. The beautiful gear-driven overhead-cam design was also included in its standard road models from 1913 through to the company's collapse in late 1916.

By 1929, only Excelsior and Indian remained strong rivals to Harley-Davidson. Excelsior's Super-X was an impressive sporting middleweight, but the Excelsior company couldn't operate its Chicago factory as efficiently as its Milwaukee and Springfield rivals. So the midsize 45 ci, 750 cc Super-X wore a higher price tag than the 61 ci, 1000 cc Harleys and Indians.

Indian had plenty of clout, but failed hugely in letting Harley-Davidson catch up with it. Among Indian's past mistakes was a proliferation of designs, including three models that lasted only one season: a belt-drive model with a complicated planetary gear pulley, an electric-start twin and a two-stroke single; a horizontally opposed twin lasted only three seasons. Those design and marketing errors were back in the 1910s, along with bad management that yielded huge losses on World War I military contracts and cost Springfield valuable dealerships. Indian's mistakes of the 1910s allowed Harley-Davidson to grow more rapidly than Indian during the critical era of weeding out the weaker companies like Merkel and Cyclone. In 1929, bad management was still the rule at the Wigwam—Indian wasn't producing to capacity despite the popularity of its Series 101 Scout.

So others had built better motorcycles on paper or had built better motorcycles that were uncompetitively priced or had built better motorcycles but in numbers too low to matter. Harley-Davidson was continuing to beat its rivals in the real world. The real world calls for practical results measured in performance, reliability and dealer support, so that riders stay happy long after they ride away on their brand-new motorcycles. Harley-Davidson had done the job, largely because it knew it had two sets of customers: dealers and riders. Dealers liked handling Harley-Davidsons, and they were able to operate efficiently because of steady management direction in Milwaukee. Riders liked owning Harley-Davidsons and had that satisfaction reinforced by good dealerships.

For Harley-Davidson, there was no time to rest on laurels, for ahead lay the continuing challenge of staying in business. This challenge would soon prove more difficult than Harley and the three Davidsons could imagine.

Chapter 3

1928–1932

Side-valve strategy

Development of the Harley-Davidson 45 ci twin probably began in 1926 at a time when the trendy British market was about evenly divided between the side valves and the increasingly popular overhead valves. Since overhead valves were the coming thing, why did Harley-Davidson switch from F-heads to side valves on its big twins? Because in the United States, Indian had redefined the technical balance with its line of highly successful 45 ci Scouts and 61 and 74 ci Chiefs, all with side-valve layout.

Over here, the switch to overhead valves in motorcycles seemed a long way off, partly because Indian side-valve racers had frequently shown their backsides to both Harley-Davidson and Indian overhead-valve racers. Although racing was important advertising in the United States, riders didn't measure engine efficiency in terms of power per cubic inch. The emphasis on big twins meant there was always power to spare in road models, so the cubic capacity was considered another variable for the designer. In other words, an

The 1929 45 ci, 750 cc side-valve twin, commonly referred to as the Forty-five. Harley-Davidson

American rider of a 74 ci, 1200 cc side-valve twin wouldn't be embarrassed to compare the performance of his mount to that of a 61 ci, 1000 cc overhead-valve twin. Performance on the road was the ultimate measurement, and from this standpoint side-valve motorcycles offered more than enough power while avoiding the problems peculiar to overhead-valve designs.

What were the problems of overhead-valve motors in the 1920s? For openers, they were noisy and messy. Manufacturing technology hadn't yet produced highly reliable valves and valve springs, so designers of overhead-valve motorcycles left the valve stems and springs exposed. The idea was to get plenty of cooling air on the valves and springs to prolong life. Motorcyclists regarded sporty exhaust pipes as musical, but valve gear sounds were just noise—noise that seemed to say things hadn't been properly thought out and put together. Because the valve stems and rocker arms were

General compactness is evident. Standard finish was olive with maroon stripes edged in black and centered in gold. A few 1929 Forty-fives and F-heads were sold with light-colored tank panels, but sales catalogs and The Enthusiast *didn't mention this option. Some models were finished in all white, another unpublicized alternative. Harley-Davidson*

79

exposed, the overhead-valve motors were noisy. As for messiness, even a new overhead would become covered with oil mist that made its way up through the valve guides. Once wear set in, there were running leaks through the guides.

Riders were also concerned about the possibility of dropping a valve in an overhead-valve motor. With an overhead-valve motorcycle, a failed valve would usually jam against the piston and stop the entire works after causing considerable damage. This wasn't a concern with a side-valve twin and in fact, a rider could thump home on one cylinder and replace only the failed valve. With an overhead-valve motorcycle, failures could also include a piston and a cylinder. Even worse, things could lock up suddenly enough to bend rods and break chains and gear teeth.

The Indian side-valve models were proving more civilized and as fast as the Harley-Davidson F-heads. A Harley-Davidson move to overhead valves would yield a performance improvement, but at the cost of magnifying the noise and mess complaints already leveled at the F-heads. The F-heads were beginning to take on an antique look. So to leave that image behind and respond to the American market, the Harley-Davidson switch to side-valve big twin layout was a logical course in 1926 when the engineering began.

Factory literature characteristically termed the middleweights simply 45. In conversation, the people

The unusual vertical generator next to the rider's left foot led Indian fans to scornfully label this model as the three-cylinder Harley. The left half of the four-tube muffler is shown. Harley-Davidson

who designed, built, sold, rode and raced these middleweights of Harley-Davidson, Indian and Excelsior manufacture always spoke of them as Forty-fives and never as Four-Fives.

1928
Debut of the Forty-five

Production of Forty-fives began in July 1928, but moved along at half the normal pace because of various technical problems. On the earliest Forty-fives, there was shearing of the key securing the countershaft sprocket to the countershaft. This problem was solved almost immediately by cutting a deeper key slot and fitting a larger key.

On the first few hundred Forty-fives, there were no lock washers for the inner front chainguard screws. In a few cases, the screws dropped out and damaged the chain, sprocket or both. Lock washers were added to production line procedures during August.

Initial production was confined to Model D machines, which had a 4.3:1 compression ratio, a ¾ in. venturi and a thirty-tooth rear sprocket. In early September, the factory began to assemble Model DL motorcycles with a 5:1 compression ratio, a ⅞ in. venturi and a twenty-eight-tooth rear sprocket.

A crossover shaft and bevel gear were used to drive the vertically mounted generator on the left side of the motor. On some early Forty-fives, the crossover shaft backed out of the left-side bevel gear and forced the right side of the shaft against the gearcase cover, resulting in a squeaking noise. This problem was cured in early September, effective with motor 29D3404, by pinning the bevel gear to the left end of the shaft.

Also effective with motor 29D3404 was a change to the crossover shaft bearing. Earlier Forty-five motors had the right end of the shaft turning in an unbushed hole—just a hole reamed out in the aluminum. This hole sometimes enlarged, and the resulting wobbly shaft action produced a bad clatter when accelerating from low speeds. The new setup featured a bronze bushing to support the right end of the shaft.

As originally equipped, the Forty-fives had a three-piece generator driveshaft consisting of two shafts and a coupling. This was handy for racing, hillclimbing and field meets because the generator drive gear could be easily removed after a cover was lifted. Manufacturing tolerances resulted in looseness in the fit of these three parts, however, and sometimes the combination of these three loose fittings caused excessive gear noise. The factory cured the noise problem by switching to a one-piece generator drive beginning in November 1928.

In some of the earliest Forty-fives, the oil slot in the end of the crankpin (crankshaft) extended a little too far out into the bearing, which resulted in inadequate oiling. This production error was eliminated by November 1928.

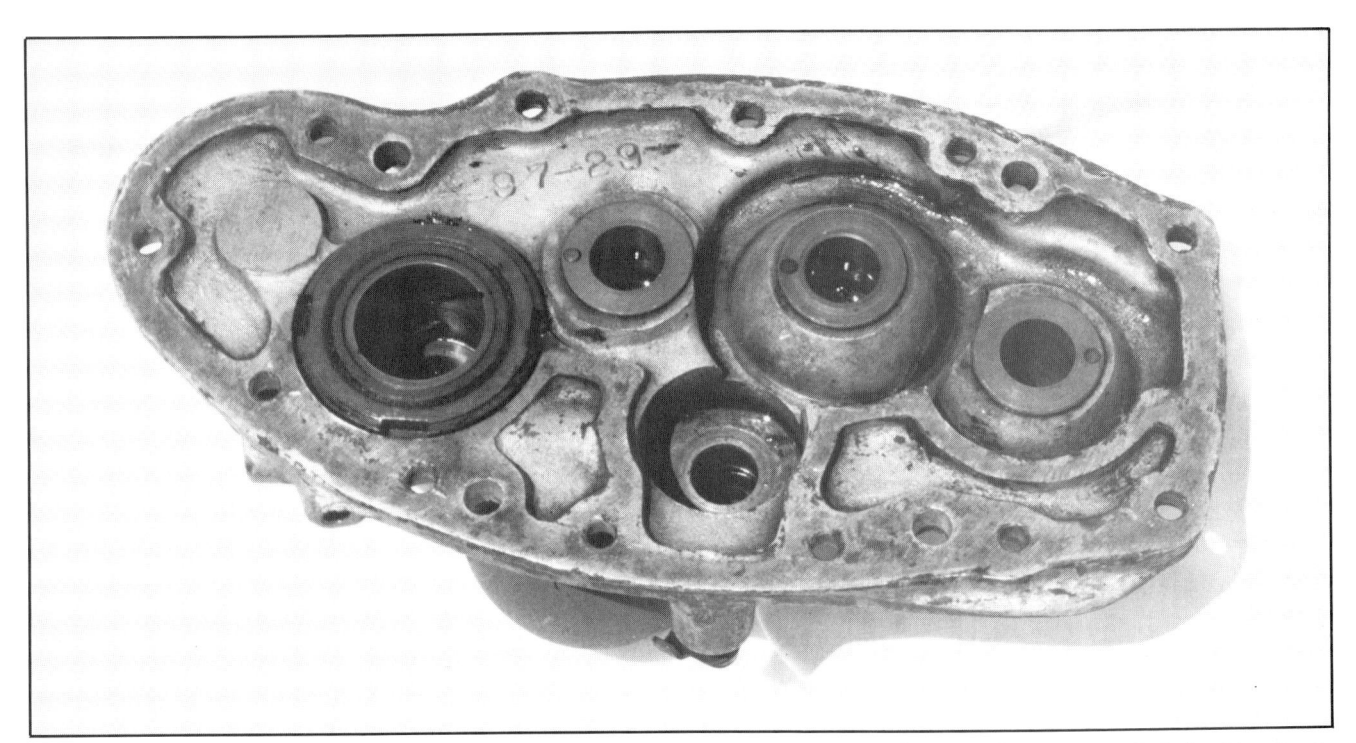

Crankcase breathing on the Forty-five differed from the F-heads with full baffles under each cylinder. Air-oil mist was transmitted through the hollow inlet camgear shafts, out through shaft ports, which registered with the bushing ports shown here, to the ported generator shaft bushing in the crankcase then alongside the horizontal generator driveshaft, to the left-side generator bevel gear housing and then through a relief tube into the primary chain guard. Troy Ross

Idling and low-speed running of early Forty-fives were poor. This was also cured by November by switching to cylinder heads with an oil deflector "dam" around the spark plug that prevented the plug from becoming oil-fouled. Swapping to the new heads immediately solved the problem with no other adjustments necessary.

When motors locked up on the earliest Forty-fives, sometimes the worst sticking rollers were right where the oil came through. This indicated the oil pump didn't put out any oil at high speeds. This was cured prior to motor 2734—the 1,734th produced—which represented about one-fourth of the eventual production of 6,222 1929 model Forty-fives. Implementation of this change came around December 1928.

By year end, four changes were incorporated into the Forty-five clutch design and the factory assembly procedures. The two asbestos friction disks were riveted to the clutch sprocket, and the clutch springs were stronger. To ensure a tight seal against oil leakage through the mainshaft keyway, shellac was added between the back clutch disk and its lock nut. Metal clutch disks were more carefully ground in order to achieve a flatter surface.

Other running changes included valve tappet bushings held down by two screws each instead of by one screw each, a gear cover with four dowel pin holes instead of two, a new rear brake rod and minor changes to the front fender. Effective dates of these changes are unknown.

Proposed V-four

During 1928, the engineering department was developing two V-four models. Although the term four cylinder appears in factory records, the term V-four doesn't appear. So why were these assuredly V-fours? Fair enough. Factory planning called for using the same frame for the new fours as for the new side-valve big twins under development, so the configuration would have to have been the V layout. Moreover, the V-fours would have been north-south: two V-twins side by side.

Development of the V-fours proceeded far enough to get at least one of the prototypes running, as William S. Harley related many years later to Tom Sifton. Harley also confirmed the V configuration and mentioned that the sound of the motor didn't please his ears. The V-fours were laid out as an 80 ci, 1300 cc chain-drive and a 90 ci, 1475 cc shaft-drive.

Regrettably, the intended valve configuration of the proposed V-fours isn't known. Normally, Harley-Davidson proceeded in new design efforts by changing only a few components at a time, which would suggest that the prototype model (or models) may have been F-heads. Whatever form the prototype had, it seems likely that the ultimate production models would have been side-valve models, since that was the evolutionary path of twin-cylinder development. Incidentally, to keep abreast of worldwide developments, the factory subscribed to and maintained bound volumes of Britain's leading motorcycle weekly, *The Motor Cycle*. Motorcycle design was highly diverse and innovative in England and Europe. It is perhaps more than coincidental that Brough-Superior exhibited a side-valve V-four at the November 1927 national motorcycle show in England.

Here's one final, exasperating and sad footnote on the proposed V-fours. The late Bill Hoecker, founder of the Southern California Chapter of the Antique Motorcycle Club of America, actually saw a circa 1928 V-four crankcase; Hoecker related this a few weeks prior to his death in 1988. The crankcase was seen in 1987 at the home of an individual who attends motorcycle swap meets but doesn't care to divulge either his name or his treasure. The V-four crankcase was spotted in the collector's shed during a search by Hoecker and the anonymous collector for standard old Harley-Davidson parts. In the ensuing discussion, the collector explained that he had the V-four crankcase because his father had worked at Harley-Davidson during the 1920s. Hoecker and the author intended to revisit the collector, whose location Hoecker knew but without having memorized

This late 1929 clutch was the fourth-generation clutch for the singles and the second-generation clutch for the Forty-fives. The 1926 singles clutch had one large centrally mounted spring; the 1927–1928 singles clutch had a heavier spring; early 1929 singles and Forty-fives had twelve springs; late 1929 singles and Forty-fives had fourteen springs as shown here. Clutch sprockets changed too. The 1926–1927 sprocket had thirty-six teeth at a ⅜ in. pitch, for a 22½ in. circumference. The 1928–1929 sprocket had forty-seven teeth at a ½ in. pitch, for a 23½ in. circumference. The clutch shown here was used from late 1929 through 1931 on singles and Forty-fives. Troy Ross

the address. Sadly, that never happened and the mystery remains unsolved. Perhaps we will yet see this long-lost piece of the prototype V-four.

1929
Forty-five versus 101 Scout

For 1929, the F-head big twins and the side-valve and overhead-valve singles continued in the lineup. The big newsmaker was the Forty-five, which was immediately compared to the Indian 101 Scout. Here's what riders saw.

The most basic difference between the Forty-five and the Indian Scout was in the valve actuation. The Scout used two cam gears, each with only one lobe, to operate all four valves through a system of pivoted cam followers. The Forty-five used four cam gears, each with its own lobe, so that each valve on the Forty-five had a dedicated cam gear and lobe. The Forty-five setup added manufacturing complexities and increased valve train noise, but offered the promise of simpler tuning than with the Indian technique of reshaping the cam followers.

Crankcase breathing on the Forty-five was a departure from F-head practice. In the F-heads, the baffling arrangement consisted of a full baffle below the front cylinder (with six drilled holes) and a half-baffle below the rear cylinder. In the Forty-five, a full baffle was below both cylinders. Earliest Forty-fives had no holes drilled in the baffles, but later 1929 Forty-fives had three holes drilled in each baffle side under the rear cylinder. In the F-heads, a single timed breather gear was used. On the Forty-five, the two hollow inlet cam gear shafts were ported, and registered with their timing case bushings, in order to pass air and oil mist at just the right time in relation to the pistons' positions. Pressure in the timing case forced the air and oil mist through the ported bushing of the horizontal generator driveshaft. The oil then flowed alongside the generator driveshaft, arrived in the left-side generator bevel gear housing and exited through a relief pipe into the front chainguard.

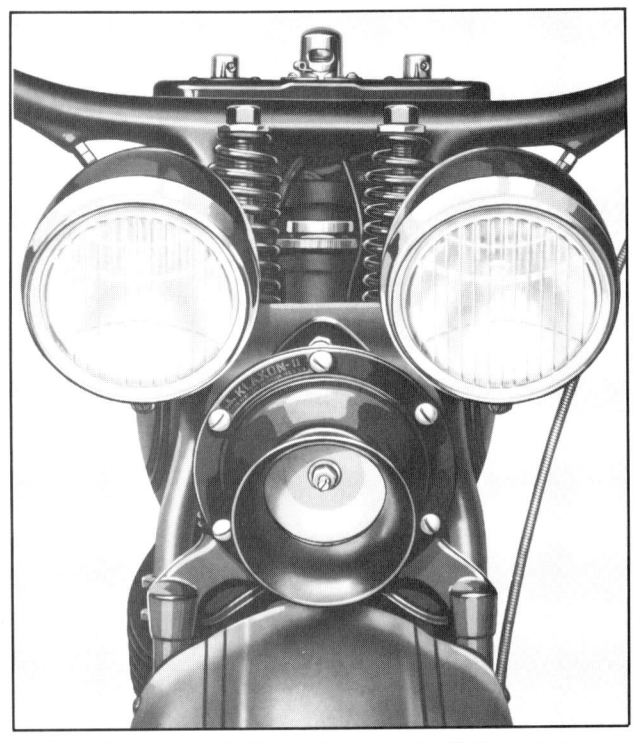

The Forty-five bore and stroke differed from the Indian Scout. On the Forty-five, bore and stroke were $2\frac{3}{4} \times 3\frac{13}{16}$ in. The Scout had a bigger bore and shorter stroke, measuring $2\frac{7}{8} \times 3\frac{1}{2}$ in. In modern eyes, the Scout has the advantage, but in those days much attention was paid to compression ratios. Theory back then said that a major limiter of side-valve performance was the inability to raise the compression ratio to levels possible in overhead-valve motors. Since the Forty-five had a smaller bore and longer stroke than the Scout, it was possible to run the Harley with a slightly higher compression ratio than was practical with the Scout.

Another distinction of the Forty-five was its generator mounting and drive. The generator was vertically mounted on the forward left crankcase. A generator drive gear in the right-side motor cam gearcase drove a long shaft that extended horizontally through the right crankcase and into the left crankcase and then spun the vertical generator through a pair of bevel gears. This permitted the use of the same frame as the 21 ci singles, which featured a straight front downtube and an overall compact look. In contrast, the Indian Scout generator was belt-driven from the clutch sprocket. Indian

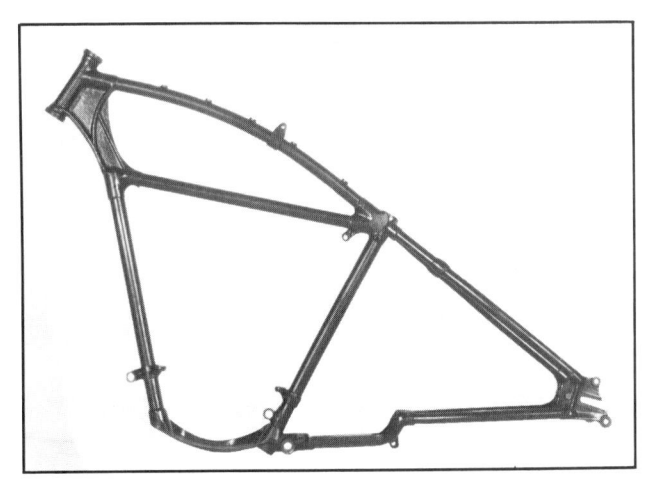

Light and narrow tubular forks on early 1929 models were lifted from the singles. In the middle of the production run of 1929 models, the tubular forks were lengthened by 1 in. to give better clearance for cornering. Harley-Davidson

This frame was also a carryover from the singles. Use of these light components suggests the prototype Harley-Davidson light twin was a 37 ci job, like the earlier Indian Scouts. Harley-Davidson

fans were quick to dub the new Harley-Davidson middleweight as the three-cylinder Harley.

The Forty-five featured roller bearings on the drive (left) side and a plain journal bearing on the pinion gear (right) side. The 101 Scout had roller bearings on both ends of the crankshaft. The Forty-five connecting rod little ends ran directly on the piston wrist pin without bushings. The 101 Scout used bushings on the little ends.

The Forty-five was the only Harley-Davidson model that had oil metering through a hole in the left crankcase. A groove in the engine sprocket bushing allowed oil to reach the sprocket, and centrifugal force carried the oil to the primary chain. In a few early motors, the bushing slipped and stopped oil flow, so all but these earliest motors had the bushing pinned in the proper location. Incidentally, the factory still recommended occasional rider-applied grease or oil for the primary chain—quite a contrast to the Indian Scout cast-aluminum oil-bath primary case.

Ignition on the Forty-five was by battery and coil, while the Scout featured magneto ignition. Both systems had pluses and minuses. Magnetos could quit in wet weather, but were unaffected by long periods of inactivity, such as winter storage.

Comparing primary drives and transmissions, the advantages went to Indian. The Scout had an indestructible oil-bath helical-gear primary drive that transmitted power to a gearbox bolted directly to the crankcase. The Forty-five had a sheet-metal-covered double-row primary chain. Both marques used sliding-gear transmissions of the crossover style, in which the primary and final drive chains were on opposite sides. This didn't matter on the Scout with its gearbox rigidly connected to the motor, but on the Forty-five the gearbox was mounted to the frame. This resulted in significant torque loading that could twist the motor, gearbox and frame out of alignment—and in fact this sometimes happened on the Forty-five. One point in favor of the Forty-five was its cushion drive sprocket, the same as used in the singles, which incorporated eight rubber blocks to absorb engine shock loading. Indian didn't have this feature.

The clutches of the Forty-five and the 101 Scout were opposite concepts. The Harley had a dry clutch and the Indian had an oil-bath clutch. The earliest Forty-fives had the twelve-spring clutch used on the singles. Later Forty-fives switched to the fourteen-spring clutch, along with the singles. The Harley clutch was smoother, but the Indian clutch was more rugged, so in this area we could call the competition close.

In the remaining areas of running gear and styling, the Forty-five fell in line with existing models. Along with sharing the single-cylinder model frame, the Forty-five used the single's tubular front fork. However, the Forty-five had 18 in. diameter wheels instead of 20 in. diameter wheels as on the singles. Consequently, the twin sometimes grounded during turns. To cure this, the mid 1929 Forty-five forks were extended 1 in. Because of the extended forks, the fender bracing geometry was changed, so the late 1929 fenders carried a different part number.

Upon initial introduction, the Forty-five was available only in the standard low-compression variant, the D. When the hotter DL was introduced, the factory also brought out a hop-up kit for the D to give it performance equal to the DL. This hop-up kit consisted of

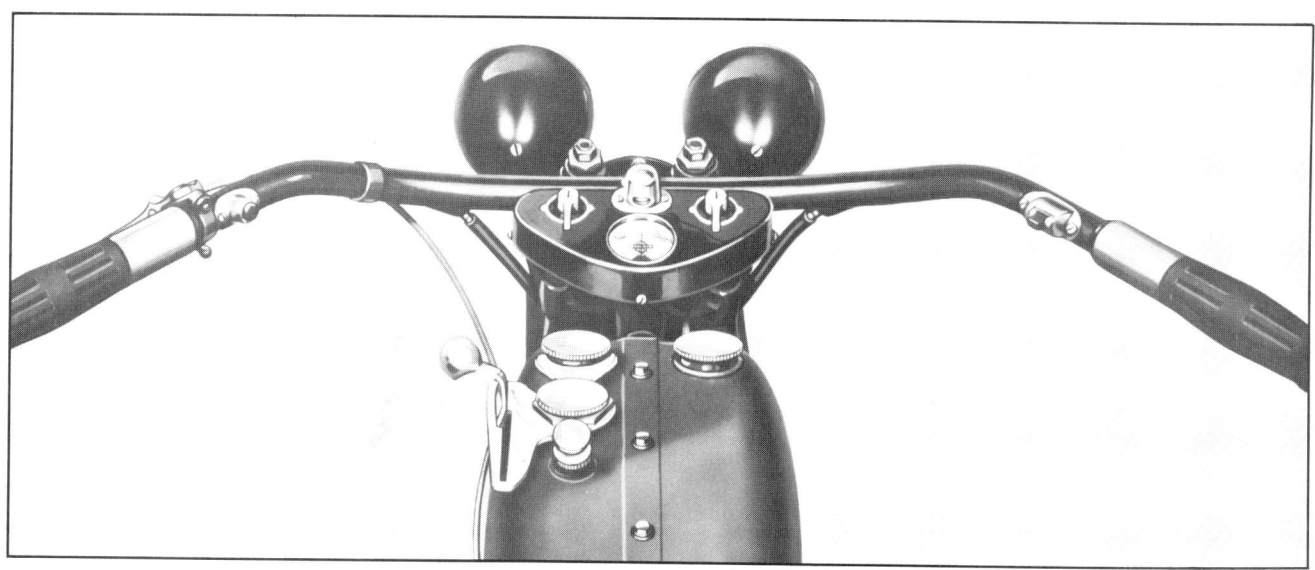

Rider's view of a 1929 Forty-five. The toggle switch on the right handlebar selected both headlights or extinguished the right light while dimming the left. The generator wasn't capable of keeping the battery charged if both lights were used for prolonged low-speed running. Harley-Davidson

high-compression cylinder heads, a ⅞ in. venturi and a twenty-eight-tooth rear sprocket.

A sidecar version of the Forty-five was offered as the Model DS. The DS featured a 4.3:1 compression ratio as in the D. The DS had a gear ratio of 5.45:1, achieved with a thirty-six-tooth rear sprocket. The DS sidecar was the Goulding Litecar, manufactured in Saginaw, Michigan.

A four-tube muffler was featured. Early Forty-fives had a (motor) gearcase cover with two dowel pin holes to mate with the two-pin right crankcase. Late 1929 models had four dowel pins on the crankcase and four mating holes in the gearcase cover. Early Forty-fives used the same tanks as the singles with a 4⅜ gallon total capacity. Late 1929 models were fitted with tanks totaling 5¼ gallons that were also used on the 30.50 ci, 500 cc single introduced in midseason. Solo or speedster handlebars were optional. The model had an appealing light look, but this lightness would soon be revealed as more of a functional problem than an aesthetic advantage. Color was the traditional olive green, although special-order one- or two-color finishes were available.

All in all, the 1929 Harley-Davidson Forty-five didn't measure up to the Indian 101 Scout when viewed by customers who had no strong brand loyalties. This was especially true during late 1928 and early 1929 when developmental problems nagged the Forty-five. The Indian 101 Scout, launched in 1928, stood in stark contrast as a motorcycle without problems because it was an evolutionary change to the original 1920 Scout—the bugs had long been worked out of the Scout series, in other words.

In January, the Forty-five and single clutch was improved. A steel collar, at first $3/16$ in. thick but later ⅜ in. thick, was installed to provide a guide for the clutch pushrod. This prevented damage under clutch-releasing loads caused by improper mating of the pushrod with the thrust cap.

In March, the Forty-five and Thirty-fifty clutch was further improved by adding two more friction disks. The thicker clutch required a longer pushrod and a spring-adjusting nut.

In the spring, the 1929 model Forty-five was discontinued, and production of Forty-fives was held up pending release of the 1930 model. During this interval, the first 30.50 ci, 500 cc side-valve singles were assembled as late 1929 models. These initial big singles used the same frame as the 21 ci singles.

Seventy-four woes

Initial shipments of the new 74 ci side-valve V and VL models were made in August. Newly established San Francisco subdealer Tom Sifton was highly enthu-

From left to right: Walter Jr., Gordon and Allan Davidson, ready for a 1929 8,000 mile transcontinental tour. Each motorcycle is outfitted with accessory lighting. Gordon's Forty-five has optional cadmium-plated wheel rims. Walter later took over publicity duties, including racing. Gordon became production manager. Allan didn't enter the company. Harley-Davidson

siastic about the new Seventy-four side-valve models, and his enthusiasm was contagious. Because of hot sales, Sifton obtained twenty extra Seventy-fours, and these were sold almost immediately. Several were sold one Saturday and ridden the next day to a race meet—and these all broke down. The problem was in the new splined hubs that had been introduced to speed up tire changes. The splines were too loose, which resulted in jerky operation, noise and loose spokes.

Dealers' complaints on the Seventy-fours began to pour into the factory. By mid-September, service manager Joe Ryan was so busy with problem investigation that he was unable to keep up with his customary dealer correspondence. The management decided to temporarily halt further shipments of V and VL models while problems were researched.

Some cases of brake-operating shaft breakage were reported. The heat-treating operation was changed on this part.

Broken or weak valve springs were caused by the inconsistent quality of the spring manufacturer's deliveries and by inadequate Harley-Davidson receipt inspection methods. Weak valve springs resulted in a dropoff of 300 to 400 rpm and 3 or 4 hp. In early October, the factory shipped replacement valve springs to dealers.

Clutch slippage was reported, but the factory's investigation indicated the real problem was a combination of other factors. Because of the combinations of clutch and engine sprockets, the new side-valve Seventy-fours had a lower starting ratio. The kicking resistance was higher on the 1930 big twins than on the 1929 big twins, and some riders weren't kicking over their motors vigorously enough. Starting was made more difficult due to lost motion on the kicking stroke prior to the starting ratchets engaging. Instead of carrying the starting momentum onward through the compression stroke, the inadequate kick, the ratchet problem and the light flywheels would combine to let the motor "bounce" backward. The effect was a feeling of clutch slippage. The factory issued starting instructions to the dealers in early October.

A tougher problem was the lack of flywheel momentum during low-speed running. Service manager Ryan advised dealers that for the present the factory had no cure, and that riders should be instructed to slip the clutch during low-speed running to avoid annoying jerks. This wasn't a satisfactory answer because the all-or-nothing fiber-plated clutch was difficult to slip. American riders were accustomed to using clutch slip to gain smooth low-speed running, but that didn't work well on the new Seventy-fours.

In mid-October, President Walter Davidson signed several hundred personal letters—one to each dealer. The letters explained the new components that would soon be shipped to solve Seventy-four V and VL problems. Foremost were heavier flywheels with an increase in outside diameter of $13/16$ in. New crankcases were necessary to accommodate the larger flywheels. Valve springs were $9/16$ in. longer and stronger. Complaints about Dow metal piston noise led to offering iron alloy pistons in V and VS models. Fiber clutch plates were replaced by steel raybestos-lined plates, the same as in the 1929 models. Clutch pressure was increased by changing from six to nine springs. A new starting ratchet (also called a starter clutch) with twenty teeth instead of twelve was provided to eliminate lost motion during kickover.

The new Seventy-four side-valve parts were shipped to dealers as a kit, and dealers had to underwrite the labor expense for conversion to the new configuration. Tom Sifton recalls that each of his two mechanics could reconfigure two Seventy-four side-valve models per day—they got plenty of experience to become efficient! The retrofit began by placing a new frame next to the motorcycle to be retrofitted. All usable old parts were then transferred from the old frame to the new frame, and then new parts were added from the retrofit kit.

Late in 1929, the mounting of the torque stud of the Seventy-four rear brake was changed to improve security. Several cases were reported of the front brake lining disintegrating because the brake action was too severe. The aluminum brake shoe was discarded in favor of an iron shoe.

After initial brisk sales, the Seventy-four side-valve models became difficult to sell because of their numerous problems. The dealer in Omaha, Nebraska, reported that one of his riders traded in a new Seventy-four for a Forty-five—he was probably not the only dealer with this tale. Yet within a few months of the retrofit program, the Seventy-four side-valves began to gain acceptance.

The year 1929 is famous for the Wall Street stock market crash that set off the Great Depression of the 1930s. Sifton recalls that he heard about the panic at the New York Stock Exchange, but didn't think it had anything to do with him. He was in California, he reasoned. Back in Milwaukee, the Harley-Davidson officers had a better understanding of Wall Street, but even they were unprepared for the depth and staying power of the economic plunge.

1930
V Series

The 74 ci side-valve twins were the 1930 catalog highlights. The 1930 models listed were the V, VL, VM and VLM, the latter two having a magneto-generator. Company literature usually referred to the Seventy-four side-valve as simply the 74, but sometimes model designations such as V or VL were used. Riders continued to call the big twin the Seventy-four as they had done with the 74 ci F-heads.

The V Series Seventy-fours had new motors, frames, front forks and clutches. Only a few F-head bits and pieces were used in these V Series major assemblies. Some of the shared items were an air cleaner and clamp, spark plugs, piston pins and bushings, roller bearings for the crankpin and crankshaft, sprocket shaft collars, starter crank, foot pedal rubbers, rear chain, keys, washers, shims, studs, springs, screws and nuts. The Model 30VL with Dow metal pistons used the same guide and cushion rings as the 1928 and 1929 F-heads with Dow metal pistons.

The new side-valve Seventy-fours were the same in principle as their Forty-five stablemates, including the total-loss lubrication system. Cylinder heads followed Forty-five practice by incorporating an anti-plug-fouling dam between the spark plug area and the main area over the piston. Individual cam gears and cams were provided for each valve. Early 1930 Seventy-fours had two-piece valve covers similar to the Forty-five covers; later 1930 Seventy-fours had three-piece covers.

Seventy-four crankcase breathing differed from Forty-five practice. Instead of full baffles under each cylinder, like the Forty-five, the Seventy-four reverted

Specifications
Year and models	1930 74, Models V, VL, VM and VLM
Engine	Side-valve 45 degree V-twin
Bore and stroke	3.424 in. (advertised as $3^{7}/_{16}$ in.) x 4 in.
Displacement	73.66 ci, 1207.07 cc
Gearbox	Three speed, sliding gear with positive gear locking
Shift	Left hand
Primary drive	Double-row chain, oil-mist lubricated
Clutch	Dry, with metal-lined disks
Clutch operation	Left foot
Wheelbase	60 in.
Wheels	Drop-center rims, quickly detachable, interchangeable, 27x4.00 in. standard (4.00 x19 in. in modern terminology), 27x4.40 in. optional (4.40x19 in. in modern terminology)
Suspension	Front: leading-link drop-forged forks; rear: rigid
Weight	529 lb.
Seat height	28 in.
Fuel consumption	35-50 mpg
Top speed	VL: 85 mph (estimated); V: 80 mph (estimated)

Talk about bad timing! Charles "Red" Wolverton opened his Reading, Pennsylvania, Harley-Davidson dealership in the summer of 1929 and soon proudly displayed these new 1930 models. In San Jose, California, Tom Sifton had the same sort of bad timing. Dealers like Wolverton and Sifton proved their mettle by staying in business throughout the Depression and World War II. Red Wolverton

to the F-head setup of a full baffle with six holes under the front cylinder, and a half-baffle under the rear cylinder. Instead of only the inlet cam gearshafts being ported for breathing as on the Forty-five, the Seventy-four also had the rear exhaust cam gearshaft ported. Routing of the crankcase blow-by was also different in the Seventy-four, which collected the air and oil mist at the bottom of the timing case, and routed the blow-by through a tube behind the engine and into the primary drive cover.

Some F-head enthusiasts were disappointed with the new Seventy-four side-valve twins, and even today there are those who argue that the side-valve big twins were inferior to their F-head predecessors. Tom Sifton, a dealer for twenty-four years, has a different view.

"Until 'twenty-eight, the competition two-cammer had just been used for racing on the track and for hillclimbers. In fact, you had to be somebody to buy one. They didn't make enough of them to give all the dealers that wanted one, a two-cammer. The Indian Scout cut such a swath, and Harley didn't have anything ready, so they put the two-cammer in a road frame for 'twenty-eight. It was a high-performance motorcycle. It used to wear out because it wasn't covered properly to keep the dirt out of the lubrication system, but those things would go!

"The 1930 selling season had started in August of 1929. When you bear in mind that the factory had taken those new 1930 side-valve Seventy-fours off the market for about four months and made all those new parts to convert those motors, those 'thirty Seventy-fours weren't too respected, and they hadn't had time to gain any respect. I had a demonstrator there that we'd done a little work on, and not too much, either. We'd cleaned the ports and took the rough edges off and matched the carburetor to the manifold. That thing would go!

"We had a guy called Red, who had an 80 in. two-cammer, which was a regular Seventy-four, stroked. It was considered a fairly fast motorcycle, and Red took pride in his ownership. Red came in on a Saturday afternoon and said, 'Tom, don't laugh at me, but I want to trade in my two-cammer on a new Seventy-four. But will it go as fast as my two-cammer?'

"I told him, 'Red, it will be in the same ballpark. I won't tell you it'll go faster, but it's not a weak motorcycle. There's only one way to settle that: let's take them

1930 V Series specifications

Model	Compression ratio	Horsepower at 4000 rpm	Pistons	Gearing
V	4:1	27 hp	Nickel-iron	4.04:1
VL	4.5:1	30 hp	Dow metal (magnesium)	4.04:1
VM	4:1	27 hp	Nickel-iron	4.04:1
VLM	4.5:1	30 hp	Dow metal (magnesium)	4.04:1

Side-valve big twins replaced the F-heads in the 1930 lineup. The new two-tube muffler was entirely on the right side. Artist retouching left too much shadow on the front of the right tank—tanks were not so squared off on the front.

Early-1930 right fuel tank was unique on the Seventy-four and Forty-five. Tank cap was fully forward, in line with left tank oil cap. Right tank had straight-down fuel hole, angled fuel tap and no indentation. Harley-Davidson

out to the stretch and find out.' There was about a mile stretch with no crossroads. I beat him fairly easy (on the V Series bike). So we turned around to run the other direction, and I beat him pretty bad.

"The JDs were not faster. That's wishful thinking, and I've straddled a lot of JDs."

Harley-Davidson sales catalogs claimed the new Seventy-four side-valve V Series had twenty percent more power than the F-head J Series. A cursory examination refutes this generalized claim. The January 1930 factory horsepower curves showed the high-performance side-valve Model VL produced about three percent more power than the Model JDH Two Cam F-head. The VL maximum was 30 hp, and the JDH maximum was 29 hp, both at 4000 rpm. The lower compression Model V had a seven-percent advantage in maximum power compared to the equivalent standard F-head Model JDL. The V put out 28 hp and the JDL 26 hp, both at 4000 rpm.

But a better comparison of V Series and J Series power is revealed by examining the shape of the horsepower curves. The VL and JDH Two Cams had almost identical torque characteristics from idle to peak horsepower at 4000 rpm, about 79 mph. However, the plot thickens between 4000 and 4800 rpm. The VL urge dropped to 29 hp at 4800 rpm while the JDH dropped to 26 hp, a twelve-percent difference. Between 4800 and 5000 rpm, the VL power fell slightly to 28.5 hp while the JDH plunged to 22 hp, a thirty-percent VL advantage over the Two Cam Seventy-four.

In short, the new side-valve Seventy-fours produced useful torque over a broader rpm range than the old F-heads, but most of this advantage was at the high end of the scale. This substantiates Sifton's comment about the relative high-speed performance of the side-valve and F-head designs.

In one of his many letters to dealers, service manager Joe Ryan stated that the typical JDH would top out at 85 mph, which was about 4300 rpm from 28 hp. The VL produced 28 hp through 4400 rpm, which implies about 87 mph on tap. To sum up, in most cases a good VL had a little more top speed than a good JDH Two Cam, while either model out of tune could be beaten by the other in average condition.

The lighter JDH naturally had better roll-on acceleration in the middle revolutions than the heavier

The sidecar was a new design featuring integrated braking. All three wheels of the rig were interchangeable. The standard finish was still olive, but striping was changed from maroon to vermilion. Black stripe edges and a center gold accent were carryovers. Special-order finishes were available. Harley-Davidson

As with the singles, advertising emphasized that side-valve V-twins were easy to decarbonize. The ridge, or dam, near the spark plug was necessary to keep the plug from fouling. Early 1930 Seventy-fours had the two-piece valve covers shown here. Late 1930 models had three-piece covers. Early 1930 Seventy-fours had head bolts with twenty threads per inch. Late 1930 Seventy-fours had bolts with sixteen threads per inch. This is an early-1930 model. Late-1930 right-side tanks on twins were indented near the rear spark plug. Harley-Davidson

VL. The JDH weighed about 408 lb. and the VL about 529 lb. As Sifton recalled, "You could ride one of those JDs around the block and it would feel real husky. They had a lot of acceleration." The JDH, therefore, had what could be called a more practical performance profile than the VL, since the latter's top speed advantage was only good for bragging rights.

On the plus side, the Seventy-four side-valve was a cleaner design than the Seventy-four F-head. Moreover, the new side-valve was at the beginning of its evolution and the F-head was at its peak, so the small horsepower edge of the VL could be expected to grow over the coming years.

What about reliability? Of the F-heads, Sifton said, "When you would take those things out on the highway and run them 70 or 75 mph, mile after mile, those things fell apart. They either overheated and went on the bum, or they shook apart. What we did, we started club runs—a hundred miles there and a hundred miles back—and our guys with Seventy-four VLs, and even our guys with our Forty-fives, they had no trouble. But

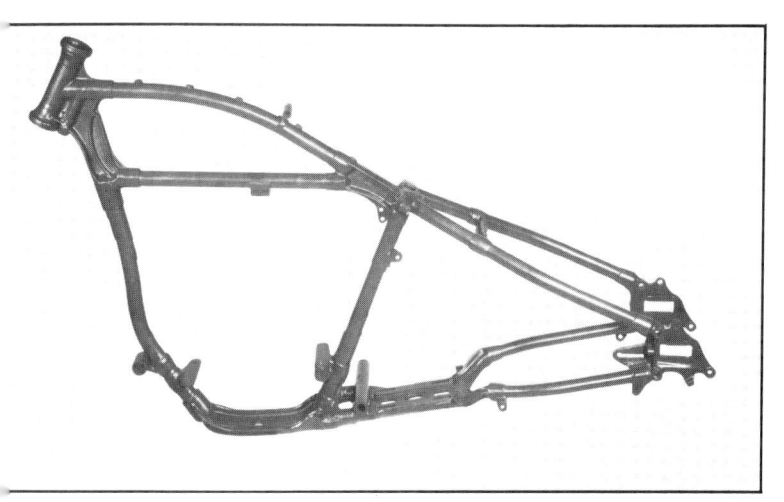

The V Series frame was rugged. The front downtube was double-butted, as with F-head twins. Harley-Davidson

Tubular forks of the F-heads were replaced by forged I-beam forks in the side-valve big twins. The Forty-five and Thirty-fifty single used similar I-beam forks. Harley-Davidson

90

Double-chain primary drive of the Seventy-four. The Forty-five twin and Thirty-fifty single also had this feature. The ported tube provided oil mist from the crankcase breather.

The clutch pullrod acted through the triangular clutch-actuating plate, which pressed against the three clutch spring nut sectors. Harley-Davidson

A new light-action six-spring clutch was installed in early 1930 Seventy-fours. The large plate area and fiber discs helped produce easy operation. An optional handclutch could be fitted, but all-or-nothing clutch action made clutch slipping difficult during slow running—and clutch slip was necessary due to flywheels that were too light. Springs were paired in spring nut sectors, a layout that began in 1912. Harley-Davidson

Very early in the production run of 1930 Seventy-fours—by October 1929—the light-action six-spring fiber-plate clutch was replaced by a stiff-action nine-spring metal-plate clutch. Harley-Davidson

all that old JD stuff fell apart. It didn't take us very long before they saw the light and we had them riding Harley side-valves."

Even staunch Two Cam fans had to concede that Two Cam reliability wasn't a strong point. As one Two Cam fan noted, the Two Cams got "terribly hot at sustained high speeds . . ." and major overhauls were required at 5,000 mile intervals due to the hot running and exposed valve gear. To be sure, there were Two Cam fans who couldn't be convinced. But most riders didn't have access to the inside circle that used Ricardo heads or Riccy chips, and in any case most riders weren't willing to trade reliability for speed. So, the side-valve Seventy-fours were an improvement in the eyes of most riders.

The new Seventy-four frame gave the rider a 2 in. lower seating position. Out front were new drop-forged I-beam forks instead of the F-head tubular type. Front and rear wheels were interchangeable and quickly detachable. Rear wheel brake operation was now by an internal expanding shoe instead of an external contracting band.

V Series power was transmitted through a double-row primary drive chain, an idea brought out with the 1929 model Forty-five. For the first time on big twins, an attempt was made to provide automatic lubrication for the primary chain. F-heads had featured a crankcase relief tube that sprayed lots of air and occasional oil onto the primary chain. The new side-valve big twins now positively metered oil to the primary chain.

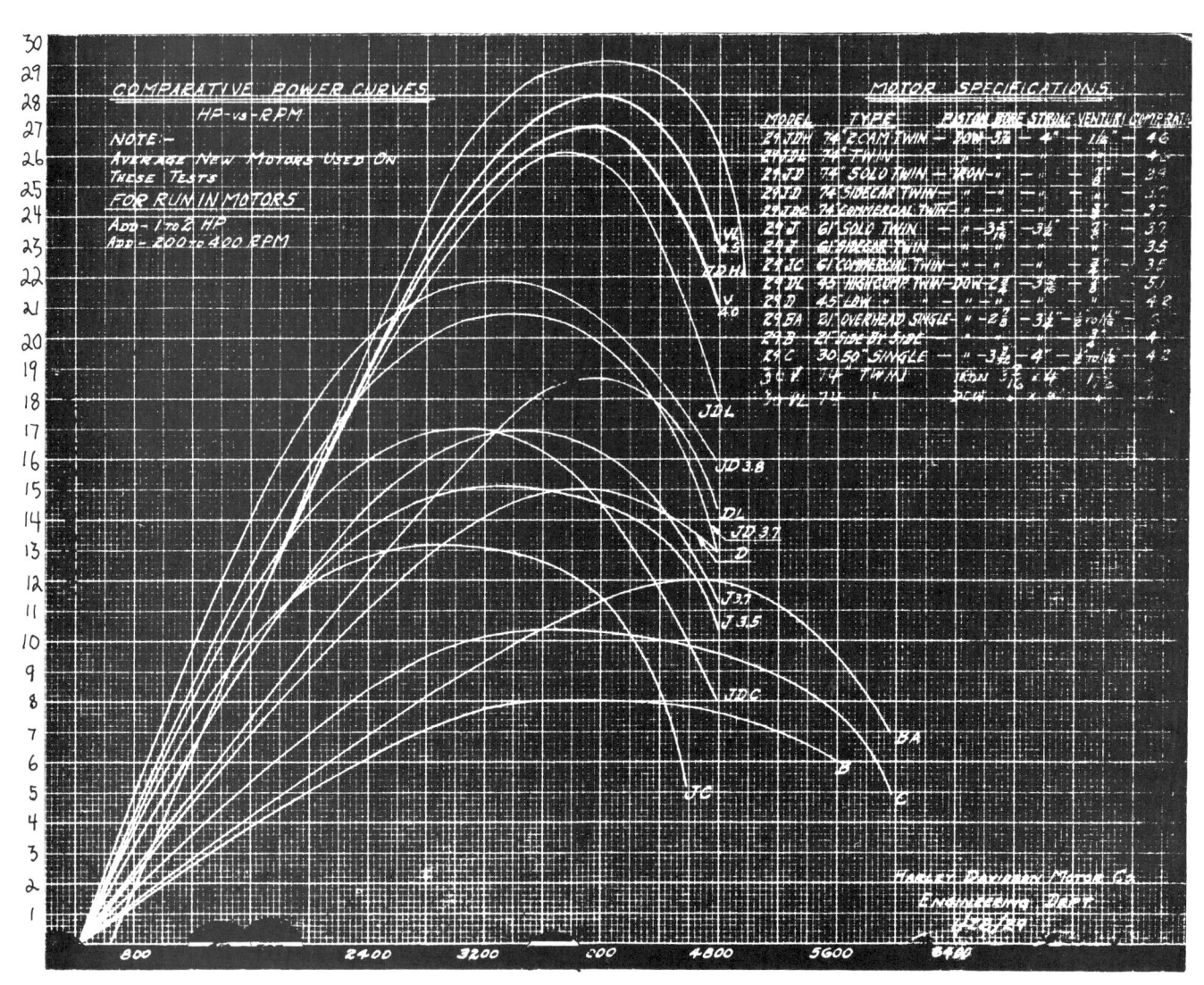

Comparison of F-head and side-valve power, January 28, 1929. The top-of-the-line VL side-valves had about the same output as the Two Cam Seventy-fours. Typical VLs had slightly higher top speed than typical Two Cam Seventy-fours. Acceleration was better on the Two Cam Seventy-fours because they weighed about 120 lb. less than the VLs. Harley-Davidson

The new V Series clutch had 220.89 sq. in. of friction surface compared to the J Series 56.35 sq. in. Six clutch springs were used as in the J Series.

The V Series transmission housing was new, but most other transmission parts were carried over from the J Series. Carryovers included the gearbox top cover, mainshaft, main drive gear, countershaft, countershaft gear and sliding gear. The transmission housing included two cast-in "ears" for mounting the inner section of the primary drive chainguard. These ears usually broke off if the rear chain was thrown.

After the ignition timing of the 1930 Seventy-fours was adjusted at the factory, the circuit breaker setting was indexed with a file mark. The riders instruction book advised that ignition timing would automatically be set correctly if the valve geartrain was properly set up. The valve geartrain was set up by aligning each gear so that its index marks aligned with the index marks of the adjacent gears. All well and good except when the circuit breaker became loose on its mounting; then it was necessary to bring the motorcycle in to the dealer for retiming of the ignition. This arrangement proved impractical and unpopular.

There were four 74 ci models. These were the low-performance V, the high-performance VL and the magneto-equipped variants of each, dubbed the VM and VLM.

The 74 ci motors above number 7290 that featured a new breather design sometimes filled the generator with oil because the factory didn't fit the oil retainer tight enough. The factory added a felt washer to fix this problem. Also effective with motor 7290, the gearcase cover, oiler, generator drive end oil retainer, and generator drive end bearing plate were changed. New seat

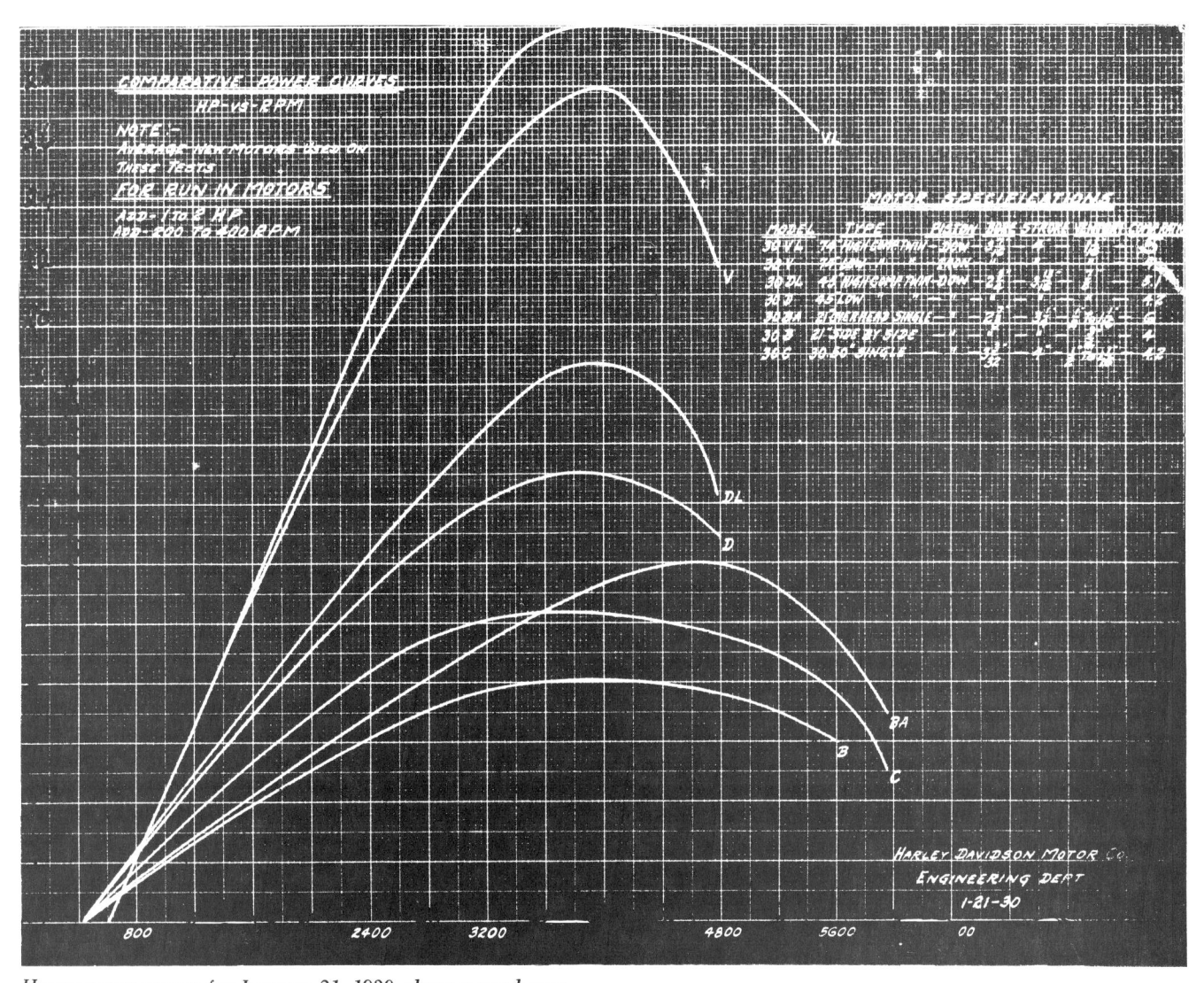

Horsepower curves for January 21, 1930, show a one horsepower increase for the V and VL. Harley-Davidson

93

Specifications

Year and models	1930 45, Models D, DL, DLD and DS
Engine	Side-valve 45 degree V-twin
Bore and stroke	2¾x3¹³⁄₁₆ in.
Displacement	45.32 ci, 746.63 cc
Gearbox	Three speed, sliding gear with positive gear locking
Shift	Left hand
Primary drive	Double-row chain, oil-mist lubricated
Clutch	Dry, fiber and metal disks
Clutch operation	Standard: left foot; optional: right hand
Wheelbase	57½ in.
Wheels	Drop center rims, quickly detachable, interchangeable, 25x4.00 in. (4.00x18 in. in modern terminology)*
Suspension	Front: leading-link drop-forged forks; rear: rigid
Weight	390 lb.
Seat height	26½ in.
Fuel consumption	60-75 mpg
Top speed	D: 60-65 mph; DL: 65-70 mph; DLD: 70-75 mph (estimated figures)

*The factory referred to the Forty-five wheels as having an 18 in. diameter, but termed the tires 25x4 in.—their math was wrong.

post springs were designed in midyear, and fork rod rattle was being attacked. During the 1930 model production run, the two-piece valve covers for the Seventy-four were replaced by three-piece covers. Other new Seventy-four parts introduced as running changes included cylinder head bolts and washers, valve springs and valve spring collars.

The rest of the lineup

The 1930 Forty-five featured a new frame and front fork. Saddle height was lowered by 2½ in., yet ground clearance was increased. The new Forty-five frame was stronger than the old frame shared with the 21.35 ci, 350 cc singles. The upper rear frame tubes were bowed out more under the seat, which gave better access to the battery. The new forged I-beam forks were similar to those used on the Seventy-four and replaced the tubular forks shared with the singles. The Forty-five and Thirty-fifty tanks were enlarged from 5¼ to 5⅝ gallons.

Experience gained with the 1929 Forty-fives proved that the front chain was inadequately lubricated by relying solely on the air-oil mist of crankcase blow-by.

For export markets, two-port 21 ci, 350 cc singles were offered as 1930 models. These were leftover 1929 machines and the only 1930 models with a single headlight. Harley-Davidson

Accordingly, on the 1930 Forty-fives a circular (banjo) fitting was placed under the oiler chamber screw of the oil pump, and from this fitting a small line bled off oil to the front chain.

The Forty-five clutch was enlarged by 23 sq. in. to become the same size as the big twin clutch. An optional hand clutch setup could be purchased.

A new sportier Forty-five called the DLD featured a 6:1 compression ratio and a twenty-eight-tooth rear sprocket. The DLD inlet port internal diameter measured 1$^{19}/_{32}$ in. The DLD carburetor was the same one used on late 1930 VL models. Like the DL, the DLD venturi measured ⅞ in. compared to the ¾ in. of the D.

The factory recommended Ethyl premium fuel for the DLD, or for better results, a fifty-fifty mixture of benzol and gasoline.

The single-cylinder line had both foreign and domestic models. In export catalogs only, the company listed 1930 models that were referred to as 350 cc models (actual displacement was 345.73 cc). These were offered as side-valves or as two-port overhead-valves. The overhead-valve models had nickel-plated exhaust pipes. The side-valve 350s had the four-tube muffler, which was no longer available on the domestic 1930 models. This and the fact that these lightweights weren't listed in domestic catalogs indicates the so-

1930 D Series specifications

Model	Compression ratio	Carburetor diameter	Horsepower	Pistons	Gearing
D	4.3:1	1 in.	15 hp at 3900	Lynite	4.54:1
DS	4.3:1	1 in.	15 hp at 3900	Lynite	5.45:1
DL	5:1	1 in.	18.5 hp at 4000	Lynite	4.54:1
DLD	6:1	1¼ in.	20 hp at 4000*	Lynite	4.24:1

*Estimated

A 1930 45 ci, 750 cc overhead-valve hillclimber with two exhaust ports per head, but only one exhaust valve. Several types of hillclimbers were built by the racing department in the late 1920s and early 1930s. The odd trailing link forks were a brief experiment. Harley-Davidson

Hillclimbing was so popular in the teens, 1920s and 1930s that Harley-Davidson and rival makes hired full-time professional riders. Joe Petrali had the distinction of winning national championships in both hillclimbing and flat track racing from the late 1920s through the mid 1930s. Harley-Davidson

Accessories were always promoted by dealers due to the high profit margin. These alligator hide saddlebags were advertised in the April 1930 issue of The Harley-Davidson Enthusiast. Harley-Davidson

called 1930 350s were 1929 leftovers lingering in overseas warehouses. These were the last of the overhead-valve singles sold for road use.

For both foreign and domestic markets, the company had a new addition, the 30.50 ci, 500 cc side-valve single. The big single was officially known as the Model C, but was usually called the Thirty-fifty in reference to its nominal displacement of 30.50 ci. The Thirty-fifty shared all running gear with the Forty-five. The bore and stroke were $3^{3}/_{32}$x4 in., for an actual displacement of 30.07 ci or 493 cc. Gearing was 5.75:1. All domestic and export models could be equipped with an optional hand clutch.

On all 1930 models, except the export-only 21 ci singles, the electrical system was revamped. Generator circuitry was changed so that two independent field coils were used on demand. One coil supplied ignition and battery charging for daytime riding; the other coil came into use when the lights were operated and provided the additional charging necessary for low-speed running with the lights on. Wheel rims were drop center instead of clincher. Handlebars were new. A two-tube muffler replaced the four-tube layout, and an optional lever-actuated steering damper was available. On the sidecars, a brake was operated in conjunction with the motorcycle rear brake.

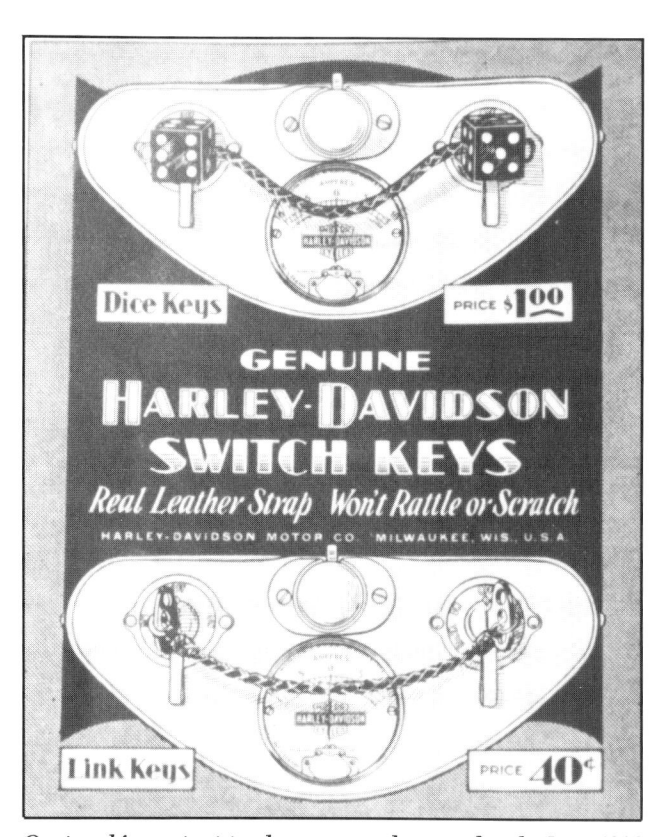

Optional fancy ignition keys were advertised in the June 1930 Enthusiast. *These key sets remained popular until 1937, when a single-key tanktop panel was introduced.* Harley-Davidson

Typical 1930 Seventy-four police model. A rear-wheel-driven siren is on the opposite side. This example has been fitted with the 1931 style air inlet cap instead of the 1928-1930 air cleaner.

There were cases in which carburetor backfire caught motorcycles on fire, so to cure this, an air deflector was later installed behind the cap. Doug Wilson

On all models, the standard finish was olive green. Tank and fender striping were changed from maroon edged in black to vermilion edged in maroon. The center gold pinstripe was retained.

Optional colors

Yes, there were optional colors for the 1930 models, although the sales catalogs and the 1930 model edition of *The Harley-Davidson Enthusiast* were silent on the issue again. For proof of the 1930 status, we have to take a momentary diversion to the 1931 new-model edition of *The Harley-Davidson Enthusiast*, the August 1930 issue, which stated: "Again, you are offered the option of dolling up the bus like a Saturday night at a very slight extra cost. There are a number of color combinations offered, besides the standard color.... Your dealer can put you straight on this color proposition." The key word is "again."

Proof has now been presented that 1928 models were available in virtually any color and that 1930 models were available in a wide variety of colors; by inference, it's clear that 1929 models were also available in a wide variety of colors. Paint colors continuously stocked since 1928 were azure blue, police blue, coach green, maroon, fawn grey and cream. Whether the factory routinely stocked motorcycles in these colors remains open to conjecture. However, any combination of these colors in one- or two-color finishes could be special-ordered at extra cost. The any-color option may also still have been in effect.

Prototypes

The factory built a few prototype 30.50 ci, 500 cc overhead-valve singles during late 1929 and 1930. These were the first Harley-Davidsons to feature dry-sump lubrication, meaning that the oil was picked up from the motor sump and returned to the oil tank for recycling. One of the 30.50 ci motors was placed in a Forty-five frame and outfitted as a road model for young Gordon Davidson, son of Walter, Sr. Gordon rode this green-and-black single during his education at the University of Pennsylvania. Reading, Pennsylvania, dealer Red Wolverton tried out Gordon's single and was so

Specifications	
Year and model	1930 Model C
Engine	Side-valve single
Bore and stroke	3³/₃₂x4 in.
Displacement	30.1 ci, 493.28 cc
Horsepower	10.4 bhp at 3600 rpm
Gearbox	Three speed, sliding gear
Shift	Left hand
Wheelbase	57½ in.
Seat height	26½ in.
Fuel consumption	45 mpg (estimated)
Top speed	60 mph (estimated)

Prototype 1930 Forty-five featuring new I-beam forks; motor number is 29D6848. A taller front end prevented grounding during cornering. The lightweight frame was reshaped to fit larger tanks and to lower the seat. The vertical generator was retained. Tank striping on this prototype has gold outer edges—a nonstandard trim. Harley-Davidson

In mid 1930, the factory began development of a commercial street painter. A problem with this first design is the rider being on the wrong side of the painted stripe! Harley-Davidson

enthused that he booked orders for two of the 30.50 ci overhead-valve singles for the next season. However, the prototype overhead-valve big single never went into full-scale production because of concern that its sales would come at the expense of the Forty-five side-valve twin.

Several of these singles were used as hillclimbers in the 1930s, and at least one was outfitted for road racing and shipped to Europe. The road racer motor was 30CAF302; one ex-hillclimber has been restored and its motor is 30SF505. The road racer and hillclimbers featured a low seating position made possible by a radical downward slope of the upper frame structure behind the cylinder. The seating position was only slightly above the top of the cylinder head. The short bean-shaped fuel tanks appeared to be made from standard tanks.

Following the Seventy-four's troublesome debut in late 1929, sales of the new side-valve big twin gained momentum in the spring of 1930. For a few weeks it seemed that the Wall Street crash had indeed been overplayed by the press. Then, just as suddenly, sales of all 1930 models began to drop off steadily. Accordingly, plans for the 1931 business year were undergoing

Comparison of sales 1929–1930

Year	Big twins	Forty-fives	Singles	Total
1929	10,842	6,222	3,882	20,946
1930	10,727	4,946	1,989	17,662

Another 1930 creation was the Cycle Tow. The outrigger "training" wheels were retracted for solo riding to the car owner who requested the car be picked up for service. The touring mechanic then lowered the outrigger wheels, hitched the motorcycle to the car rear bumper, and drove the car and captive motorcycle back to the garage. Not many Cycle Tows were built and sold, but they inspired the Servi-Car, destined to be a Harley-Davidson staple for a generation. Harley-Davidson

continual rewriting. By mid 1930, the projected 1931 schedule called for a one-third drop in production to 12,000 units.

After a survey indicating promising results, the company began producing a single-cylinder 3 hp industrial engine adaptable for a number of uses. Harley-Davidson also began development of a three-wheeler that would paint signal lines on streets and highways.

1931 V Series specifications

Model	Compression ratio	Horsepower* at 4000 rpm	Pistons	Gearing
V	4:1	28 hp	Aluminum or optional nickel-iron	4.04:1
VL	4.5:1	30 hp	Dow metal (magnesium)	4.04:1
VM	4:1	28 hp	Nickel-iron	4.04:1
VMG	4:1	28 hp	Dow metal (magnesium)	4.04:1
VS	3.6:1	25 hp	Aluminum or optional nickel-iron	4.89:1
VC	3.6:1	25 hp	Nickel-iron	4.89:1
VCR	3.6:1	25 hp	Nickel-iron	6.67:1

*V and VL horsepower ratings are from factory power curves. VM and VMG horsepower ratings are by inference (they have the same compression ratio as the V, so they should have the same horsepower). VS, VC and VCR horsepower ratings are estimates.

The factory sometimes shipped experimental equipment to dealers and requested the dealers report the results of use. For example, a different piston cushion ring group with heavier expanders was shipped to dealers in June.

A used-machine sales contest in September and October helped push used-motorcycle sales to 3,200 during this typically slow part of the season. This was gratifying because every possible sales dollar was needed to keep the dealer network solvent through the oncoming winter.

Business was off about fifteen percent for the 1930 business year ending November 30, 1930. Even so, the company probably didn't yet realize that the economic setback of the Wall Street stock market crash would linger for the next several years. A more apparent problem was the overnight nosedive of the markets in Australia and New Zealand because of new restrictive tariffs. Single-cylinder sales were about half of the previous year's. Nevertheless, total foreign sales of 7,630 represented forty-three percent of total factory output.

1931
Numerous changes

Three changes were common to all 1931 models. On the front fork, a toolbox with a wedge-shaped cross section replaced the cylindrical toolbox. A chrome-faced disk horn superseded the black Klaxon horn. A

A 1931 30.50 ci, 500 cc Model C side-valve single. This model was commonly called the Thirty-fifty. The single headlight and wedge-shaped toolbox were new for domestic models.

The Model C used the same running gear as the Forty-five. Harley-Davidson single 7 in. headlamp with a flat (nonconvex) diffusing lens replaced the dual headlamps. Called the John Brown Motolamp, the headlight rim had a distinctive shape.

The 1931 Forty-five and Thirty-fifty shared a new rear brake, which was the same brake used on the 1929 F-head big twin. The new stopper was thirty-one percent larger than the previous unit. These two models were also outfitted with a gear lock to keep the transmission from jumping out of gear. Both the Forty-five and Thirty-fifty got new handlebars, either in standard or the shorter speedster configurations. No other changes were incorporated on the Thirty-fifty, but the Forty-five had a new single-tube muffler in place of the two-tube design, and a die-cast Schebler carburetor. The die-casting process consisted of pouring molten metal into a steel mold instead of a sand mold. Die casting produced more uniform interior surfaces.

On most 1931 model Forty-fives, a new generator drive gear set was installed. This change started with motor 31D 1786 in September 1930. The new set consisted of the following new parts: generator drive gear, generator driveshaft and generator driveshaft bevel gear with pin. The new configuration was heavier and had fewer but larger teeth. This setup was offered to dealers as a retrofit kit for 1930 and 1931 models. Retrofitting wasn't possible on the 1929 models because the earlier generator had a different-size armature shaft.

A new Forty-five clutch was introduced on the top-of-the-line DLD only, while existing stocks of older clutches were expended on the other Forty-fives. The new DLD clutch assembly had a different sprocket, inner roller race and bearing washers, key ring and outer clutch disk. The combination included one more steel plate and one more fiber plate.

As usual, a number of small parts were changed. Just to give an idea of the continual rollover of parts, the following are some of the new items for the 1931 model Forty-five twin: valve spring covers, piston pin bushings (there were none on the earlier Forty-fives), crankcase relief pipe, gear cover and oiler, oil pump assembly, seat post cushion springs, windshield bits and pieces, police siren and oil pump assembly. The new oil pump dispensed with the banjo fitting for the oil bleeder to the front chain. Instead, the bleeder line came directly out of the oil pump body.

Visually, the most notable changes to the 1931 Seventy-fours were a new single-tube Burgess muffler and a single headlight. A die-cast Schebler carburetor was a new feature. A three-speed transmission with reverse was offered in the 1931 models—this was a running change later publicized as a 1932 advancement.

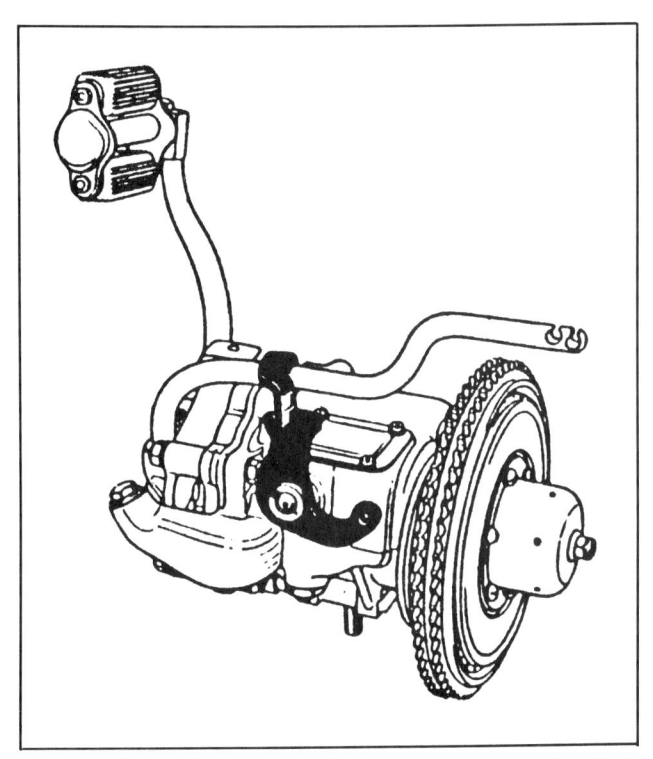

A gear lock was added to the Forty-five transmission for 1931. The same transmission was used in the Thirty-fifty. Harley-Davidson

Winter-equipped 1931 police Seventy-four. The standard olive finish had broad vermilion striping centered in gold and edged in maroon. The clutch and brake pedals were cadmium plated instead of parkerized in flat black. The pedals kept this finish up to and including the 1937 models. The Burgess muffler was a new feature of 1931 Seventy-fours. Harley-Davidson

William H. Davidson, later to become company president, in the process of winning the rugged 500 mile Jack Pine national championship enduro of 1930. His 1931 Forty-five sports one of the optional extra-charge paint jobs not explained by the sales catalogs. The optional colors were explained in a dealers special color brochure that included sample paint chips. The 1931 "standardized special colors" combinations were as follows: black and vermilion with one fine gold stripe and one broad gold stripe; solid white with one broad gold stripe bounded by two fine gold stripes; maroon and cream with one broad vermilion stripe and one fine gold stripe; police blue and fawn gray with one broad vermilion stripe and one fine gold stripe; and olive green and vermilion with one broad maroon stripe and one fine gold stripe. Gold striping bounded a smaller area "inside" the larger area bounded by the non-gold stripe. Harley-Davidson

A new method of ignition timing was provided for the 1931 Seventy-fours. A removable plug was provided on the left side of the crankcase, through which the flywheel could be observed. The circuit breaker could be adjusted to open at the proper time as indicated by the flywheel index notch.

New Seventy-four piston cushion rings (expanders behind the guide rings) were thicker. This required correspondingly thinner piston guide rings.

A midproduction change introduced new piston pin lock rings for all models. Pistons assembled from December 1930 and on incorporated the new lock rings.

Another midproduction change followed close behind. On the Seventy-four, a new constant-mesh starter design was incorporated, which prevented gears from jamming during starting or backfiring and made kickover easier due to smoother operation.

Numerous small parts were changed in the carburetor, saddle and front forks. New linings and other bits and pieces were incorporated in the brakes.

Four new 1931 models were introduced: the VC commercial model, the VCR road-marking model, the Model VMG with a magneto-generator and the VS sidecar model. The VC and VCR models featured pistons that were 1/16 in. shorter than normal, which lowered the compression ratio on these models to 3.6:1. The high-performance magneto-equipped VLM was dropped.

More optional colors

On all models, the standard paint job remained olive green with vermilion striping edged in maroon

For 1931, this special-shaped tank panel was offered. Two other examples appeared in The Harley-Davidson Enthusiast. *This was the first year of chromium plating on small parts. This motorcycle is fitted with optional cadmium-plated wheel rims.* Harley-Davidson

and centered in gold. The sales catalogs followed the tradition of being mute concerning the availability of optional finishes. For a change, however, the 1931 model edition of *The Harley-Davidson Enthusiast*, (August 1930) stated that optional finishes were available at extra cost—but without explaining what the extra-cost optional finishes were.

A 1931 Forty-five, showing the new single-tube muffler. This was the first year of catalog-referenced extra-cost color options—but the catalog didn't tell you what the colors were! Harley-Davidson

Clarification or confusion—take your choice—is added by the March 1931 issue of *The Harley-Davidson Enthusiast*, which mentions cerulean blue as a stock color, then goes on to mention several other finishes. Nonstandard finishes mentioned were red (vermilion) and copper, mauve, blue and silver, and red and gold. All of this "discussion" takes place in a back-cover cartoon panel that relates a rider's dreams, so the verbage could be tongue in cheek. Moreover, cerulean blue and mauve don't show up in the several period accessories catalogs reviewed by the author, and copper first makes the scene in 1934 (with stock number 11647-34A, signifying the year).

But now comes the clincher. *Shop Dope*, number 73S, dated April 13, 1931, lays out the prices for re-enameling. The color categories mentioned were "standard color" and "standard optional & all other colors." Harley-Davidson was continuing its any-color option and—in the author's opinion—the any-color option was available from 1928 through 1931. "Standard optional colors" were those that the factory carried in stock, azure blue for example. "All other colors" seems clear enough. Like the guy in the cartoon, you just "dreamed up" any colors you wanted and special-ordered them through your local Harley-Davidson dealer.

A new finish option was a flamboyant scroll pattern for the fuel tanks, but neither the regular motorcycle catalogs nor *The Harley-Davidson Enthusiast* mentions the availability of the 1931 scroll tanks. The scroll tank was rarely chosen, as evidenced by its appearance in only one photo in the 1931 issues of *The Harley-Davidson Enthusiast*. The July 1931 caption labels the motorcycle a "brand new 1931 special color 45 Harley-Davidson." The same 1931 style panel shows up on another motorcycle in a 1935 issue.

Chromium plating made its first appearance and was used on a number of small parts. Cadmium-plated wheel rims were an extra-charge option on the 1931 models. The clutch and brake pedal finishes were changed from a flat black Parkerized finish to cadmium plating. The foot pedals would retain this finish up to and including the 1937 models.

Other orders of business

In April 1931, the board discussed the building of a 21 ci, 350 cc single, primarily for the benefit of the export market. Engineering Chief William S. Harley recommended that the factory build about 500 of the singles from material in stock. Sales Chief Arthur Davidson felt the proposed singles should be painted in some distinctive color combination, such as red and black, to attract the younger set. Harley agreed to make up one of the proposed singles for thorough testing before the management would commit itself to more 21 ci single-cylinder production.

This is probably a styling exercise depicting the prototype 65 ci, 1065 cc twin as viewed by the company officers in July 1931. Or this styling may have been under consideration across the board. This was Harley-Davidson's first attempt at an integrated instrument panel. The front forks have side bracing. Valve covers are of a three-piece style introduced in the middle of the 1930 model production run. The frame is double-loop cradle style, similar to that later used on the 61 OHV. Since this was a styling mockup, the gas and oil lines, throttle and brakes weren't hooked up. The engine looks suspiciously like silver-painted wood. Harley-Davidson

The following month, the board decided to try out the proposed 21 ci single for another year before manufacturing 500 of them. Optimism continued to grow about the prospects of a continued 21 ci line, so in June the management decided to definitely offer a 1932 21 ci model and increase the projected 1932 21 ci single schedule to 1,000 units.

In July, Walter Davidson notified the Courtesy Car firm that no further Servi-Car work would be sent to them. Instead, Harley-Davidson was committed to doing its own Servi-Car engineering and production, even to the extent of running overtime on Servi-Car development.

The engineering department prepared a styling mockup of a proposed 65 ci side-valve twin during July. The mockup showed the factory's interest in further streamlining and apparently featured an all-welded lugless frame. William S. Harley favored going into production on this frame and using it for both the 65 ci motor and the 74 ci motor, but Walter Davidson didn't agree. Arthur Davidson didn't like the idea of a 65 ci twin at all. After a few weeks of discussion, the Sixty-five side-valve proposal was rejected.

Two different sizes of industrial motors were built during this period. Further testing of these two motors was agreed on before designing an additional model.

Tom Sifton journeyed to the factory in July and picked up the first 1932 Forty-five built. Before leaving the plant, he met with William S. Harley, who asked Sifton what problems he had been experiencing on Harley-Davidsons. Sifton related that he welded a reinforcement to the frame of every Forty-five before selling it. Harley summoned Assistant Superintendent George Nortman and instructed him to install the Sifton modification on Sifton's new 1932 motorcycle before Sifton rode it out of Milwaukee to San Francisco. Harley also said he wanted every 1932 Forty-five already built to get the Sifton treatment and to continue to modify the Forty-five side-valve frames until a heavier forging was designed to replace the existing weak component.

Board approval for the 61 OHV

In August, William S. Harley reported the engineering department would soon be ready to go ahead with the development of a "new sump oiler motor" and asked for the board's concurrence with continued effort on this project. Approval was granted and the engineering department began preparing design drawings for a 61 ci overhead-valve twin that would eventually become famous as the Model 61 OHV.

When drafting began on the 61 ci overhead-valve motor in 1931, conventional wisdom dictated no attempt at all toward valve enclosure. Leading British overhead-valve designs in 1931 invariably featured full exposure of the rocker arms and valve stems in order to get plenty of cooling air to unreliable valve springs. For example, the most expensive of all British bikes, the Brough-Superior SS100 favored by Lawrence of Arabia, had fully exposed valve stems and springs. So Harley-Davidson gave no thought to valve stem enclosure.

Among the earliest design decisions on the proposed 61 ci overhead-valve twin was the selection of bore and stroke dimensions. The bore and stroke selected were $3^5/_{16}$x$3½$ in., for a ratio of 0.946:1. By comparison, the JAP (J. A. Prestwich) V-twin powerplant of the 1931 Brough-Superior SS100, measured 80x90 mm, for a ratio of 0.888:1. (In the 1920s, JAP had built 61 ci motors with bore larger than stroke.) Long strokes had long been favored by motorcyclists for their good low end punch, but with improving roads and ever higher speeds came the march of engineering toward ever bigger bores and shorter strokes. Bigger bores meant bigger valves, and shorter strokes meant higher revolutions without risking overheating. In short, 61 OHV development was proceeding in line with the latest engineering trends.

Tightening the belt

During the year, the factory worked on a reduced hourly schedule. The management felt it was more fair to spread the hourly work out than to lay off hourly workers. All salaried employees making $60 a month or less took salary reductions of twenty-one percent. Higher paid employees took pay cuts too, of varying percentages.

Because of the drastically reduced sales, competition for police sales became intense; author Harry Sucher discusses this at some length in *Milwaukee Marvel*. The Schwinn family had stopped building the Super-X V-twin and Henderson four-cylinder, leaving American riders in a two-brand world: Harley-Davidson or Indian. In that situation, rider loyalty ran deep, and policemen were no exception. During the course of trying to convert a particular police department from Indians to Harley-Davidsons, dealer Tom Sifton heard the motorcycling police chief state he would never ride a Harley-Davidson on his police duties. Sifton convinced the town mayor to convert to Harley-Davidsons anyway, but the chief kept his word by switching his rounds to an automobile!

During a visit to the factory in the summer of 1931, Sifton ran into a most disappointing, even shocking, matter. Service manager Joe Ryan was known for his prompt responses to all queries from dealers and for his lengthy and detailed letters that exhibited both in-depth knowledge and genuine concern for the dealers. To Sifton and many other dealers, Ryan personified Harley-Davidson. In Sifton's mind, Ryan was up on a pedestal.

Joe Ryan invited Sifton to the Ryan home for dinner one evening. Dinner was delayed somewhat because Mrs. Ryan was late getting home from work. She had taken on a job as a scrub woman so that the Ryan household could make ends meet during the era of pay cuts at Harley-Davidson!

Sales during the 1931 business year totaled 10,500 units compared to the original plan for 12,000 units. Foreign sales were hardest hit, dropping from the 1930 total of 7,630 to 3,831. Planned production of 1932 models was reduced to 9,000 motorcycles, less than half of the 1929 and 1930 sales—and less than all motorcycles sold in 1912.

On December 21, Walter Davidson submitted a somber letter to the board of directors. To convey the seriousness of the situation, here are the words of the company president:

"In order to discuss our future plans I have outlined some of the things I think we must consider. First, there can be no question in anyone's mind that our business is showing a continual shrinkage.... The industrial motor,

Here's a little trivia. The rider is William H. Davidson. The Forty-five is a 1931 model because it has a vertical generator. An artist retouched this photo, which then went on the cover of the 1932 catalog! The headlight is a John Brown Motolamp, which was used in 1931 and 1932. Harley-Davidson

that we hoped would possibly help us somewhat, has naturally not come through, largely because of industrial conditions that did not permit its sale.

"Our foreign business has shown a very great decrease in the last several years, and it would almost seem that it is going to be a very small part of our business in the future. There does not seem to be anything much we can do about it.

"We then come back to the question as to whether this company can exist on the very decreased motorcycle business that we apparently face for some time in the future.... With this greatly decreased business in sight it then becomes the duty of our directors to decide what the future policy of our company is going to be.

"First, can we reduce our costs sufficiently to meet our decreased income and still make a profit?... At the present time we are in a wonderfully liquid condition and certainly do not want to take our surplus that we have accumulated and dissipate it in losses in the next few years. If we decide we should continue in business, can the officers of the company honestly say to themselves that we can get our costs down to the point where we can show a profit?... This is a question we should all begin to think about because between now and next spring we will have to formulate definite plans as to the future of this company."

1932
Onslaught of the Great Depression

After a two-year absence from the domestic lineup and a one-year absence from the export group, the Model B 21 ci side-valve single was re-introduced in the United States for 1932. Between 500 and 1,000 Model Bs were built up from excess stocks that had languished in the factory in the two years since the collapse of sales to Australia and New Zealand. Harley-Davidson claimed the 1932 Model B was the lowest priced motorcycle ever sold by the company. The $195 price of the

The protype 1932 Forty-five with a horizontal generator and double-curved front downtube. A new method controlled the air-oil mist expelled from the crankcase. The timing gear cover was shaped to move the air-oil mist to the middle of the oil slinger mounted on the end of the generator drive gear. The oil was then separated from the air by centrifugal force. This feature was not incorporated in the side-valve big twins until 1937. On right-side tank of twins, angled fuel hole and straight fuel tap were phased-in on late-1931 models. Harley-Davidson

San Francisco dealer Tom Sifton takes delivery of the first 1932 Forty-five from William S. Harley. Sifton had the frame reinforced before leaving, and William S. Harley incorporated the Sifton fix in production models. With the oil pump delivery turned way up, Sifton rode 70 mph for long stretches of his 2,460 mile journey. Harley-Davidson

A 1932 small single, referred to as the Twenty-one due to the nominal displacement of 21 ci, 350 cc. These were built up from surplus stocks that had been stored for two years. The $195 price was the lowest ever offered by Harley-Davidson. Harley-Davidson

A 1932 Seventy-four VL, as pictured in the sales catalog and in the new-model announcements in The Harley-Davidson Enthusiast. *The 1932 Burgess muffler was longer and smaller in diameter than the 1931 Burgess unit. Tank plain panels were part of the standard no-extra-charge configuration. The new-model announcement in* The New American Motorcyclist and Bicyclist *gives incomplete color information. Plain-panel color choices were vermilion with gold striping; white with gold striping; delft blue with gold striping; and police blue. Period photos indicate broad light-colored striping centered in gold and edged in a dark color—probably maroon.* Harley-Davidson

Model B probably meant these singles were sold at a loss, but this was preferable to the even greater loss of scrapping all Model B stock.

The 1932 Model B frame seat post tube was shortened 1 in., so the seat was 1 in. lower than on previous singles. The starter pedal was now a bicycle style instead of the single-tube style. The ammeter was dropped from the new switch panel, which had ignition and light switches. A stronger rear axle with tapered roller bearings was fitted. A two-tube muffler was used instead of the previous four-tube muffler.

The Forty-five was the most changed of the 1932 models. The D Series gave way to the R Series with a horizontally mounted generator. Models listed were the R and RS (sidecar model) with 4.3:1 compression ratios, the RL with 5.1:1 compression ratio and the RLD with 6:1 compression ratio. The RS had a sidecar gear ratio of 5.45:1, the R and RL were geared at 4.54:1 and the RLD was geared at 4.57:1. As with the former top-of-the-line DLD, the new RLD featured a 1¼ in. diameter carburetor instead of the 1 in. diameter carburetor of the less sporting Forty-fives.

Larger flywheels for the Forty-five were installed in new crankcases. New cylinders provided an air space between the exhaust ports and the barrels. Under each cylinder was a full baffle, and the rear baffle had six drilled holes, three on each side. This was a continuation of DL practice.

Aluminum pistons replaced the former Lynite variety. Piston pin lock rings were new. Thicker cushion rings of chrome-vanadium steel were combined with thinner guide rings, a change introduced a year earlier on the Seventy-four. Longer connecting rods had bronze bush upper bearings. Stronger valve springs and an improved crankcase breathing design were introduced. Inlet and exhaust cam gears and shafts were new. As in the DL Series, the cam gearshafts were used to handle crankcase air and oil mist blow-by. But instead of using only the inlet cam gearshafts for breathing, the RL also used the rear exhaust cam gearshaft. This was the same setup as in the Seventy-fours.

A new Forty-five oil pump with redesigned internals also had a different mounting so the pump could be removed without removing the new gearcase cover. The oil pump body was reinforced to prevent distortion, and the gearcase cover was redesigned to accommodate the new pump. The gearcase cover also featured an air-venting section designed to work with the new combined generator drive gear and oil slinger. The oil slinger spun in the air-oil mist and by centrifugal force pushed the oil out through holes in the periphery of the slinger. Meanwhile, the air was expelled from the center section of the slinger through a venting passage to the outside. The gearcase cover venting section was shaped to facilitate air-oil separation.

A new four-plate clutch on the Forty-five replaced the previous clutch. The Forty-five front chainguard was new.

An air scoop and gasoline strainer were new features for 1932, as shown on this Seventy-four motor. Harley-Davidson

The new Forty-five frame had a bowed front downtube to accommodate the new generator mounting, so the Forty-five took on the look of the big twin. Heavier forgings and tubing were used for the new frame, and the front fork was strengthened.

The Forty-five shared a new generator with the Seventy-four. The generator featured larger brushes to produce more uniform output and cooler running. A stronger bearing housing was incorporated, and the generator gear-side ball bearing run operated in an oil bath. Outside generator terminal connections were provided.

Changes in the Forty-five's rear brake anchorage made the rear wheel more readily removable. Rear axle bearings were changed from cup-and-cone style to two tapered roller bearings. The muffler was changed from a straight tube to a Burgess silencer similar to the big twin muffler.

The Thirty-fifty frame retained the straight front downtube, but the frame tubing was strengthened as in the Forty-five. Likewise, the Thirty-fifty shared the Forty-five's improvements in the oil pump, brakes and rear axle.

Cylinders on the Seventy-four were redesigned to provide airflow between the exhaust ports and the barrels, as on the Forty-five. Piston pin lock rings were new. A longer Burgess muffler was fitted. The big twin starter was changed to constant-mesh operation. Front forks were strengthened. The Seventy-four got the new generator also used on the Forty-five. Oil sealing was improved between the cam case and the generator, and a new oil pump assembly was installed. Although the oil pump was advertised as a 1932 feature, the pump was phased in with the late 1931 models. Oil pump improvements included a stronger disk hinge pin and lighter plunger spring for easier throttle operation.

For the Seventy-four, a new transmission countershaft and countershaft gear replaced the previous type, which had been used since 1916. Earlier Seventy-four gearboxes featured front and rear cast-in ears for mounting the inner section of the primary chainguard (which the factory simply called the inner chainguard). In the earlier design, a thrown rear chain could jam between the inner chainguard and the gearbox and break off the forward gearbox ear. In 1932 model Seventy-fours, the forward gearbox ear was removed, and a stamped metal bracket was substituted. The bracket attached to the top front transmission cover studs.

Four changes were common to the Forty-five and Seventy-four. A longer air intake pipe was chrome plated, and a fuel strainer was incorporated on the carburetor. Anti-score front brake lining was featured. Lighter oil pump plunger springs reduced operational effort.

Radios were first made available for police use. These were receiving units only and were built by Harley-Davidson. The company regarded radio manufacture as a necessary nuisance, which it tolerated in order to maintain police sales in the face of increasing competition from radio-equipped squad cars.

At some time during the 1932 model production run, a three-wheeled version of the Forty-five was

This three-wheeler wasn't cataloged, so the specifications are unknown. Such rigs were popular in Japan. Harley-Davidson

110

introduced. Known as the Servi-Car, this unit would be advertised the following sales season as a new 1933 advancement and would remain a Harley-Davidson staple for more than thirty years. Earlier, the Courtesy Car Company had built tricycles powered by Harley-Davidson single-cylinder engines.

A new accessory called the Safety Guard was first offered. Safety Guard remained the official term, but riders generally called the item the Crash Guard. The Safety Guard was a frame-mounted tubular brace that protruded to either side of the motorcycle. In a fall, the guard prevented the weight of the motorcycle from trapping the rider's legs.

Special color finishes for 1932 weren't mentioned in the sales catalogs, but were mentioned in the annual new-model edition of *The Harley-Davidson Enthusiast*. Specific colors, however, weren't listed. But from the July 1931 edition of *The New American Motorcyclist and Bicyclist*, we learn that Harley-Davidson offered seven optional extra-cost finishes for 1932 in addition to the long-running standard of olive green. The optional colors were vermilion with gold striping, white with gold striping, delft blue with gold striping, police blue, vermilion and black, delft blue and turquoise, and police blue and cream. The magazine didn't explain how the colors were divided on the two-color motorcycles. On factory orders, customers could specify cadmium and chromium plating on selected parts.

Still, there was some mystery. None of the previous sources disclosed that special scroll or tank panels were available. The December 1931 issue of *The Harley-Davidson Enthusiast* cleared this up by advertising optional scroll or plain tank panels for an extra charge of $2.85.

Production reductions

The company started the 1932 business year in November 1931 with a production schedule of 9,000 1932 models, which seemed a conservative judgment compared to the previous two years' totals of 17,662 and 10,500. By early 1932, however, the current production schedule began to undergo periodic reductions.

In February 1932, Walter Davidson recommended the elimination of the industrial motor program. William A. Davidson disagreed because of the company's considerable investment in the program and because he felt that there was still a chance that these motors could be sold once business conditions returned to normal.

In March, the outlook for industrial motors wasn't any better, which prompted Plant Superintendent William A. Davidson to suggest that the firm continue to push the sale of the existing supply of industrial motors and use up the materials on hand. Sales Manager Arthur Davidson didn't see any kind of significant market for

Police radios were first available in 1932. These were receiving units only. This speaker style didn't go into production. Harley-Davidson

Here's the production style of the 1932 radio. The motorcycle in this and the previous photo may not have been finished in any of the standard plain-panel choices because optional special finishes could be ordered by police departments. Gold lettering of city name, police department and vehicle number was commonly ordered as extra-charge options. Harley-Davidson

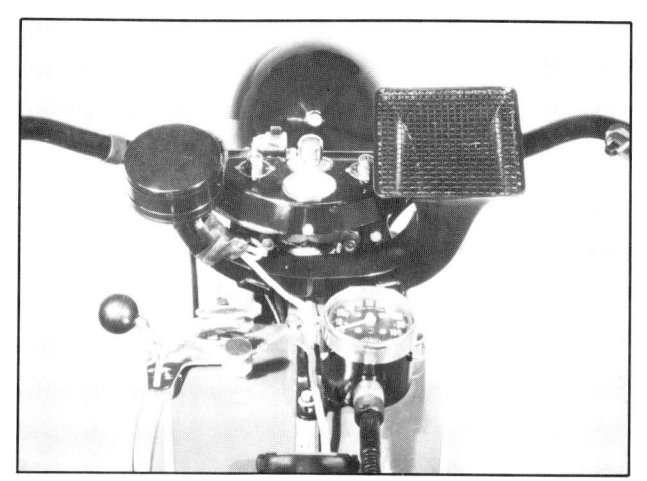

Rider's view of a radio-equipped model. Harley-Davidson

such motors. President Walter Davidson said the industrial motor engineer, Mr. Thanger, had been too optimistic on the matter, and Walter recommended the immediate cancellation of the industrial motor project. Other topics discussed included the manufacture of one-way police radios and a reverse gear for the Forty-five, both of which were approved for continued production.

Overhead cost reductions began to get more and more attention. Arthur Davidson recommended that the industrial motor engineer be released prior to laying off any administrative personnel. Walter Davidson recommended continuing the two-man factory competition team of Joe Petrali and Herb Reiber, but after some discussion the board decided to lay off Reiber.

Orders for industrial motors were still being honored in June, but only twenty-three units had been sold so far that month. The second generation's William H. Davidson traveled to Chicago to visit Sears & Roebuck concerning their possible order for 2,500 industrial motors to be used in garden tractors. The order didn't materialize because Sears & Roebuck needed a larger motor than what Harley-Davidson was building.

Overhead costs were again the dominant topic in July. All shop foremen had been laid off for a month, including annual vacation time, and in some instances these foremen would not be called back. The board debated the question of permanent layoffs of foremen and decided that further study was needed before a final decision. Sales Manager Arthur Davidson recommended the elimination of the racing department, effective the day after the traditional season ending on Labor Day with the flat track races at Syracuse, New York.

By August, scheduled 1933 model production was cut to 3,700 units. Recommendations were made to combine the racing and testing departments, to combine the sales and advertising departments, and to

This photo from the April 1932 Enthusiast *shows an interesting sunburst tank design. The photo was taken in Arizona. In another issue, an identical tank design appeared on another motorcycle in Saskatchewan, Canada! Apparently, the factory was experimenting with this optional paint style during 1932. Harley-Davidson*

Optional tank swirl panels weren't mentioned in sales literature or in The Enthusiast, *but based on the photos of owners' steeds appearing in the latter, most of the 1932 models had the swirl panels. Optional extra-charge two-color finishes for the swirl-panel models were vermilion and black; delft blue and turquoise blue; and police blue and cream. The second-named color appeared in the center of fenders and on tank swirl panels. Another option was two-color swirl panels with solid-color fenders. Striping was usually gold, but other striping colors could be ordered. Extra chromium and cadmium plating could be had on special order. Harley-Davidson*

The factory operated at about ten percent of capacity during 1931 and 1932. To take up the slack, Harley-Davidson built V-twin, opposed-twin and single-cylinder industrial engines. Sales were poor, and the program lasted less than two years. This is the V-twin. Harley-Davidson

Another variation of the V-twin. Harley-Davidson

The opposed-twin industrial engine. Harley-Davidson

The single-cylinder industrial engine. Harley-Davidson

locate the parts, accessories and service departments together. Walter Davidson again urged the dropping of the industrial motor program, and the directors unanimously concurred, thus killing off one of Harley-Davidson's rare excursions into nonmotorcycle production.

In October, all office salaries over $100 were lowered by ten percent. Well, not quite all. Salaries of the founding four were cut in half.

The management decided to enter into an unusual arrangement with their Japanese affiliates, A. R. Child and the Sankyo family. Harley-Davidson contracted to furnish a complete set of blueprints for the 74, 45, 30.50 and 21 ci models for a fee of $3,000, which covered cost. The Japanese connection was to pay a royalty fee of $5,000 for the first year, $8,000 for the second year and $10,000 for the third year. The fees also obligated Harley-Davidson to provide engineering services to Japan. The company reasoned that the unfavorable exchange rate between the dollar and the yen had ruined a once-lucrative market and that the modest fees would help keep a few members of its administrative and engineering staffs on board during these troubled times.

Among the engineering projects still hanging on was the so-called sump-oiler motor, later to become the famous Model 61 OHV. The sump-oiler motor probably stayed alive for two reasons. First, a minimal engineering staff had to be on board as long as the company was in business. The sump-oiler motor project may have fit into the available time for this staff, due to the leveling off of the Forty-five and Seventy-four side-valve problems. Second, the Seventy-four side-valve probably didn't measure up to expectations. Piston problems nagged the big side-valve, and an overhead-valve big twin looked like the way out.

For the 1932 model year, production totaled 6,841, of which 1,974 were for foreign markets and 110 were for the US Army. The estimated break-even production rate was 6,000 motorcycles per year, provided additional cost-cutting measures were taken. The production for the upcoming 1933 model year was changed to 4,050 motorcycles, about half the 1931 total and about one-fourth the 1930 total. The 1933 production schedule was the lowest since 1910. Only 500 motorcycles or twelve percent were for export, compared to a forty-percent export rate over a number of previous years.

Despite substantial cost reductions, the company had an operating loss of $321,670 compared to a $17,000 loss the previous year. Among the reduction measures were a number of layoffs of long-time employees, a situation that was occurring throughout American industry. Periodic economic downturns had always been around in the United States, but young workers had traditionally endured these setbacks on the way to obtaining job security through seniority. In reaching deep into the ranks for layoffs, American industry was sowing seeds that within five years would reap the harvest of unionization. Older hands could no longer feel secure and without their traditional company loyalty, unionization was inevitable.

Would you believe a Harley-Davidson tractor? This one has the single-cylinder engine shown in the previous figure. Harley-Davidson

The second street painter design got all the works on the proper side of the center stripe. This configuration went into limited production as the Model VCR. The motorcycle engine was the same as in the regular commercial model VC, with a 3.8:1 compression ratio. A Harley-Davidson industrial motor powered the compressor. Pinstriping was nonstandard. Note the huge rear sprocket. Harley-Davidson

Chapter 4

1933–1935

Hedging the side-valve bet

1933

Few technical changes were incorporated into ongoing models for 1933 due to the serious financial status of the company. Late 1933 models were outfitted with Linkert die-cast brass carburetors instead of the Schebler die-cast brass carburetors that had been fitted beginning in 1931.

The Buddy Seat made its debut as an accessory item and would henceforth remain the most popular of all optional equipment items. Indian soon had to follow suit.

Another new accessory item, introduced in late 1932, was the front fork Ride Control, a device consisting of a pair of slotted channels through which a sliding

First-offered in 1929, these lightweight sidecars for the Forty-five were built by the Goulding company of Saginaw, Michigan. This is a 1933 example. Harley-Davidson

member moved up and down. The Ride Control was supposed to be a sort of shock absorber, but it offered equal resistance to fork movement in either direction, not just on recoil. Friction of the Ride Control was adjustable by a knob on the right side.

Harley-Davidson offered three new models. These were the VLE, VLD and CB. The VLE was basically a VL fitted with magnesium alloy (formerly called Dow metal) pistons. The new VLD had the magnesium alloy pistons plus a Y-shaped intake manifold, new cylinders and new cylinder heads that yielded a 5:1 compression ratio. Maximum VLD power was 36 hp at 4500 rpm, a twenty-percent increase over the 1930 VL's 30 hp. With this change, the top-of-the-line VLD side-valve had low- and mid-range acceleration about the same as the old two-cam JDH F-heads. Meanwhile, VL power had been increased to 32 hp. Other new V Series parts included an oiler bleeder pipe, carburetor and generator oil retainer.

The CB single featured the Thirty-fifty motor in the Twenty-one frame, so parts differences were minor, if any. The CB was announced in the November 1932 issue of *The Harley-Davidson Enthusiast*, three months into the new-model season.

As mentioned, the Servi-Car originally appeared as a mid-1932 model. The 1933 Forty-five three-wheeler came with either small or large body.

A new deal for the 1933 Servi-Car was a constant-mesh three-speed plus reverse transmission. This called for a number of new parts, including gearbox, low gear, second gear, reverse gear, shifter guide, bell crank rod, shifter shaft, shifter fork and shifter clutch for low and reverse, shifter fork and shifter clutch for second and high, and gear lock plate. The shifting mechanism on the three-speed plus reverse transmission, was different from all previous Harley-Davidson layouts. Above the gearbox was a slotted drum, which was rotated by movement of the gearshift lever. The drum slot registered with a vertical stud, which protruded from a lower piece that encircled the sliding gearshaft somewhat like a hand encircles a baseball bat. Together, the hand and stud were termed the shifter finger. The rotating drum slots caused the shifter finger to move laterally, and to shift the sliding gears into the selected ratio.

Gone was the standard solid olive green finish that had characterized Harley-Davidsons since the late

The hot-stuff VLD model debuted in 1933 with a Y-shaped inlet manifold. These "TNT" motors had 36 hp, six more than the standard big twins. The oil pump is representative of the early 1930s for the Thirty-fifty, Forty-five and Seventy-four. The double-plunger principle was still used. Harley-Davidson

Ride Control was a new accessory for 1933. The rider turned a knob to adjust stiffness of suspension. Its practicality was questionable since rebound action was equally affected by the control knob—not a true shock absorber, in other words. However, the device was popular. Harley-Davidson

1910s. The singles were available in silver and turquoise only, with black and gold striping. Twins were offered in the following colors: silver and turquoise with black and gold striping, black and mandarin red with gold striping, sunshine blue and white with gold striping, olive and brilliant green with brilliant green striping, and police blue and white with gold striping. Regardless of colors used on the tanks and fenders, black was used on the frames, forks and chainguards. This continued henceforth. A stylized tank panel with a bird motif completed the facelift of standard paint finishes. This was the first year for mandatory black frames and forks.

An optional extra-cost chrome-plating package was offered, including the handlebars, generator end cover, exhaust system, seat bar assembly, oiler cover, chainguard cover, valve spring covers, intake pipe nut, front brake control and coil clamp. Appearance and function of the headlights on all models were changed by the new convex diffusing lens, which replaced the flat diffusing type.

Meanwhile, arch-rival Indian had been purchased by E. Paul DuPont, so Indians were now available in

This 1933 Forty-five shows off popular accessories: front fender eagle, Safety Guard (commonly called a Crash Guard), Ride Control, handlebar crossbar, Little King spotlight, fancy gearshift ball, speedometer, buddy seat and buddy seat cover. The 1933 style scroll tank design could be supplied for earlier-model tanks returned for painting. Harley-Davidson

The 1933 models featured a bird motif on the tanks. This was the first year of no-extra-charge paint options. The gal on the Forty-five is perched on a buddy seat, which was first offered that year. The 1933 models were the first with convex headlight lenses. Harley-Davidson

119

many one- and two-color combinations of DuPont finishes. The resulting color war between Harley-Davidson and Indian would continue throughout the decade.

In February 1933, Plant Superintendent William A. Davidson requested that 100 350 cc and 500 cc side-valve singles be built in excess of estimated requirements in order to use up all materials on hand. He further estimated that the direct labor and material costs on the singles would amount to about $65 per motorcycle. President Walter Davidson, however, expressed his view that it would be better to offer a reduced price of $250 on the Forty-five and forget the single. No decision was reached on these matters, but the board agreed to continue development of the new 61 ci overhead-valve twin and introduce new fenders on the 1934 models.

In March, the management agreed to hire rider Joe Petrali for the racing season ahead, but the terms were Spartan. Petrali was to be offered a $100 per month straight salary plus expenses and equipment, but there was to be no guarantee of a full season's employment. Instead, Petrali would in essence be working one month at a time, an approach that not only minimized factory commitment but was doubtlessly intended to motivate the jockey! Petrali later accepted the arrangement.

President Franklin Roosevelt closed all of the nation's banks right in the heart of the spring sales campaign, which greatly curtailed the confidence of both dealers and prospective customers. Sales of the single-cylinder models continued to wither away, and by April the total orders for the past six months had included only fifty-five Twenty-ones and ninety-eight Thirty-fifties. Arthur Davidson wondered whether there might be more demand for both the singles and the Forty-five twin if their weights could be reduced, but no conclusion was reached. He next proposed several sales economies, including salary reductions and the release of several traveling men and their replacement by office staff members.

In May, the board decided to accept the Japanese arrangement for production of Harley-Davidsons in Japan under license. The management concluded that the top-of-the-line model for 1935 would be the new 61 OHV with a four-speed gearbox and new clutch, and that this motor would be installed in the new single-top-tube frame, which had already been designed for the 74 ci side-valve twin. The Seventy-four was to be phased out in favor of the new Sixty-one overhead-valve. Arthur Davidson reported that his previously proposed economies in the sales department had been initiated and that the savings had been even more than the $1,000 per month anticipated.

Walter Davidson met in New York with officials of the Indian company to discuss the National Industrial Code as applied to the motorcycle business. The two firms agreed there was no reason for action on the political front at this time.

During the week of Labor Day, the first finished parts for the new Sixty-one overhead-valve were turned over by the tool room to the experimental department. Testing began shortly thereafter, and oil leakages were among the first problems encountered.

In November, Walter Davidson told the stockholders that a 30.50 ci overhead-valve single was under consideration. The following month, the Thirty-fifty overhead was officially added to the proposed 1935 lineup.

Foreign currency exchange rates became favorable during the past year; for example, the British pound sterling had doubled in value compared to the dollar. Foreign sales were on the upswing because of suddenly more affordable Harley-Davidsons on the show room floors of foreign dealerships. Consequently,

Fun and Games Department. No wonder Harley-Davidson didn't use this photo in their advertisements! Optional finishes for twins were silver and turquoise with black and gold striping; black and mandarin red with gold striping; sunshine blue and white with gold striping; and police blue and white with gold striping. Singles were available in silver and turquoise only, with gold striping. The second-named color was for the tank side panel and the centers of fenders. Black frames and forks were fitted to all models beginning in 1933. Harley-Davidson

2,200 motorcycles were being projected for foreign sales as compared with the previous season's 500.

Although Harley-Davidson was still on shaky ground, Indian was in even worse shape. As well as sharing Milwaukee's struggle against the depressed economy, Springfield had compounded its worries by building unsuccessful nonmotorcycle products, such as automobile shock absorbers and outboard motors. According to Red Wolverton, during 1933 Arthur Davidson tried to get his brothers and William S. Harley to agree to buy out Indian. Arthur believed the Indian company could be had for a song, but because of Harley-Davidson's own perilous circumstances, the others wouldn't go along with Arthur's proposal.

Sales of 1933 models totaled 3,703 instead of the targeted 4,050. Production was thus averaging about twenty percent of full factory capacity for single-shift operation. The Depression was at its bottom, with total stock values on the New York exchange falling to eleven percent of the precrash 1929 level.

Because of the severe financial picture, Harley-Davidson and Indian collaborated to invent a new class of motorcycle competition, Class C. This class featured racing and hillclimbing events limited to stock motorcycles, which was an effort by both factories to get out of the expensive Class A game involving factory specials. Competition was limited to 45 ci, 750 cc sidevalve motors and 30.50 ci, 500 cc overhead-valve motors in road racing and flat track racing. For TT events (predecessor of the motocross) and hillclimbs, 61, 74 and 80 ci motorcycles were also allowed, with big twin competition having its own class. All racing motorcycles had to be "same as you can buy," with that aspect being controlled by stipulating minimum production figures for each eligible model.

Class C debuted in the 1933 competition rules book, but didn't start to make a dent until the 1934 season. The new racing game would eventually bring both factories back into racing in a big way, but that was some years in the future due to the current survival efforts by both Harley-Davidson and Indian.

Ongoing Depression

A lot of motorcycle dealers didn't hold on throughout the Depression. One who did was Tom Sifton. He talks about how tough it was to keep his San Francisco dealership alive:

"I used to stay open until ten o'clock at night, and I wouldn't come down to work until nine or ten in the morning. You didn't sell motorcycles in the daytime because a guy who had any money to buy a motorcycle was working, but he was free at night.

The oil pump was completely redesigned for 1934. A year earlier, Indian brought out dry-sump oiling with recirculating oil. Harley-Davidson countered by stressing that only clean oil was used in the total-loss system. Harley-Davidson

The 1934-1940 Forty-five clutch. Late 1929 through 1933 Forty-five clutches used fourteen small springs, the same as used in the singles. The 1934-1940 Forty-five clutches used twelve larger springs. Troy Ross

"We did various things. They'd be sitting around here and all of a sudden one of the guys would say, 'Well, let's go to Palo Alto and get a milkshake.' Palo Alto is about twenty-seven miles from San Francisco, and they'd ride twenty-seven miles down there to get a milkshake. And they raced all the way down there, too.

"We were open six days a week, and on Sundays we went on club runs—we worked seven days a week. In those days, motorcycles used to break down on the road. If a guy broke his motorcycle, I'd put my foot on his rear fender and push him all the way home. Stella was on behind me, and she didn't enjoy that. Well, when I pushed it home, I pushed it to my shop, and we started on it Monday morning to fix it. Once I pushed a motorcycle from Bijou, near Lake Tahoe, Nevada—about 240 miles!

"In 1930, Moms and I got married. We were going to get ourselves a nice apartment, but things were too tight. I had a little two-room apartment above my motorcycle shop that I'd been 'baching' in, and we moved in there. We lived on $50 a month through the Depression.

"Lots of guys were working on lawn mowers and things like that to supplement their income, and they would maybe work cheaper than we would. We only dealt in motorcycles, but we survived. We managed to keep the San Francisco Motorcycle Club going through it. A lot of married people in San Jose rode motorcycles. A guy and his wife would come down to the shop, and while he had some work done and bought some accessories or something, his wife would go up and have coffee with my wife, and we existed fine. The shop paid the utilities and the rent and took in about $50 a month for groceries, and that was it."

Better days were around the corner, according to Harley-Davidson management. The 1934 business year production schedule was set at 7,800 units, more than double the 1933 actual production of 3,700 units.

1934
Upgrades

A year earlier, Indian had come out with dry-sump oiling, so for 1934 Harley-Davidson felt the need to upgrade its total-loss lubrication system. The Harley response was a new oil pump on the Forty-five and Seventy-four. This pump was supposed to have better oil control over a wide speed range and a better adjustment for oil to the front chain. Company advertisements proclaimed the superiority of total-loss oiling because only clean oil arrived at vital points. The new pump required a new gearcase cover.

Frames and forks on all models were subjected to new heat-treating operations. The company claimed the new heat treating made the frames and forks fifty percent stronger.

The Forty-five and Seventy-four were fitted with Linkert die-cast brass-bodied carburetors in lieu of the die-cast Schebler mixers; this was a running change made during production of the late 1933 models. VC commercial Seventy-fours and all Forty-fives but the RLD featured a 1 in. Linkert carburetor. Other V Series models and the RLD used a 1¼ in. Linkert.

Problems were experienced with the 1¼ in. mixer. The carburetor caused a flat spot when accelerating from low speed and uneven running and popping back through the carburetor when running with a slightly opened throttle.

New low-expansion aluminum alloy pistons replaced magnesium alloy pistons on the Forty-five and Seventy-four. The aluminum pistons were more reliable than the magnesium pistons and were only slightly heavier.

On the Forty-five, the fourteen-spring clutch was replaced by a twelve-spring setup. The larger springs were the same as those in the Seventy-four clutch. This modification was made to prevent setting of the clutch springs when hot. Several other new parts were incorporated into the Forty-five clutch, including the clutch gear, outer clutch disk, clutch spring collar and thrust cap.

Late 1934 Forty-fives with reverse-gear transmission had new shifting arms, one for low and reverse, the other for second and high. A new front stand was available on the Forty-five, but this was almost exclusively used on export models. The Servi-Car was now offered in four variants: small box without towbar, small box with towbar, large box without towbar, and large box with towbar, air tank and combination bumper-and-tire carrier.

The Seventy-fours could be fitted with a new front stand, although few domestic models were so equipped. The big twins had a new lower backside section for the primary chainguard. All Seventy-fours had the Y-manifold introduced on last year's VLD.

New styling features shared by the 1934 Forty-five and Seventy-four were the Airflow taillight, High-flo muffler, new saddle and streamlined fenders. The new bucket saddle was studded with shiny rivets and mounted to a new gloss black enameled seat bar. White handlebar grips were standard, but black grips were

New, more stylish fenders graced the 1934 twins. Photo layouts like this were translated into advertisements showing the rider seemingly flying through the air. Standard color combinations for the Forty-five, Seventy-four, Package Truck and sidecar were teak red with black tank panels and fender sides; and silver with teak red tank panels and fender sides. For the Forty-five and Seventy-four, three no-extra-charge options were available but not carried in stock. These were seafoam blue with silver tank centers and fender centers; black with orlando orange tank centers and fender centers; and black with olive green tank centers and fender centers. Striping colors weren't specified. For a limited period, a Summer Color Special was offered at no extra charge for the twins. This consisted of a copper enameled main section with vermilion tank centers and fender centers. Harley-Davidson

The 1934 Forty-five had a rear fender unique to that year. The fender valance on later Forty-fives extended below the chainguard. This was the last year of the fork-mounted toolbox. The High-flo tailpipe was new for 1934. Harley-Davidson

available. As in 1933, an extra-cost chrome-plating package was offered on two-wheelers, covering handlebars, generator end cover, exhaust pipes, saddle bar assembly, muffler, tailpipe, oiler and timer cover, intake pipe clamp nuts, valve spring covers and front brake control clamp.

Harley-Davidson singles were offered for the last time, in both 21 and 30.50 ci sizes. These were the last models to feature the old two-tube muffler. For all models, completing the styling makeover were a new tank panel and new color combinations.

By January 1934, the 61 ci overhead-valve twin was three-fourths finished, but the 30.50 ci overhead-valve single was just under way. Sales Manager Arthur Davidson favored bringing out the single first, but Engineering Manager William S. Harley recommended bringing out each model as soon as they were ready.

Over the next several weeks, the prototype Sixty-one was plagued by oil leaks, so some parts were redesigned. The production parts for the Sixty-one were finished in March, and Harley forecasted completion of the final-configuration prototype by the end of April.

Design efforts continued on both the Sixty-one and the Thirty-fifty, and by mid-April the gearbox for the single was designed and ready for detailing. Progress on both models was slower than expected, partly because the factory workweek had been cut from forty-four to forty hours as a result of the new National Recovery Act. Harley extended his estimate of Sixty-one completion from the end of April to the end of May.

In early May, two Sixty-one frames were painted and the first finished motor was installed. Testing of the first complete 61 ci motorcycle began immediately, and oil leakage persisted. Oil leaks continued through mid-June despite constant efforts to seal up the large number of joints. On the other hand, some parts were getting too much oil. The problems with the Sixty-one were delaying drawing completion, testing and ordering of forgings, castings and other materials.

Late in the 1934 model production run, the traditional tapered-bore cylinders were abandoned in favor of straight-bore cylinders. In combination with the straight bores were new T-slot aluminum pistons. These changes were introduced effective with Forty-fives from serial number 34-R-4000 and with big twins from serial number 34-VL-9000.

The new models were customarily introduced over the Labor Day holiday. This year, however, the company decided to move the launch date for the 1935 models back to mid-December. The Sixty-one no longer figured in plans for the seasonal kickoff. By the third week of July, the Sixty-one was again ready for road testing. However, the Thirty-fifty single was still being designed and bench tested.

The hoped-for overhead-valve models continued to lag behind their development schedule. Consequently, in October the management decided to cancel the Sixty-one and Thirty-fifty as 1935 models.

The 1934 models were carried in stock by dealers throughout the year, so the 1934 model sales period was about sixteen months. This move was made to clear 1934 stocks when sales didn't improve as much as had been forecasted. Still, the sale of about 10,000 1934 models over sixteen months, or 6,250 per year, represented a seventy percent rise in business compared to 1933 sales of 3,700 units.

1935
Arrival of straight-bore cylinders

The most significant mechanical change for 1935 was the switch from tapered-bore cylinders and round pistons to straight-bore cylinders and cam-ground (elliptical) T-slot pistons. Harley-Davidson had been

Police machines show off new fenders and Airflow taillight. Harley-Davidson

The left side of this Seventy-four shows the new rear chainguard, which extended farther back over the rear sprocket. The sidestand was taken out by the artist to improve the appearance of this retouched photo. Harley-Davidson

The Servi-Car, now in its third year, was immediately popular with police departments. Civilian models were available in one finish only, silver with black frame and forks. Harley-Davidson

Quarter-mile cinder-track speedway racing became popular. This 1934 two-port 30.50 ci, 500 cc example is one of Harley-Davidson's first speedway models. Other variants were built in the next few years, but production was limited. Harley-Davidson

alone in its use of tapered bores from 1914 through 1934. The new straight-bore cylinders were honed to a "gun barrel" finish. The T-slot pistons featured two diagonally cut (formerly called slot cut) compression rings. These changes were advertised as 1935 model improvements, although they were incorporated late in the 1934 model production run. For the Forty-five and Seventy-four, the company advertised a higher grade of steel for the crankpins.

The RLDR was a new Forty-five model designed for Class C racing and hillclimbing. Because Class C required riders to ride their stock motorcycles to the events, full road equipment was still included. A separate parts book supplement was published for the RLDR. The RLDR was fitted with looser clearances in the major motor assemblies.

The first Harley-Davidson Eighties were available as 1935 models. The 1935 Eighties didn't appear in 1935 press releases or sales literature because of their late arrival. The Eighties were included on the 1935 Season Order Blank as Models VLDD "Sport Solo, Solo Bars," and VDDS "Low Compres., Sidecar Gearing and Bars." Another under-publicized big twin was the VLDJ, a 74 ci "Twin, Competition Special, Solo Bars." The VLDJ doesn't appear in any of the new-model announcements or catalogs.

On the Seventy-fours and Eighties, an adjustable circuit breaker stop screw was provided to simplify ignition timing. Earlier V Series timing was accomplished simply by loosening and shifting the advance/retard plate, and was thus inaccurate.

The Forty-five Solo models featured the constant-mesh transmission that made its debut on the 1933 Servi-Cars. The transmission featured the slotted shifting drum (termed a shifting cam by the factory).

The Forty-five was given a quickly detachable rear wheel, a hub-driven speedometer and an internal expanding rear brake. Sprocket combinations of the Forty-five were changed, but without altering the gear ratios. This resulted in both the primary drive and final drive chains moving faster, but with less torque load and with the intention of reducing chain wear.

On the Servi-Car, double-acting internal and external rear brakes were continued after the running change made during the production of 1934 models. On Servi-Cars without a towbar, the toolbox was moved from the front fork to the body. The rear axle housing was fitted with a tie rod for added strength.

On the Forty-five and Seventy-four, an adjustable brake shoe pivot stud enabled brake adjustment for maximum contact between the shoe and brake lining. This was accomplished by loosening the pivot stud nut, then applying the brake. The stud would then move within an oblong mounting hole until the stud reached the ideal location and then was secured by tightening the stud nut. The adjustable brake shoe pivot stud was particularly useful as the motorcycle accumulated mileage, since without the stud, one shoe would wear more than the other and ideal shoe-to-drum contact could not be maintained. Although billed as a 1935 improvement, the adjustable stud was phased in during the latter part of the 1934 model production. Brake drums were carburized to harden them, and linings were hardened to improve braking. Carburizing was a process of heating iron in contact with carbon, thus forming case-hardened steel.

Both models got a prefocused headlight. The prefocused feature referred to the more accurate location of bulb filaments and the new bayonet bulb mounting, which ensured that the bulb could be located only at the ideal depth within the reflector. The bayonet base also was adjustable by a screw in the back of the headlight shell. Earlier headlight bulbs had been screwed in, with hit-or-miss results in light beam output.

There were a few appearance changes. These included shorter handlebar grips, large filler caps, new carburetor air intake, gas-deflecting muffler end, new toolbox location, new horn mounting and beehive taillight lens.

You have to wonder about advertising. The 1935 sales literature claimed easier starting on the Seventy-fours due to a higher starter ratio. There was no change in the starter mechanism, but the effective ratio was changed by a switch from a twenty-three- to a twenty-two-tooth motor sprocket. This change lowered the starter ratio—the opposite of the claim—and increased

The last year of the singles came in 1934; this is a Twenty-one. For the Twenty-one and Thirty-fifty, the standard color combination was silver with teak red tank panels and fender sides. Olive green with black tank panels and fender sides was a no-extra-charge option, but was not carried in stock for these two singles. However, olive green with black tank panels and fender sides was the standard color combination for the CB single, the model with the 30.50 ci motor in the 21 ci frame. Harley-Davidson

128

kicking resistance instead of decreasing it. Oh well, maybe the new setup did make starting more consistent by spinning the motor over faster.

In January, the new 1935 side-valve models began to appear in the show rooms. By the end of the month, the factory was responding to a few dealer complaints

Unpaved roads became smoother during the 1930s, and militaristic riding garb gained popularity. Advertising boosted the buddy seat with many such photos. The fender paint scheme on the 1934 twins featured a narrow section of contrasting color, tapering to a point on each end. Harley-Davidson

Advertised as a 1935 feature, straight-bore cylinders first appeared late in the 1934 model production run. Harley-Davidson

about new motors locking up. Reports of locked-up motors became more frequent during February, and a vigorous effort began to locate the cause of the problem.

A cost analysis in March indicated the proposed 1936 Thirty-fifty overhead-valve single would have an unacceptably high selling price if the standard profit margin was included. William H. Davidson suggested the model be subsidized in order to sell for $295.

During the next several weeks, the 30.50 ci overhead-valve single was subjected to comparative testing against a 30.50 ci overhead-valve BSA single. The two motorcycles had about the same top speed, but the American job was about 60 lb. heavier with consequently less acceleration. Because of the disappointing test results, the proposed overhead-valve single was boxed up in April, and no further development was planned.

The factory at last determined the cause of motor lockups in the new Forty-fives and Seventy-fours. When lower ends were replaced by dealers, invariably there were no more problems, thus confirming that 1934 and earlier replacement parts were not deficient. Investigation traced the origin of the lower end problems to a change in the heat treating of bearing retainers

Cam-ground (elliptic) T-slot pistons were used with the new straight-bore cylinders. These pistons occasionally broke between the bottom of the T and the bottom of the skirt.

Never fear: the artist removed the scratches for the advertising copy! Harley-Davidson

Most obvious of the 1935 changes were the new tank panels and the wide section of contrasting color in fender centers. Harley-Davidson

New for 1935 was the constant-mesh transmission on the Forty-five. Above the gearbox is the slotted drum that functioned as a shifter cam. This debuted on the 1933 Forty-fives with reverse transmission, but was first used on solo models in 1935. Because the cam is turned away in this photo, only a small part of the slot can be seen on the right end. Harley-Davidson

used in the connecting rods. When the connecting rod bearing retainers were heated and then quenched, the open end shrinked to result in a slight conical shape of the retainer instead of the proper cylindrical shape. The conical shape shifted the bearing rollers sideways a few thousandths of an inch so that, instead of rolling freely, there was a creeping and dragging effect. Elimination of the deficient bearing retainers from factory inventory ended the problem. Replacement retainers were identified with a groove around the outside diameter. The solution had come none too soon, because some dealers had to overhaul half of the 1935 models they sold prior to the production line fix.

Aluminum cylinder heads were first tried on sidevalve models in March, with samples being provided to Los Angeles dealer Rich Budelier and two other dealers, Egloff and Goodwin. The three dealers reported unfavorably on the aluminum heads, which cracked and didn't seem to produce better performance than the standard cast-iron heads. These reports and the extra cost of the aluminum heads led to discontinuing these field tests in April. Incidentally, the aluminum heads tried by the three dealers may have been samples of those made by a Portland, Oregon, firm.

A 1935 Forty-five with the new gas-deflecting muffler end, a feature also used on the Seventy-four and Eighty. Standard 1935 finishes were teak red and black; venetian blue and silver; verdant green and black; Egyptian ivory and regent brown; olive green and black; and silver and black for police use only. For a brief period, another option was cameo cream with dawn gray panels and potomac blue striping. The second-named color was applied to the small panel on the tank front and to the side panels of the fenders. New features shown are shorter handlebar grips, carburetor air intake styling, horn mounting, frame-mounting toolbox and beehive taillight lens. The 1935 models were the first with the Cycle-ray headlight with prefocused bulb. Harley-Davidson

This firm used regular Harley-Davidson iron heads for patterns, then machined the aluminum heads to obtain the desired compression ratio.

Although the aluminum heads did not work out, factory tests of new iron cylinder heads resulted in improved power and smoothness on the Forty-five, Seventy-four and Eighty. Management decided to incorporate these improvements into the 1935 models as soon as possible instead of waiting for the 1936 season.

Going ahead with the 61 OHV

The 61 ci overhead-valve twin, henceforth referred to by its eventual production title the 61 OHV, was nearly ready for production. Although earlier canceled from the 1935 lineup, management was now debating the option of introducing about 200 61 OHVs in the summer of 1935. The engineering department suggested this approach to prove the design before entering into large-scale production. However, the sales department argued against introducing the 61 OHV until dealers could sell out the 1935 Seventy-four side-valves on hand. A compromise release date of September 1 was discussed, but no decision was reached in the April board meeting.

At about this time, a running change was made to the grounding setup for 1935 models. Up to this time, the grounding circuit was completed through the fork fittings and frame head bearings, with the occasional result of burned-out bulbs or ignition points due to poor grounding. The problem was cured by running a ground wire directly from the ammeter to the frame.

The new side-valve cylinder heads continued to perform well in final tests conducted in May. Management decided, however, that it was too late in the 1935 model production run to introduce these new iron heads, as had earlier been their plan, so the new iron cylinder heads were delayed until production of the 1936 models. Because of the success with iron head experiments, management again became interested in experimenting with aluminum cylinder heads.

The Thirty-fifty single was formally canceled as a 1935 model.

The question of bringing out the 61 OHV in September 1935 or in January 1936 came up for consider-

The 1935 Forty-fives were the first with a quickly detachable rear wheel—Seventy-fours got this feature in 1930. Harley-Davidson

Rider's view shows new larger filler caps for 1935. Harley-Davidson

133

able discussion in the May board meeting. Certain board members even questioned the wisdom of bringing out the 61 OHV at all! Since a majority of the required tools for the 61 OHV had already been made, the idea of killing it was short lived. Perhaps the negative second thoughts on the 61 OHV arose from continued developmental problems, since the test model had experienced excessive wear on the chains and the brake linings wore too rapidly. Walter Davidson recommended testing with different sizes of sprockets to see if this would reduce wear.

By June, Walter Davidson's suggestion had proven sound. The board timidly endorsed the beleaguered 61 OHV by noting, "we will probably go ahead with the job."

Board business

Following some complaints on Linkert carburetors, Mr. Linkert came to the factory in July to present ideas for improvements. One of Linkert's ideas was a new carburetor that featured a slide that opened a port over the venturi. While this slide was rather clumsy when separately operated, the experimental carburetor did yield faster running and better acceleration above 40 mph in high gear. The experimental carburetor was taken back to Linkert's factory in Indianapolis for further tests.

William H. Davidson traveled to the East Coast in July to visit the Atlantic City, New Jersey, police convention, the Keene, New Hampshire, motorcycle races and the Indian factory. Davidson was pleased by the police convention because there was less squad car talk and more interest in the motorcycle exhibit than at previous conventions.

At Springfield, Davidson was surprised at the apparent efficiency of the Indian plant, which operated with a far smaller labor force than did Harley-Davidson. The Indian office force was only about one-

Earl and Dot Robinson set a transcontinental record in this outfit, which featured a Goulding sidecar manufactured by Dot's family. For a while, Harley-Davidson considered buying all of their sidecars from Goulding. Harley-Davidson

third the Harley-Davidson office force, yet Indian General Manager Joe Hosley got a complete record of all changes in cost every week. Davidson was impressed that Indian didn't build up large stocks of motors and enameled parts like Harley-Davidson, as the carrying of large inventories of these items was expensive.

The Indian engineering department consisted of only six men, including the drafting department, while the experimental room was manned by just three persons. Although a small organization, Indian engineering had recently completed the design of a new four-cylinder engine that had just gone into production and was dealing with continual updates of existing two- and three-wheelers as well. Davidson didn't realize how lucky Harley-Davidson was, because the 1936 Indian Four would soon prove to be one of Indian's worst and Harley-Davidson would simultaneously be bringing out one of its all-time best models, the 61 OHV.

Back in Milwaukee, no feasible method had been devised to adapt the experimental Linkert carburetor because the concept depended on two-handed operation, so this idea was dropped in August. Meanwhile, tests on the 61 OHV continued, with the outlook that these tests would end in a few days and complete all remaining engineering effort prior to production.

William H. Davidson suggested at the September board meeting that the company use the new 61 OHV to go after the American speed record held for some years by Indian. The 1936 production schedule for the 61 OHV was set deliberately slow in order to learn what problems the riders would encounter while enabling the factory to correct these problems with less adverse publicity than with an all-out production program. The concensus was that a speed record attempt would be wiser after this process resulted in a perfected 61 OHV.

Young Davidson next made a case for both an improved 45 ci side-valve motor and a 30.50 ci overhead-valve model. As a considerable amount of money had already been spent on the latter, he felt it might be worth spending a little more to complete development.

A mock dealership was displayed at the factory for many years. Most dealers didn't have such spacious show rooms. Harley-Davidson

The board was made aware of the Forty-five sidevalve's unpopular reception by Harley-Davidson dealers, who didn't want to order the Forty-five because it didn't have the speed it should.

Assistant Plant Superintendent George Nortman believed that greater standardization was needed. A wide variety of equipment options as well as color choices complicated the manufacturing job beyond the days of all-olive or all-gray motorcycles. Nortman also recommended that the company launch a cheaper model to appeal to the bicycle trade. This point led into a lengthy discussion about the prospects for such a lightweight.

William S. Harley suggested that a revival of the discarded 21 ci single, perhaps with a new frame, might be attractive, but only in the United States, as the company couldn't hope to compete anymore in foreign markets because of labor costs and tariffs. Walter Davidson concurred, and William A. Davidson felt the engineering department might be able to do something with the old overhead-valve single. With that, the board adjourned after one of their busiest sessions ever.

Partly due to the thirty-percent tariff on American motorcycles, Canadian police departments tried British big twins during the early 1930s. The British big twins apparently proved less satisfactory than Harley-Davidsons because 1935 saw increasing Canadian police orders for Harley-Davidsons despite the punitive tariff.

Preproduction 61 OHVs

By October, standardization somewhat improved by grouping certain accessories and charging a flat fee for them and also by simplifying colors. The management continued to consider the advisability of bringing out a 21 ci single, but Sales Manager Arthur Davidson was a key opponent of a revived Twenty-one, feeling such a model wouldn't have enough power to satisfy American riders. The 61 OHV was finally officially added to the program for 1936, and the production schedule called for 1,600 of this model.

The development difficulties of the 61 OHV and the resulting one-year delay in getting the model to the dealers took away whatever secrecy had ever been attached to the 61 OHV project. Dealers had already heard so much through the grapevine that the management couldn't avoid showing them a prototype 61 OHV during the National Dealers' Convention in late November. The rave dealer reception was encouraging, but the management maintained a conservative outlook by refusing to confirm the availability of the 61 OHV at any particular time. A few weeks later, the December 2 bulletin to dealers included the following unusual quote:

"WHAT ABOUT THE 61 OVERHEAD MODEL? . . . our engineering staff has been working for a long time on a model of new and original design and their efforts finally reached the stage where such a motorcycle, a 61 cubic inch overhead, was shown to the dealers in attendance at the National Dealers' Convention. However, production on this model will necessarily be extremely limited and we are therefore in no position to make a public announcement at this time. . . . Under no circumstances should this model be ordered as a demonstrator!"

In mid-December, the first preproduction 61 OHVs rolled off the assembly line. These were assembled to check the flow of parts through the various buildup levels, the assembly procedures for motors and transmissions, and the procedures for the final motorcycle assembly line. Additionally, the preproduction models offered the last chance to make minor improvements prior to "freezing" the design for full-scale production.

The first ten or fifteen motors, after being assembled into complete motorcycles, were returned to Ed Kieckbusch and the engineering department for road testing. Most of these first production 61 OHVs were returned to the motor assembly section for reworking. Accordingly, the routine was changed so that only the motors were sent to the engineering department for block testing. Upon passing the block tests, the motors were then sent to the motorcycle assembly line, and the complete motorcycles were subsequently road-tested by a separate section outside the engineering department. Most reworking was by this

Speculation: During 1935, the factory experimented with a single-cylinder 30.50 ci, 500 cc overhead-valve roadster. The proposed new single may have been a takeoff on this 1930 racer layout. The motor number is 30SF505. Harley-Davidson

time sufficiently infrequent and minor to be accomplished on the assembly line.

Another "new" 1936 model was an 80 ci side-valve twin. Although 1936 was to be the formal launching of the Eighty, these machines had been available as 1935 models.

A photo described as the first production 61 OHV (actually a preproduction model) surrounded by the founders has been repeatedly published over the years, and the author gives the picture another encore. The pleasant expressions of the four founders gave no hint of the difficulties that caused this model to be a year behind schedule! In the months ahead, they would smile often about the 61 OHV. They had a hit on their hands.

This widely reproduced photo supposedly shows the first-production 61 OHV. Actually, this model is a preproduction example used to check out factory personnel. Close examination of the original photo—not this reproduced halftone—reveals the lack of exhaust valve spring covers, which were fitted to production models. Another clue is the lack of other 61 OHV models moving down the assembly line. Full-scale production was probably in batches, not in the salt-and-pepper approach. The photo was developed on December 12, 1935, within days of the factory photo session. By December 16—perhaps a week after the photo was taken—at least "ten or fifteen" more preproduction models had rolled off the line and were turned over to testers. Harley-Davidson

137

Chapter 5

1936–1938

A new image

1936

The 61 OHV was a styling masterpiece. The integrated tank-top instrument panel was particularly artistic, and more than fifty years later the tank-top panel still has many fans. Oil was carried in a separate tank between the seat post tube and the rear fender instead of in a compartment in the main tanks. The total layout fitted in with the British idea that sunlight finds few paths through the profile of a good-looking big twin.

The fuel tanks represented a manufacturing departure, as they were welded rather than soldered. The double-loop frame added to the substantial look. Tubular chrome-molybdenum forks looked more modern than the forged I-beam forks of the side-valve models.

The 61 OHV styling was masterful. All of the spaces were filled with machinery. Many parts were unique to the 1936 61 OHV, such as the air intake horn and the covers over the ends of the rocker shafts. Harley-Davidson

The clutch pedal was changed to an underslung layout with a balancing spring. The 61 OHV styling drew immediate and strong praise from Harley-Davidson customers.

Mechanical design of the 61 OHV

Unlike earlier Harley-Davidson overhead-valve engines, the 61 OHV was not an upper end conversion sitting on a base designed for an F-head or a side-valve engine. In a fresh overhead-valve design, there was no need for a system of two or four cam gears. Accordingly, all four cam lobes were placed on a single camshaft.

The single-camshaft configuration offered more accurate valve timing because there was less concern over timing gear backlash than when dealing with two- or four-camshaft designs. The single-camshaft design also was quieter than a two- or four-camshaft design for two reasons. First, there were less gears spinning. Second, there was no distortion of the valve geartrain due to heating and cooling of the crankcase and timing chest. Such thermal gradients could cause properly fitted cam gears in the F-head and side-valve models to become too tight, too loose or out of alignment. Another advantage of the single-camshaft layout was easier manufacturing.

The 1936 61 OHVs featured valve stems and springs with only the slightest attempt at enclosure, a

```
Specifications
Year and model ......................... 1936 61 OHV
Engine ................ Overhead-valve 45 degree V-twin
Bore and stroke ............................ 3 5/16 x 3 1/2 in.
Displacement ....................... 60.33 ci, 988.56 cc
Compression ratio ............. Solo: E, 6.5:1, and EL, 7:1;
   sidecar: E, 5.5:1, and EL, 6:1
Horsepower .......... E: 37 bhp at 4800 rpm; EL: 40 bhp at
   4800 rpm
Gearbox ..................... Four speed, constant mesh
Shift ............................................. Left hand
Clutch ............... Dry, multiple disk, left foot actuated
Wheelbase ...................................... 59 1/2 in.
Wheels and tires .............................. 4 1/2 x 18 in.
Suspension ................. Front: leading link; rear: rigid
Weight ... 515 lb. (includes 15 1/2 lb. for standard solo group)
Seat height ...................................... 26 in.
Fuel consumption ........................... 35-50 mpg
Top speed ................. E: 85-90 mph; EL: 90-95 mph
```

point that drew predictable criticism. A small two-piece sheet-metal cylinder about the size of a baby food jar fitted over each set of double valve springs, each set commonly referred to as a spring. The valve spring cover was attached to the cylinder head by the valve guide. The guide was pushed through a hole in the floor of the spring cover until an annular ring on the valve guide—sort of a hat brim—bottomed out the cover on

The 1936 Safety Guard was bolted to the sidecar mounts; 1937 and later guards were bolted to the footboard mounts. The 1936 rear chainguard brace hung down from the fender; 1937 and later braces extended up from the frame. Note the front chainguard. Unlike production models, a screw fits through the right and left corners of the diamond-shaped embossed guard stiffener. These screws probably held a felt noise suppressor. The motor number is 35E1002, the second 61 OHV built. Harley-Davidson

139

the cylinder head surface. The top and bottom sections of the valve spring covers had slightly different diameters and were press-fitted, hardly a positive arrangement on a motorcycle destined for high-speed running. The top section of the valve spring cover was canted away from the rocker arm so that the rocker arm of a fully closed valve would still be somewhat within the enclosure when the rocker arm was at its highest perch. A slot was provided in the top section of the enclosure to provide access to the rocker arm.

Some veteran riders believe the earliest 61 OHV models were delivered without the small valve spring covers. Quite possibly, some of the preproduction models without the covers made their way to favored dealers. This would've been entirely within the Harley-Davidson tradition of using dealers to check out designs and could explain the stories about riders getting their laps full of oil. No *Shop Dope* installments have surfaced with retrofit instructions concerning the early small covers, which seems to say that few, if any, 61 OHV models were delivered without the small valve spring covers.

Although lacking suitable valve enclosure, the 61 OHV was still ahead of foreign overhead-valve motorcycles on that score. In 1936, fully exposed valve stems were still commonplace across the Atlantic. Foreign models using fully exposed valve stems included the latest Brough-Superior SS100 flagship. At least Harley-Davidson was attempting to cover the valve stems successfully.

Apart from Harley-Davidson, most of the world's overhead-valve big twins were manufactured in England by JAP or AMC (AJS-Matchless). These engines were used in several makes of motorcycles, including England's most expensive mount, the Brough-Superior. A comparison of the 61 OHV with the Brough-Superior is therefore appropriate.

The 61 OHV's bore and stroke were $3\frac{5}{16}$x$3\frac{1}{2}$ in., for a ratio of 0.946:1. Because bigger bores and shorter strokes were the trend, these dimensions put the 61 OHV close to the front. By comparison, the 1936 Brough-Superior SS100 was available with either a 59.9 ci JAP engine of 3.15x3.90 in. dimensions (a 0.808:1 ratio) or a 59.9 ci AMC engine of 3.37x3.37 in. dimensions (a square 1:1 ratio).

No factory archive photo exists for the 1936 instrument panel, so this 1937 shot will have to do. The 1936 61 OHV models had a 100 mph speedometer instead of this 120 mph instrument. The 1936 fork top piece was chrome-plated steel; 1937 and later pieces were stainless steel. The 1936 piece had four inexplicable holes visible to the rider; 1937 and later pieces had no visible holes. Early 1936 61 OHVs had black parkerized nuts on top of the fork springs instead of chromed acorn nuts like late 1936 and subsequent models. The 1936 models didn't have the speedometer light toggle switch at the base of the instrument panel. The 1936 gearshift lever had a round cross section, and the tankside shifter gate didn't have notches. Harley-Davidson

Single-camshaft design was possible because the 61 OHV didn't spring from side-valve roots. Its layout was quieter than the four-camshaft style. There was no oil slinger on the generator drive gear; instead, much of the oil was scraped from the flywheels and diverted to the scavenge sump, which is the knobby protrusion over which the ignition cable is hanging. Another departure was the gear-type feed pump combined with a gear-type scavenge pump. The pump is mounted sideways on the crankcase behind the timing case. Harley-Davidson

As for cylinder head internals, the 61 OHV and both varieties of the Brough-Superior SS100 were identical in concept. All three had 90 degree included valve angles, constituting the classic hemispherical combustion chamber. Claimed output of the 61 OHV with a 7:1 compression ratio and one carburetor was 40 hp at 4800 rpm. Factory power curves for the Brough-Superior SS100 with a JAP standard overhead-valve engine having a 6.4:1 compression ratio and two carburetors showed 43.7 hp at 4800 rpm. To sum up, the 61 OHV's power was delivered in a mild state of tune and its performance was typical of such engines.

The 61 OHV's power was transmitted to the gearbox through a new clutch. Spring tension adjustment was through a single large nut in the center of the clutch hub, as on the side-valve models. The hub center was larger than that on the V Series and had six splines for mounting the outer disk and spring assembly. (On the side-valve models, the outer disk and spring assembly were secured by alignment over a locking key segment placed in a notch in the hub center.)

The new four-speed transmission was a state-of-the-art constant-mesh design, a vast improvement over the old sliding-gear layout that Indian continued to use. Technically, gear shifting was now a misleading term because gear ratios were changed by shifting central dogs (sometimes called shifter clutches) instead of by sliding gears back and forth along shafts. Rider input was translated into internal gearbox motion through a slotted cylindrical drum, or cam drum, mounted in the

Note the style of the timing cover; this was made smoother during the 1936 model production run. The oil tank top is nonrecessed, and oil line fittings are welded to the tank; later production models differed. The tubular cross-section gearshift lever was for 1936 only. No exhaust valve spring covers were fitted to the prototypes and preproduction models.

Rocker arm housings had no provision for external oil lines. Cylinder head fins of prototypes differed in detail from production items. The cylinder head on the left has been rotated 180 degrees for photo purposes. The rocker arm shaft is bolted on a cylinder head tab on one end and to the rocker arm cover on the other end. Harley-Davidson

roof of the gearbox. The constant-mesh design prevented chipping and excessive wear along the gear teeth edges. The new transmission also had a spiral gear drive for the speedometer, thus dispensing with the troublesome chore of aligning the rear-wheel-driven speedometer when changing rear tires.

The 61 OHV's lubrication system was by dry sump, meaning oil was continuously circulated between the oil tank and engine. Oil drained by gravity from the oil tank to the feed section of the dual feed-scavenge gear-type pump, located at the rear of the right-side timing gearcase. The oil pressure from the feed section was regulated by adjusting a screw to vary spring compression against a seated ball. Any tendency for oil pressure to exceed 15 psi was overcome by the ball unseating and bypassing oil back to the timing gearcase.

From the pump feed section, oil was fed to the crankshaft bearings, big end bearings and upper end. A small amount of oil was bypassed through an adjustable valve to the front chain. Oil from the lower end either collected on the flywheels and then was scraped off or was slung by the crankshaft, connecting rods and flywheels to the cylinder bores.

Meanwhile, oil for the upper end flowed through a vertical external tube to the upper cylinder area and then branched off through a Y-fitting to each of the cylinder heads. Oil entered the inlet side of each cast-aluminum rocker housing and passed through a drilled passage toward the inlet valve rocker shaft. No oil was diverted to the pushrod end of the rocker, that is, the ball stud that received the upper end of the pushrod. A cork ring sandwiched between two thin steel washers provided a seal where the inlet rocker arm and its internal shaft exited the housing.

The amount of oil supplied to the inlet rocker shaft was adjustable by varying the position of the rocker shaft in the rocker cover. The oil arrived at the shaft through a groove cut around the circumference. This groove was cut eccentrically. The rocker shaft could be rotated clockwise or counterclockwise to expose the incoming oil to deeper or shallower portions of the inlet groove. This regulated the amount of oil entering the shaft. After adjustment, the inlet rocker arm shaft was tightened against the rocker housing. Oil moved horizontally along a groove in the bottom of the rocker arm shaft to form a boundary layer between the stationary inlet rocker arm shaft and the moving inlet rocker arm.

From the housing, the inlet rocker arm and shaft protruded to the left side of the cylinder head, at which point the shaft was bolted to a heavy tab integral with the cylinder head casting. No oil gasket or seal was provided on this end of the shaft, because the oil met less resistance by seeking out various passages. Meanwhile, pressurized oil had flowed horizontally through the hollow center of the rocker arm shaft and entered either of two short passages. Some oil was metered to the rocker arm pad, that is, the fulcrum that pushed against the valve stem. The remaining oil flowed through drilled passages of the cylinder head tab to the inlet valve guide.

A portion of the oil that had entered the rocker housing bypassed the inlet valve system, moved through a drilled passage in the housing, and then lubricated the exhaust rocker arm and rocker pad in the same manner as for the inlet valve system. There was one difference in the case of the exhaust valve system: no oil passage was provided for the exhaust valve guide, which instead got its lubrication from combustion chamber blow-by. As with the inlet valve system, no oil was

This mockup for photo purposes shows the rear cylinder head with 1936 and 1937 production-model two-piece valve covers. Messy, but better than the British practice of no covers at all. The inlet valve is to the left, exhaust to the right. The inlet rocker arm shaft has been inserted backwards to show the eccentric groove cut in the inlet rocker arm shaft. This groove is visible just behind the inlet rocker arm shaft mounting tab. When installed properly, the groove—which would be on the opposite end, within the rocker arm housing—mated with a port drilled in the rocker arm housing. Oil flow was regulated by rotating this shaft to align the deeper or shallower cross section with the feed hole drilled in the rocker arm housing. The top section of the inlet valve cover was omitted to show that a simple press fit arrangement was used to hold top and lower sections together. Oil lines provided vacuum return of oil from the valve covers to the rocker arm housings. Because these small lines would eventually become clogged, an air nipple was placed on the front rocker cover beginning with late 1936 models. Air could then be used to blow out both the front and rear valve spring cover lines. No air nipple was needed on the rear cover as it was connected to the front cover through the oil supply lines. Chris Haynes

diverted to the exhaust rocker ball stud, which acted against the pushrod.

From each valve spring cover, an external tube allowed oil to return from the cover to the floor of its rocker housing. Oil from the floor of each housing was returned through the pushrod tubes. The method of oil return was by vacuum, caused by piston motion in combination with baffle plates and a timed gear-driven crankcase breather valve. On the upward strokes of the pistons, the breather valve closed. Under the cylinders were the baffle plates. The connecting rods moved through slots in the baffles to form a vacuum under the pistons on the upstroke. This resulting vacuum retrieved the oil to the crankcase and also drew oil mist into the cylinder bores. The 61 OHV had a full baffle under the front cylinder and a half-baffle under the rear cylinder, which was time-honored Harley-Davidson practice.

The lowest of the three rings on the rear piston was an oil-control ring. This ring had an oil-scraper channel at the bottom edge of the ring. The oil ring assisted the half-baffles in warding off excess oil sling.

The crankcase contained oil that had been pumped through the lower end as well as oil that had been sucked down from the upper end. On the downward strokes of the pistons, the rotary crankcase breather valve opened, which expelled excess crankcase oil and air into the timing gearcase.

In the timing gearcase, the oil pumped there by crankcase pressure joined the oil bypassed by the feed pump regulator spring. The timing case contents were

The 61 OHV clutch was a new design, along the general lines of the clutches used on the singles and Forty-fives. Mounted against clutch spring pressure, a single circular spring collar replaced the three spring nut sectors used on big twins from 1912 through 1935. Ten evenly spaced springs replaced the nine springs grouped in three sets of three. A circular pushrod thrust plate, lower center of photo, replaced the triangular actuating plate. A splined clutch hub was featured in all Harley-Davidson twins from 1912 through 1940. Splines appear to be milled into the hub, but construction is actually two-piece, with a core inner section riveted to the outer hub. The inner section has thirty tabs that mate with the five notched fiber discs. Harley-Davidson

now picked up by the scavenge section of the oil pump and returned to the tank. Crankcase air escaped the timing gearcase through an outside breather passage terminating in the front chainguard.

Oil control to the cylinder walls was accomplished by the previously mentioned crankcase baffles and by the piston ring configuration. Under the front cylinder, the full baffle plates maximized the vacuum under the front piston during the upstroke, thus drawing as much oil vapor as possible into the front barrel. This was necessary because the rotation of the crankshaft (or crankpin), connecting rods and flywheels resulted in most oil sling being directed into the rear cylinder. No oil-control ring was used on the front piston.

Under the rear cylinder, the half-baffle plates reduced the cylinder vacuum on the piston upstroke and reduced the pull-up of oil vapor. This was necessary because oil was also provided to the rear cylinder by the oil sling of the crankshaft, connecting rods and flywheels. The flywheels were constantly saturated with oil from the air-oil vapor in the crankcase and with oil pumped through the crankshaft and connecting rod big ends. Centrifugal force carried the oil on the flywheels toward the outer circumference. Under the rear cylinder was a scraper cast into the crankcase. This scraper picked up oil from the flywheels and deflected it to the scavenging sump, located at the upper rear of the crankcase. From this sump, the scavenge pump returned the oil to the tank. The lubrication cycle was thus completed.

The 61 OHV was offered in two models: the E with a 6:1 compression ratio and the EL with a 7:1 compression ratio. For sidecar use, cylinder shims were available that lowered E and EL compression ratios to 5.5:1 and 6.5:1, respectively.

Early 61 OHV modifications

Oil mileage was a problem on the first 61 OHVs sold. In the middle of the production run of nearly 2,000 1936 model 61 OHVs, a change was made in the pinion gear shaft through which oil passed to the motor. This

Four-speed constant-mesh transmission was standard in the 61 OHV and optional in the 1936 Seventy-four and Eighty. Shift action was through the new slotted drum "cam" above the gearbox. Transmission drove the speedometer, which simplified tire changes. The early 1936 L-shaped bracket under the kickstarter had an adjustable shock-absorbing bolt that rested on top of the lower frame tube. The bracket was redesigned for late 1936 models, then on late 1937 models was replaced by a cast-in boss on the gearbox bottom. Harley-Davidson

change was effective with serial number 36EL1729, the 729th 61 OHV produced, and with sixty-two other motors with lower numbers. As a result, oil mileage was improved to somewhere between 200 and 400 miles per quart.

Early 61 OHV models used a kickstarter combination of a fourteen-tooth mainshaft and a twenty-six-tooth starter crank gear. This combination was changed to a sixteen-tooth mainshaft and a twenty-four-tooth crank gear in order to spin the engine over faster during starting.

During the course of 1936 model production, the timing case cover was made smoother, and then smoother again. Thus three different covers appeared on the 1936 models.

Three combinations of oil tanks and oil line fittings were also used on the 1936 61 OHV models. The original oil tanks had a smooth top, with oil line fittings gas-welded into the tank. A production change added raised embossed sections to the tank top to increase rigidity, with oil line fittings still welded to the tank. The third combination was the embossed tank top with oil line fittings swaged into the tanks. On each of the 1936 oil tanks, the oil supply (or takeoff) line was from the rear of the tank.

Cylinder head castings of the prototype 61 OHVs had part numbers that were raised, that is, male numbers formed by a female pattern in the casting molds. Production cylinder part numbers were sunken, that is, female numbers formed by a male pattern in the casting molds. Cylinder head fins were slightly different on prototypes than on production models. On the first series of production models, the cylinder head reinforcing ribs were short and oil passages were provided to the inlet valve guides. On the second series of production models, the reinforcing ribs were longer and no inlet valve guide passages were provided. The prototype 61 OHVs had no valve enclosure at all, but the production models had the two-piece "baby food jar" covers.

On all 61 OHV models (and 74 OHV models) through 1947, the left end of each rocker arm shaft was secured to the cylinder head by a nut. The right end of each rocker arm shaft was secured to the rocker housing by a nut backed by an oil seal. As earlier noted, oil flow to each rocker arm shaft was adjustable by positioning

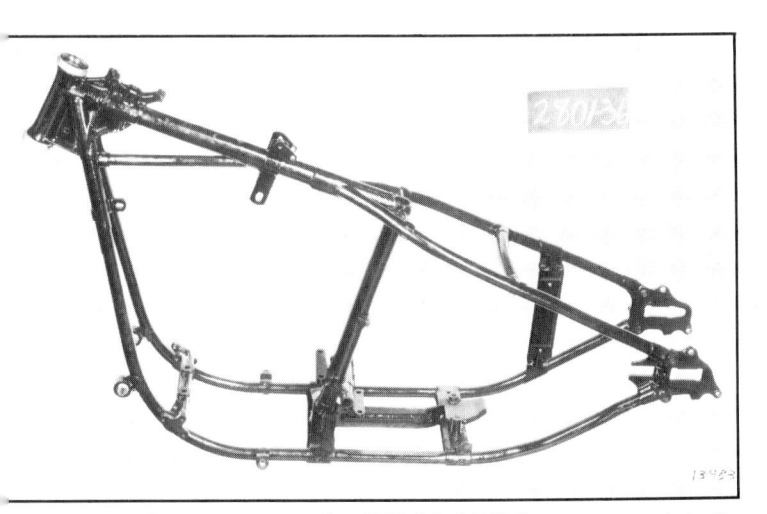

Believe it or not, the 1936 61 OHV frame was originally designed for the side-valve big twins. When the 61 OHV was threatened with cancellation, the frame was separately considered and appeared more likely to continue in production. The 1936 frame had single-butted, double-diameter front downtubes, similar to the double-butted frames of F-heads and side-valves. Note that there are no forgings at the bottom of each front downtube; front downtubes curve into the horizontal section. Front downtubes, horizontal lower tubes and lower rear tubes are actually one continuous tube for each side. Top rear frame tubes bend in gradually to the main backbone. Harley-Davidson

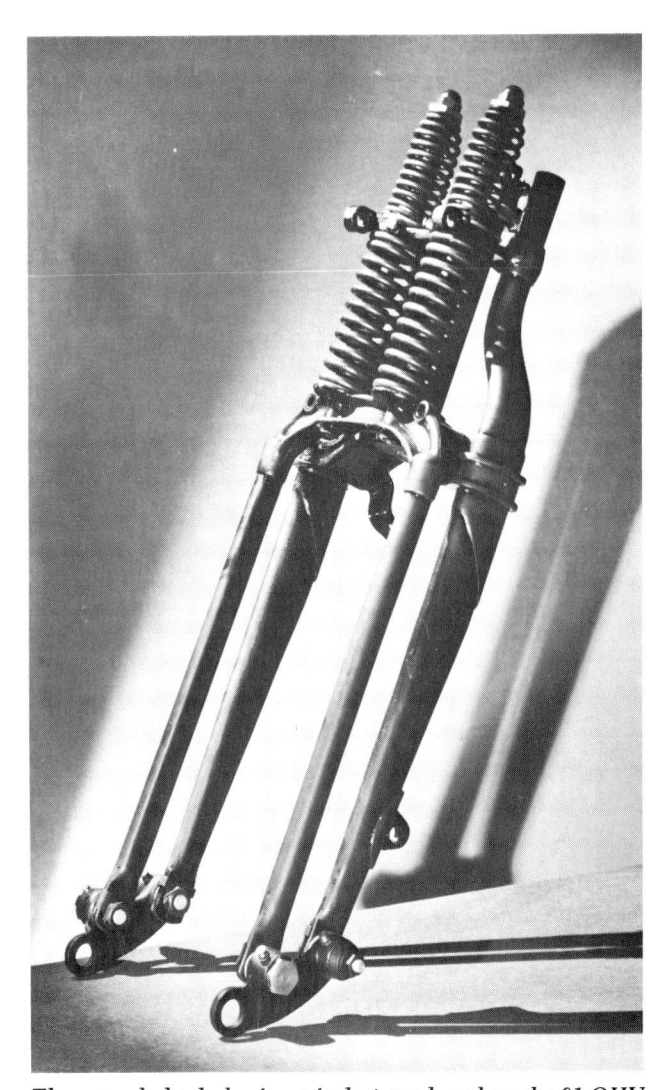

The extruded tubular front forks introduced on the 61 OHV were considered more stylish and were probably cheaper than the drop-forged I-beam forks of the side-valve big twins. Harley-Davidson

each shaft in the rocker housing. This required the end of each rocker arm shaft to protrude through the rocker housing.

On the first 1,000 or so 61 OHV models, the end of each rocker arm shaft and retaining nut was covered by a domed cap secured by a central screw. Mid 1936 and later 61 OHV and 74 OHV models combined the cosmetic and oil-sealing duties by using a large nut to cover each rocker arm shaft end and bear against the oil seal. Late-production rocker arm covers had bosses for the

A full-dress 1936 61 OHV. Strapped to the front right downtube is a tire pump, an accessory that is seldom seen on restored models. This photo was never previously published because the negative was misfiled by the factory photo studio. Supersleuth Chris Haynes rediscovered this gem. Harley-Davidson/Chris Haynes

oil lines, but early production and prototype models had no bosses.

In the Harley-Davidson tradition, the 61 OHV had no distributor, so both spark plugs fired at the same time. Because of complaints about backfiring during starting, the ignition timing was advanced from 3/8 in. before top dead center to 7/16 in. This problem and solution was similar to that applied to the original twin-spark ignition system introduced on the 1927 models.

Front chainguards of the prototypes apparently had internal felt noise suppressors, but production models didn't. There were also minor differences between prototype and early production kickstarter covers compared to late-production covers. By the middle of the 1936 production run, the 61 OHV configuration stabilized for the balance of the 1936 series.

On the Forty-five, a Y-shaped inlet manifold offered the promise of improved performance while enhancing the model's appearance. Cylinder cooling fins were larger and wrapped around the Y-manifold. The RL and RLD inlet manifolds were increased from 1 to 1 1/4 in. and the carburetor venturi increased from 7/8 to 1 1/16 in. Cylinder heads were changed from a seven-bolt to an eight-bolt pattern, and cylinder head cooling fins were larger. Internal cylinder head shape was changed for better combustion. More responsive handling was provided by reducing the fork rake about 2 degrees and reducing the fork trail by 1/2 in.

The Forty-five used the same clutch pushrod bearing setup as the 61 OHV. Until now, Forty-fives had an open slot in the center of the clutch hub section of the front chainguard to provide for clutch adjustment. This slot was now covered by a removable chrome-plated disk. Additionally, a guard was now fitted to the clutch release.

The Forty-five rear chainguard was extended farther around the rear sprocket, and the guard mounting was improved. Molded brake shoe linings were increased to a 7/32 in. thickness to extend life, provide more positive rider feel and reduce adjustment frequency.

Transmission oil seals on the Forty-five were improved by redesigning the left and right oil retainers. The retainer in the left-side inner clutch disk was formed from a leather cup with a special oil-resisting rubber cushion held in place by a steel washer. This

This late 1936 61 OHV shows changes phased into production. The rocker shafts are secured by new larger nuts. The timing case cover has been smoothed out. The Safety Guard is reshaped and bolted to the footboard mounts instead of to the sidecar mounts. Harley-Davidson

147

A keen eye or rote memory was required to distinguish the Forty-five from the Seventy-four and Eighty big twins. The Forty-five had the rear chain on the right; the Seventy-four and Eighty had it on the left. On the Seventy-four and Eighty, the optional four-speed transmission had shifting actuation through a rotary plate or disc instead of through a cylindrical cam. This was for 1936 only. Harley-Davidson transmission-clutch seal replaced the former cork washer. The right-side oil retainer behind the transmission sprocket was changed from a felt to a leather-and-steel washer combination.

The Servi-Car was fitted with an auxiliary towbar safety cable in compliance with numerous state laws. A chrome-plated spring latch was substituted for the two trunk locks on the cover. The cover stop featured a safety grip, and the body snubbers were improved by adding two more springs.

The Eighty side-valve was officially cataloged for the first time, but the 80 ci side-valves had been available by special order during most of the 1935 season. On the Seventy-four and Eighty, nine-bolt cylinder heads replaced the seven-bolt heads. As on the Forty-five, changes to the internal cylinder head shape improved combustion on the Seventy-four and Eighty, while cylinder and cylinder head cooling fins were larger. The new Seventy-four and Eighty heads were available in two compression ratios, 5.3:1 or 5.5:1. Cylinder fins were carried around over the inlet ports.

The back of the front chainguard was changed from two-piece construction to one-piece. Greater lateral clearance was provided in the guard to prevent the chain from rubbing. Standard equipment for the Seventy-four and Eighty included the old three-speed sliding-gear transmission, but the new four-speed constant-mesh transmission was obtainable on special order. A new clutch pedal and mounting provided greater room for mounting an oversized radio generator. The new pedal was claimed to provide smoother clutch action.

Styling changes included new tank transfers, a fork spring shield on the side-valve models, a tubular

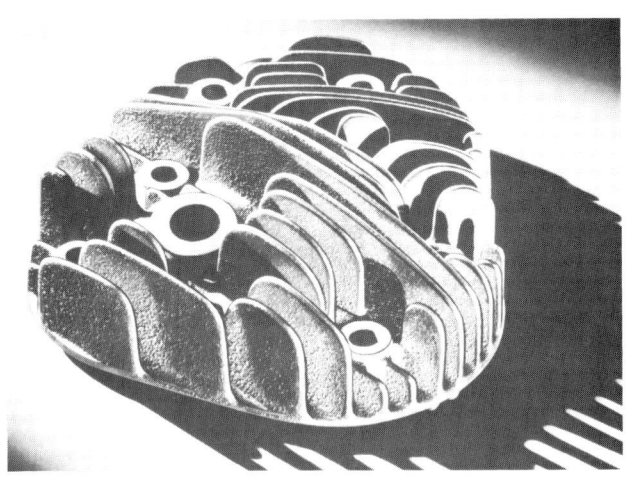

Photographers and artists could transform parts into objets d'art, as with this 1936 cylinder head. Harley-Davidson

A Y-manifold was a new feature on the 1936 Forty-five. Cylinders and heads had deeper fins. Harley-Davidson

A fork spring shield was incorporated on the 1936 side-valve models. The shield was dropped from the side-valve big twins the following year, but continued on the Forty-five through 1939. Harley-Davidson

149

rear stand and a chrome-plated air inlet. The sidecar was also completely restyled. The ammeters now had a stronger mounting arrangement and a damped pointer needle of heavier gauge.

Quality control

In the racing realm, Indians benefited from the use of Harley-Davidson parts, recalled Tom Sifton. "Red Fenwick built some of the best racing Indians that were made—they all had Harley lower ends. He didn't fool with and wait for the Indian stuff to blow up. He would take it out of there and put Harley parts in." Fenwick was a prominent Indian tuner, not just an average guy. Two of Fenwick's Indians, ridden by Fred Ludlow, set Class C 45 and 74 ci records at Bonneville.

Sifton continued, "We used to say that Indian pistons were made out of lead. They were made out of an aluminum alloy that was not very light; it was heavy, and it was not strong—it was no good. The Indian Forty-fives were the same bore as the Harley 21 in. single. When you bought a Harley single you could get Dow metal—which was magnesium—pistons, or regular Lynite. The Dow metal pistons were light, well designed and stayed together. All the good Indian Scouts and Sport Scouts in this area [northern California], and I understand in the Los Angeles area too, were running Harley single pistons."

Indian's top star Ed Kretz echoed this theme. "Indian rollers—you could buy a thousand rollers and get about 300 different sizes in it. But I miked every roller that I put in.

"The metal at that time wasn't good. I even put a Harley crankpin in the bottom end of my Sport Scout. I had to do a lot of changing, but I put it in there and I never had any more problems. It was a little heavier, but I never [again] had a bottom end go out."

The company mailed their advertising copy to *Motorcyclist* in time for the March issue. The March ad illustrated all models instead of headlining the new 61 OHV. Next to the 61 OHV illustration was simply the reserved comment that this was an all-new model. A dribble of 61 OHV deliveries began in March. Harley-Davidson was cautiously testing the waters with the 61 OHV, not wishing to get caught up in a repeat of the new-model launching problems of 1929 and 1930.

In March, George Nortman again requested that some of the special color options be eliminated in order to reduce costs. William S. Harley told the board that "something decidedly new" should be featured in Harley-Davidsons every two years in order to increase

A 1936 Seventy-four. All side-valve models got a new air horn—the Forty-five air horn was shorter than the big twin air horn. Optional finishes for 1936 were sherwood green and silver; teak red and black; dusk gray and royal buff; venetian blue and croydon cream; and maroon and nile green. The second-listed color was used on the wheels, except that the teak red and black combination had red wheels. At no extra charge, black wheel rims could be furnished on request. For the first time, accessories were sold in groups installed at the factory. The 1936 choices were called the standard and deluxe groups. Harley-Davidson

demand and concurrently provide more time for development by sticking to a plan.

To improve quality and production and lower costs, Arthur Davidson suggested that a group of five or six mechanics be selected and given the job of correcting troubles arising from either design or manufacture. These men, as he saw it, would have the ability to both identify the troubles and correct them, and would in addition have direct lines of communication with the management.

William H. Davidson again brought up the question of going for records on the 61 OHV, but Walter Davidson concluded that the coming fall season would be better because the factory wouldn't be so busy filling orders. He also pointed out that they would know more about the 61 OHV by then.

In the latter part of the 1936 model production run, changes were incorporated into the 61 OHV frame. The earliest 61 OHV models had the gearbox secured to the transmission mounting plate by four studs on the bottom of the gearbox. Additionally, an adjustable bolt was threaded into a bracket that bolted to the bottom of the kicker cover. The adjustable bolt absorbed the starting shock loads. The head of this bolt rested on the top of the frame tube, so primary chain adjustment didn't require attention to this bolt when relocating the gearbox—the bolt simply moved with the gearbox.

The engineering staff decided to beef up the right-side gearbox support on the 61 OHV and incorporate this change on the 1936 models. This was first done by devising two brackets, one fitted to the gearbox kicker cover and the other welded to the frame. A cap screw was threaded through these brackets. The late 1936 61 OHVs now had the transmission secured at five points instead of four.

Between March and August, business was surprisingly good. In fact, success got out of hand. William H. Davidson reported in August that the situation on 1936 models was "desperate" in that more orders for 1936 models were coming in than could be honored except for 61 OHVs. His request for the early release of 1937 models, however, was vetoed by sales manager Arthur

Bill Connelly, rider, and Fred Dauria, passenger, swapped jobs while lowering the transcontinental sidecar record from 89 hr., 58 min. to 69 hr., 46 min. The sidecar was the new 1936 model. The can of gasoline on the rear of the sidecar was not standard! Harley-Davidson

Davidson, who ensured that new models were stored after assembly until October 1. Arthur believed early shipment of the 1937 models would handicap dealers in selling off the remaining 1936 motorcycles.

Harley-Davidson suffered some embarrassment in Class C stock motorcycle racing because the old Two Cam F-heads were outperforming the VL side-valve Seventy-fours. In the 1935 season, a Two Cam won the New England TT (miniature road race) Championship, and a Two Cam finished third in the National TT Championship at Marion, Indiana. In southern California's Muroc Dry Lake speed trials of 1936, two of the Two Cams bettered the fastest 61 OHV by 7 and 4 mph.

In October, William H. Davidson traveled to the East Coast to attend the Atlantic City National Safety Council Convention and visit dealers there and en route. His October report had both good and bad news. The Harley-Davidson police motorcycle exhibit at the convention he judged as successful as Indian's display, despite the latter's inclusion of two machines to Harley-Davidson's one.

From dealers he learned that the standard brown finish of the 1937 models was generally unpopular. The Columbus, Ohio, dealer, upon seeing his first standard brown shipment, had immediately changed the colors of all motorcycles on order to either red or some special color. (Here again is a reference to unpublicized but obtainable special colors.) As a result of this criticism, Delphine blue with Teak red striping was added as a standard 1937 color. Two New York dealers complained about the Harley-Davidson ignition lock and remarked that the Indian steering head lock was a better anti-theft device, which was especially appreciated in New York because of its high theft rate.

All dealers objected to the Servi-Car, which they considered less attractive than the Indian Dispatch-Tow. The Indian three-wheeler was a better size, they stated, and also had a better means of stowing the towbar by folding it up over the front fork when not in use. Conversely, the Harley-Davidson towbar had to be stowed in the box, reducing usable carrying capacity.

The status of the Forty-five was a greater concern. The rival Indian Sport Scout Forty-five had been cleaning up on racetracks all over the country, including two consecutive wins in the era's most publicized race, the 100 Mile National Championship run on a long dirt track in Langhorne, Pennsylvania. Young Davidson had to endure Harley-Davidson dealers' praise of the Sport Scout. Back home, he filed his report. After noting the

The 1936 Servi-Car with fold-up towbar was in response to dealer complaints about the previous need to store the towbar in the box. Harley-Davidson dealers also compared the styling unfavorably with the Indian Dispatch-Tow. Harley-Davidson

competition successes of the Indian Forty-five, William H. Davidson stated that the Sport Scout "seemed to be a better job than ours." He concluded on a note of optimism, "But in spite of all circumstances the universal cry of our dealers seemed to be, 'When do we get some machines?'"

The low-key advertising of the 61 OHV continued. In the October *Motorcyclist*, two small 61 OHV photos appeared in the middle of an ad headlining Harley-Davidson performance in the national championship Jack Pine Enduro. This was the 61 OHV's first appearance in *Motorcyclist* ads since the March issue and also its last appearance in 1936 *Motorcyclist* ads.

Harley-Davidson manufactured its own police radios in the 1930s. Radio companies were unwilling to do the job, fearful that rough treatment of the sets and the resulting failures could be more harmful to reputations than helpful to profits. Harley-Davidson again regarded radio manufacture as a necessary nuisance, which it tolerated in order to maintain police sales in the face of competition from radio-equipped squad cars. The factory negotiated with RCA in the autumn, with the view of getting that company to take over its radio building. RCA was favorably impressed with the new saddlebag radio mounting, as their previous experience had been with radios attached to the luggage carrier. RCA agreed that if it made radios available to Indian as well as Harley-Davidson, the latter would be granted a price concession for its development work up to this point.

Caught between two forces

In November, Walter Davidson stressed that the uncertain economic situation called for the greatest caution and that money should be spent sparingly on new developments. He envisioned the four-speed transmission as an item to be dropped from standard specifications and offered only as an extra-cost option.

The engineering department was working on the inlet oil pump used on all models except the 61 OHV. The pump was erratic, sometimes oversupplying and sometimes undersupplying. Late in the year, the 61 OHV rocker housing oil seal was changed from cork to rubber. This was implemented on the 1937 model production line effective with motor 37E1672 plus twenty-eight lower motor numbers. Production of 1937 models was roughly one-third completed at that point.

The company was saving money by rationalizing production through the use of common frames, tanks and wheels for the 1937 model 61 OHVs, Seventy-four side-valves and Eighty side-valves entering production. Increased costs had mandated higher prices, which were accepted without fanfare in the United States but bitterly opposed by foreign dealers. Consequently, the foreign schedule had to be reduced by 1,100 motorcycles. The growing cost problem led Walter Davidson to generalize about it and the nature of manufacturing:

"The one thing we are quite concerned about is the fact that we apparently have reached the limit at which we can price our motorcycles, but we haven't reached the limit of what a motorcycle can cost to produce. Our pay costs keep going up and our material costs keep increasing . . . therefore, the Harley-Davidson Motor Company is caught pretty much between two forces, one that we can't raise our prices, and the other that we can't control our costs."

For the 1936 model sales year, the 61 OHV turned out to be a smash hit. Original production planning called for 1,600 of the 1936 model 61 OHVs, but sales totaled 1,836 through the business year ending September 30, 1936. The total number of 1936 model 61 OHVs produced was nearly 2,000 according to company statements, and serial numbers have been spotted that substantiate that at least 1,945 were built. The six-percent difference between 1936 model production and 1936 business-year sales represented the normal end-of-season inventory, which was sold alongside the latest models for a few weeks.

The 61 OHV was a landmark motorcycle that steered American big twin competition into a new era. Before this model, Harley-Davidson had used better management, better manufacturing quality and a better dealer network to offset the design advantages of Indians. But from 1936 on, Harley-Davidson also had the technical lead over Indian in the big twin field, which accounted for most of the sales of both companies.

Until the debut of the 61 OHV, Harley-Davidson trailed Indian in most design details, but the Milwaukee factory had long been ahead of Indian in quality control. Harold Mathewson, an Indian dealer from 1927 through 1942, recalled a lack of interest at the Indian factory in his complaints about design and quality of manufacturing. Among the complaints that found a deaf ear in Springfield were exploding flywheels and clutch action so harsh as to destroy transmissions within a few hundred miles. He remembers that when observing a group of approaching night riders, it was always easy to distinguish the Harley-Davidsons from the Indians—the Indians were the ones with poor lights.

For the first time, Harley-Davidson accessories were sold in groups installed at the factory. These accessory packages were termed the standard and deluxe accessory groups. The standard group for the Forty-five, Seventy-four and Eighty consisted of a Safety Guard, a Jiffy side stand, a lighted speedometer with a maximum-speed-attained hand, Ride Control and steering damper. The Sixty-one had the built-in speedometer, which wasn't an accessory, but otherwise had the same equipment in its standard solo group.

The deluxe solo group for the Sixty-one differed from the deluxe solo group for the other models because of the differences between switch panels. The Forty-five, Seventy-four and Eighty models had two switch keys on the switch panel, so their deluxe solo groups included decorative dice heads for the switch keys. The Sixty-one deluxe group had only one key without the optional dice head, but added foot lever (pedal) rubbers. On all models, the other deluxe solo group items were a chrome-plated group, fender lamp, stoplight, dice shift knob, saddlebags and hangers.

1937
Further modifications

The 1937 model side-valves were completely restyled to obtain the 61 OHV look. The Seventy-fours and Eighties got the double-loop frame and tubular front forks used on the 61 OHV, plus the 61 OHV welded steel tanks. On the Forty-five, the welded steel tanks were styled like the big twins. All side-valve models were fitted with the same streamlined instrument panel as on the 61 OHV. The Seventy-four and Eighty were fitted with the same Ride Control as on the 61 OHV, except for minor hardware. The Forty-five got its own Ride Control. Unlike the big twin Ride Control, the Forty-five mechanism had the adjustment knob on the left so the rider could adjust the setting without removing a hand from the throttle.

Dry-sump lubrication was incorporated on all three side-valve models. The side-valve system differed from the 61 OHV. The 61 OHV oil feed pump was a gear type driven from the pinion gear shaft and mounted to the crankcase; the side-valve feed pump was a vane type driven by the rear exhaust cam gear shaft and mounted on the outside of the gearcase cover. After circulating through the motor bearings, oil-air mist was forced from the crankcase through a vertical

A 1937 Eighty. All side-valve models got the 61 OHV styling. Three color options were offered: bronze with delphine blue stripes edged in yellow; teak red with black stripes edged in gold; and delphine blue with teak red stripes. The latter combination didn't appear in press releases or catalogs, but was listed on the dealers order form. The finish of delphine blue with teak red stripes was added because the bronze combination proved unpopular. The instrument panel was black. This was the only prewar year in which the oil tank was painted to match the fuel tanks and fenders—black was the mandatory color for the 1936 61 OHV and for the 1938-1942 big twins. Harley-Davidson

breather valve into the gear compartment. With these changes, the 45 ci twins became the W Series and the 74 and 80 ci twins became the U Series. Sub-designated models like the WLDR and UL were comparable to the previous RLDR and VL, and so on.

On the Forty-five motor, the gear shaft main bearing was changed from plain to a roller type, making the Forty-five motor fully roller-mounted. Cam gears were changed to a one-piece design. Drilling of the oil passage in the crankpin (crankshaft) was changed. The crankpin installed in new 1937 and later motors had only one newly located oil passage. Crankpins installed and issued as spares by the parts department had two holes drilled so that these crankpins were usable in any Forty-five. Horizontal cooling fins were added to the left side of the crankcase and to the timing gearcase. WLDR models had a 1⁵⁄₁₆ in. intake port; other Forty-fives kept the 1¼ in. intake port. WLDR and subsequent W Series racers had spare parts explained in a supplement to the regular spare parts book.

The 1937 side-valve big twins had a new timing case cover shaped to assist in moving the crankcase air-oil mist to the new oil slinger (centrifuge) on the generator drive gear. The oil pump was changed from a rotary piston plunger to a vane type and moved from the middle to the rear of the timing case cover. The oil feed pump drive was taken off the rear exhaust cam gear. The vane pump consisted of two spring-loaded vanes revolving in a ported eccentric chamber. Troy Ross

This 1937 frame was used on the 61 OHV, Seventy-four and Eighty. The new frame had double-thickness sections throughout instead of sections of smaller diameter tubing fitted into sections of larger diameter tubing. The bottom of each front downtube fit into a forging. The front downtubes are separate from the single tubes, which form the right and left horizontal and lower rear sections. The arc between the front downtubes and the lower section has been replaced by a short straight section. The upper rear tubes turn more abruptly into the backbone than on the 1936 frame. Harley-Davidson

A 1937 side-valve big twin. Timing gears, cam lobes and camshafts on the side-valve big twins were changed to a one-piece construction. On the rear cylinder exhaust cam gear are two tabs that drive the timing case-mounted oil feed pump. The right side of the crankshaft, termed the pinion shaft, is seen at the bottom of the timing case, directly below the V formed by the cylinders. From the pinion shaft, a spiral gear drives the vertical driveshaft of the gear-type scavenge pump located at the bottom of the crankcase. The scavenge pump vertical driveshaft was slotted to act as a timed crankcase breather valve. Harley-Davidson

The Servi-Car was given two individual rear brakes, one for each wheel. A stronger brake lock and large hubcaps were added. An apron extended from the front of the bottom of the box to the battery and seat post area.

Most functional changes applied to the Seventy-four and Eighty. The 61 OHV style clutch was fitted. The pinion gear shaft bearing was changed from plain to a roller-bearing type, so the big side-valve twins were now fully roller-bearing mounted. The crankpin diameter was increased from 1 to 1⅛ in. New connecting rods of stronger steel were fitted to mate with the new crankpin.

The Seventy-four and Eighty flywheel diameter was increased from 8 to 8 9/32 in. Flywheel balancing was changed to provide smoother running at high speeds. The stroke of the Seventy-four was changed from 4 to 4 9/32 in., the same as on the Eighty. The bore of the Seventy-four was reduced from 3 7/16 to 3 5/16 in., the same as on the 61 OHV. These changes simplified manufacturing and spare parts upkeep by having the Seventy-four use the Eighty flywheels and the 61 OHV pistons and rings.

New cylinders on the Seventy-four and Eighty had thicker walls with deeper cooling fins that extended all the way to the base. The thicker 1937 and later cylinders were satisfactory on the Eighty, but didn't work well on the Seventy-four side-valve in the opinion of the late Red Wolverton. The Wolverton dealership experienced numerous overheating problems on the 1937 and later Seventy-four side-valve models, which he attributed to the factory's use of the same cylinder castings for both the Seventy-fours and Eighties.

Timing gears, cam lobes and shafts on the big side-valve twins were now of integral construction. Outside the timing gearcase, a vertically mounted ignition timer simplified maintenance. The dimmer switch and horn button on the Seventy-four and Eighty exchanged handlebars, so the dimmer switch was on the left and the horn on the right, as on the 61 OHV.

The inlet and exhaust valves of the Seventy-four and Eighty were made ¼ in. longer. Other new parts on the Seventy-four and Eighty included an upper valve spring cover, pistons, piston rings, oil feed pump, oil feed line, gearcase cover, crankcases, carburetor, starter crank bushing (late 1937), transmission mainshaft (late 1937), transmission outer bearing race, main gear spacer and key, and cylinder bracket.

Big twin frames were strengthened. Front members were of heavier gauge steel with 6 in. reinforcements

Late 1937 big twin transmissions had a boss cast into the gearbox bottom, which eliminated the need for the L-shaped gearbox bracket previously mounted to the kicker cover. Harley-Davidson

that tied into a drop forging at the bottom that could be used to attach a sidecar or a Harley-Davidson Package Truck. The top frame member was given an 11 in. reinforcement between the seat post and the seat bar connection, and the rear stays were of heavier gauge steel. A stronger transmission mounting bracket and a hardened steel stabilizer bushing in the seat post rounded out the frame alterations for all big twins. However, even with these improvements, the 1937 frame was still flexible enough to cause severe rear brake chatter. An underslung clutch pedal with balancing spring was fitted, the same as on the 61 OHV.

The big twin oil tank was changed. The oil supply (or takeoff) line was moved from the back of the tank to the center of the drain plug. A check valve kept oil from immediately spilling when the supply line was disconnected. The rider then had time to remove the drain plug if required or perform other maintenance. The reason for this change isn't known to the author, but there's no doubt that the new system complicated oil changes. The other 1937 oil tank features were common to the late 1936 oil tanks: an embossed tank top for rigidity and swaged fittings for the oil lines. This oil tank style was used in 1937 only.

All new big twins featured a new two-piece bushing on the kickstarter instead of the earlier long one-piece bushing. In the new setup, a neoprene seal installed between each bushing piece eliminated leak-

Forty-five motors for 1937 were given ribbed timing case covers. Like the Seventy-four and Eighty, the Forty-five featured a new vane-type oil feed pump and a gear-type scavenge pump. Forty-five oil pump drive arrangements and vertical rotary breather valve were the same style as in the side-valve big twins. Harley-Davidson

A 1937 Forty-five. The 1937 standard solo accessory group for side-valve models included Ride Control. In other words, this feature was now mandatory for the side-valves as it had been on the 61 OHV since inception. A left-side adjustment knob on the Forty-five made the Ride Control easy to use while motoring; big twins stuck to the less practical right-side knob. Harley-Davidson

157

age. On late 1937 big twins, the gearbox bracket used to absorb starter loads was dispensed, and a boss was cast into the gearbox bottom; the frame bracket was unchanged.

On the 61 OHV, a new larger rear brake was the same as the one used on the Seventy-four and Eighty. The gearshift gate was changed to include positive stops like the side-valve models. The gearshift lever was changed from a round cross section to a flat-sided style to work with the new shifter gate.

On all models, a new small-base spark plug replaced the earlier big-base plug. Two changes were common to all big twins. An additional terminal post located near the seat post mast permitted the use of a short wire to the battery and simplified maintenance. Clevis ends were incorporated on the brake operating rod (the one attached to the pedal). A new chrome air horn was fitted to each side-valve model, and a mirror image version was fitted to the 61 OHV. New sidecar parts included a top spring leaf, spring shackle and brake lock.

About ninety percent of the 1937 models were ordered with either the standard or deluxe accessory groups. The standard accessory group consisted of Ride Control, front Safety Guard, steering damper, trip odometer, fender light (previously offered in the deluxe group) and Jiffy stand (side stand). Also part of the 1937 standard solo group was the stoplight, which made 1937 the first lineup with stoplights throughout. The deluxe accessory group included the standard solo group plus a colored shift knob (round, not dice as in 1936), foot lever (pedal) rubbers, chrome-plated group, license plate frame, air cleaner and deluxe saddlebags with Concho tapered-streamer trim.

Two mid-production running changes were made in January. These changes concerned the rear brake and the oil tank on 1937 model big twins.

Since 1931, no bushing had been provided for the rear brake-operating camshaft. Over the years, sporadic complaints of rear brake chatter were finally traced to excessive wear of the brake-operating shaft. This wear resulted in an inadvertent, sudden servo action—too much braking too soon—and produced the noisy and rough chatter. The cure was to return to the use of a brake-operating shaft bushing that could be replaced when wearing induced chatter. This change

The 1937 61 OHV got a new air intake horn, a mirror image of the 1936 air horn used on the Seventy-four and Eighty. The oil tank takeoff (supply) line was combined with the drain plug. The takeoff line had to be removed to drain the oil, while a check valve was supposed to keep oil from draining until it was overridden by adjustment. This setup proved cumbersome, so 1937 was its only year. Harley-Davidson

was effective with all big twins shipped from the factory after January 11, or roughly halfway through the 1937 model production run.

The oil tank screening capability was deleted on 1937 models. Some earlier motors had been oil-starved in winter operation due to condensation freezing in the screen and oil flow blockage to the feed pipe. To prevent this problem, motorcycles shipped from the factory on January 20 and after had the screen cut and opened up; later, the screen was eliminated from the production flow.

Other big twin changes were phased in during the production run of 1937 models, although documentation doesn't pinpoint when these changes were made. These parts were described as late 1937 in the parts books and included a transmission mainshaft, transmission outer bearing race, main gear spacer and key, clutch lock nut (on the mainshaft), starter crank bushing, starter crank oil seal, larger seat bar bushing and 61 OHV motor oil pump feed line.

Although no new part number was created, another running change was made to the 1937 61 OHV. In the 1936 and early 1937 models, a single oil passage in each rocker arm fed the rocker pad, which actuated the valve. In late 1937 models, a second passage was drilled in each rocker arm to channel oil to the ball stud, which received the pushrod thrust. The effectiveness of this change was not specified. Curiously, the company never advertised this improvement in later sales literature, as was the custom.

In March 1937, the famous Joe Petrali rode a special 61 OHV to a new American record of 136.183 mph. Fancy tail streamlining had to be discarded during the record run because of handling problems. The magneto ignition of the record setter wasn't available on stock 61 OHV machines. Forks were circa 1915 to keep the frontal area small. Initial planning gave this record-setting model the name "Blue Bird," but this idea was discarded because England's Malcolm Campbell used the same name for a record-setting car. Harley-Davidson

In March, Joe Petrali piloted a 61 OHV to a new American speed record of 136.183 mph at Daytona Beach. The record had been held by Indian since 1926. In April, police officer Fred Ham set the twenty-four-hour American record on a 61 OHV. Riding over the sands of California's Muroc Dry Lake and doing all the riding himself, Ham motored 1,825.2 miles. The American twenty-four-hour record had been held by the defunct Henderson Four since 1922. The Harley-Davidson side-valve big twins were known as rugged but somewhat conservative motorcycles. The records of Petrali and Ham on the 61 OHV brought a new high-performance image to Harley-Davidson.

Unionization and board successors

Two major events in 1937 altered Harley-Davidson history. In March, the company workforce unionized. Worker's formed their union without opposition from Harley and the Davidsons. In April, cofounder and manufacturing chief William A. Davidson died.

President Walter Davidson chose as his future successor not one of his sons, but his nephew William H. Davidson, son of the late production boss. Over the years, some have speculated that this decision was due to the relative stockholding of the different branches; this speculation is erroneous. William H. Davidson was chosen as the new vice president because he was the readiest of the second generation to ascend to expanded leadership. Key management decisions would continue to be formalized by the board, but for years most of these decisions had actually crystallized during informal discussions among William S. Harley and the three cofounding Davidson brothers. William H. Davidson now became a member of the inner circle of four officers in order to be exposed to the full breadth of company matters.

A new clutch cushion spring was incorporated near the end of the 1937 model production run. Big twins shipped after May 1 had a new design of sprung disk, with the purpose of producing smoother clutch operation.

Lightweight motorcycles were discussed in May, beginning with the suggestion that something on the order of the German Sachs machine would be a good model. William S. Harley said he didn't believe American riders would go for such a small model. Arthur Davidson felt there was no market for a single, but that a lightweight twin might be salable. William H. Davidson wanted to know what might be done with a 30.50 ci twin to make it less expensive than the current Forty-five side-valve model, and added that the company should purchase a BSA small twin for examination. Walter Davidson recommended purchase of a sample Auto-Lite generator used on Indians to see whether it would be practical to adapt to Harley-Davidsons.

William S. Harley suggested in June that the company should undertake design of a 45 ci overhead-valve twin by installing new cylinders and heads on the standard side-valve base. He felt this would be more worthwhile than trying to improve the Seventy-four and Eighty side-valve twins.

Harley followed up in August with more specific ideas on a Forty-five overhead. The Forty-five side-valve model's frame would have to be altered and strengthened. The most powerful of the current Forty-five side-valve models was the WLDR, which produced up to 27 hp. Harley's proposed Forty-five overhead was targeted for 30 hp in a mild state of tune that could be later revised for more power. Even in the 30 hp version, Harley reasoned, the performance would be on a par with the Seventy-four side-valve due to the smaller motorcycle's lighter weight. The manufacturing cost of the Forty-five overhead would be about the same as for the Seventy-four side-valve, but the Forty-five overhead would be more reliable than the Seventy-four side-valve as proven by experience with the 61 OHV. Harley concluded by announcing that a rideable preliminary model had already been built up from an overhead-valve hillclimber and was ready for examination. Displacing 43 ci, the test model produced 29 hp.

In September, Arthur Davidson suggested the company concentrate on the 61 OHV and reduce production of the Forty-five, Seventy-four and Eighty side-valve twins. This would increase efficiency and enable the factory to build a smaller motorcycle of new design considerably cheaper than the 61 OHV. William S. Harley countered that at least two years of design lead time would be required for a completely new Forty-five, and that the company would save money by converting the side-valve Forty-five to the overhead-valve configuration.

Walter Davidson entered the discussion by stating that the Forty-five side-valve transmission had never been thoroughly satisfactory to dealers and riders, and he doubted the transmission would hold up to the additional horsepower of a Forty-five overhead-valve motor. The Forty-five side-valve powerplant had the primary chain on the left, a frame-mounted transmission and the rear chain on the right, subjecting the gearbox and frame to heavy twisting loads. Walter believed an entirely new transmission would be required on an overhead and that the crossover feature would have to be eliminated on such a model. He was impressed by the Indian Sport Scout Forty-five side-valve, believing it had the advantages of light weight and economic production. Walter felt the Forty-five side-valve Harley-Davidson should be continued unchanged and that an entirely new Forty-five overhead-valve or 50 ci overhead-valve should be considered.

One of the reasons William S. Harley had been pushing for a Forty-five overhead-valve was a continual piston problem on the side-valve motors. Between 1914 and 1934, all Harley-Davidson motors had featured tapered cylinder bores. Heat distortion was caused by the normal temperature gradient between the top and bottom of a cylinder, as in any engine design, and was aggravated by the eccentric cylinder head porting of the F-head and side-valve layouts. The theory behind the tapered cylinder bore was that heat distortion would warp the barrels into the proper shape. But the theory was not working well in practice and had resulted in excessive piston failure. Effective with the 1934 models, the factory accordingly had been using a new piston design in conjunction with straight cylinder bores. Nevertheless, piston problems persisted until yet another redesign. The minutes of the September board of directors meeting are illuminating.

"At the time this Forty-five overhead-valve motor was suggested, we were apparently at our wit's end in regard to pistons in our Seventy-four and Eighty motors, and it was felt we would have to come to an overhead-valve motor to replace these side-valve motors. Since that time, a new piston has been developed which seems to be the answer to our troubles. If this proves to be correct, the necessity for overhead-valve motors to replace the side-valve motors is not so great. The one outstanding difference between the overhead-valve motor and the side-valve motor is that the overhead costs considerably more to make." The new piston design referenced here was the steel-strutted type. Steel-strutted pistons would be incorporated on Seventy-four and Eighty twins in the latter part of 1938 model production run and cataloged as new features of the 1939 model Seventy-four and Eighty.

Discussions on the proposed Forty-five overhead-valve continued into November without producing a concensus. William S. Harley proposed the building of fifteen to twenty special Forty-five side-valve competition motorcycles in order to compete against the Indian Sport Scout.

William H. Davidson brought up the idea of a lightweight motorcycle, which he believed should be subsidized in order to be offered at an attractive price. The board agreed that there was a demand for a lighter motorcycle; however, the design and fabrication of the tools to manufacture a lightweight were estimated to cost $75,000 to $100,000, so further study was deemed necessary.

Three new board members attended the December meeting. Robert P. Nortman, William J. Harley and Gordon Davidson, all sons of directors, had entered the management ranks. The Forty-five overhead-valve dialogue continued with William S. Harley repeating his earlier rationale. A revival of the 30.50 ci side-valve single was discussed, but Arthur Davidson's opposition ended this idea. William H. Davidson again suggested a subsidy program, this time intended for the Forty-five side-valve, which he believed too expensive. Arthur agreed this might be a good idea if the price of the projected Forty-five overhead-valve was kept up, thus ensuring a meaningful gap between the prices of the two different Forty-fives.

1938
Big twin improvements

The most publicized 1938 improvement was full valve enclosure on the 61 OHV. This was accomplished

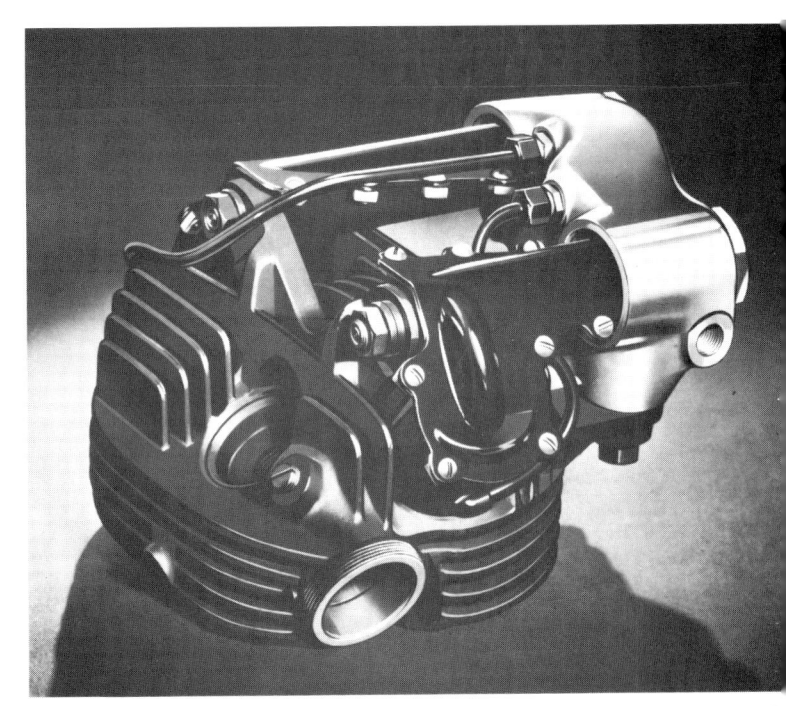

A headline feature of the 1938 catalog was valve enclosure on the 61 OHV. Harley-Davidson

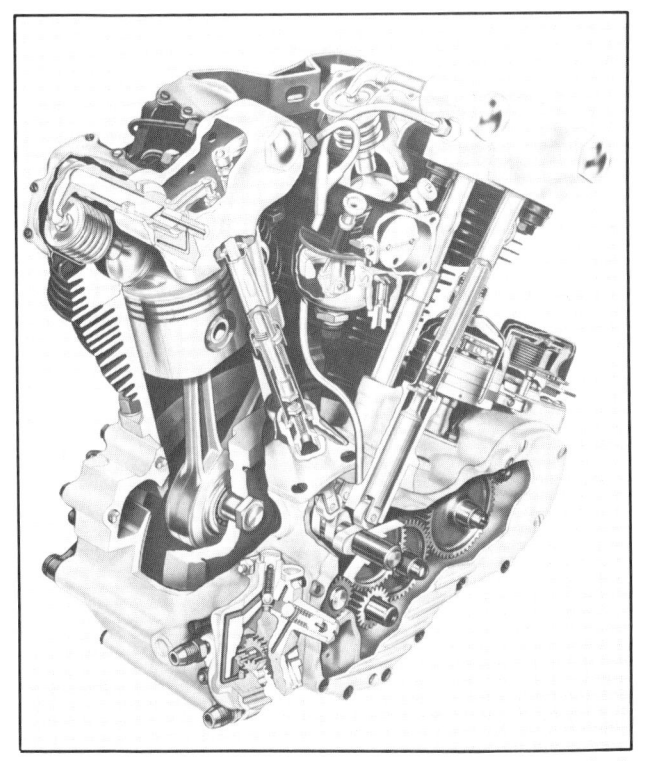

Phantom view of the Knucklehead 61 OHV motor. A little cheating here, as this is a 1947 motor, but the 1938 motor looked the same except for the absence of the timing case cover's decorative horizontal ribs and a different oil pump. Oil passage to the pushrod upper ends was phased in with the late 1937 models. Harley-Davidson

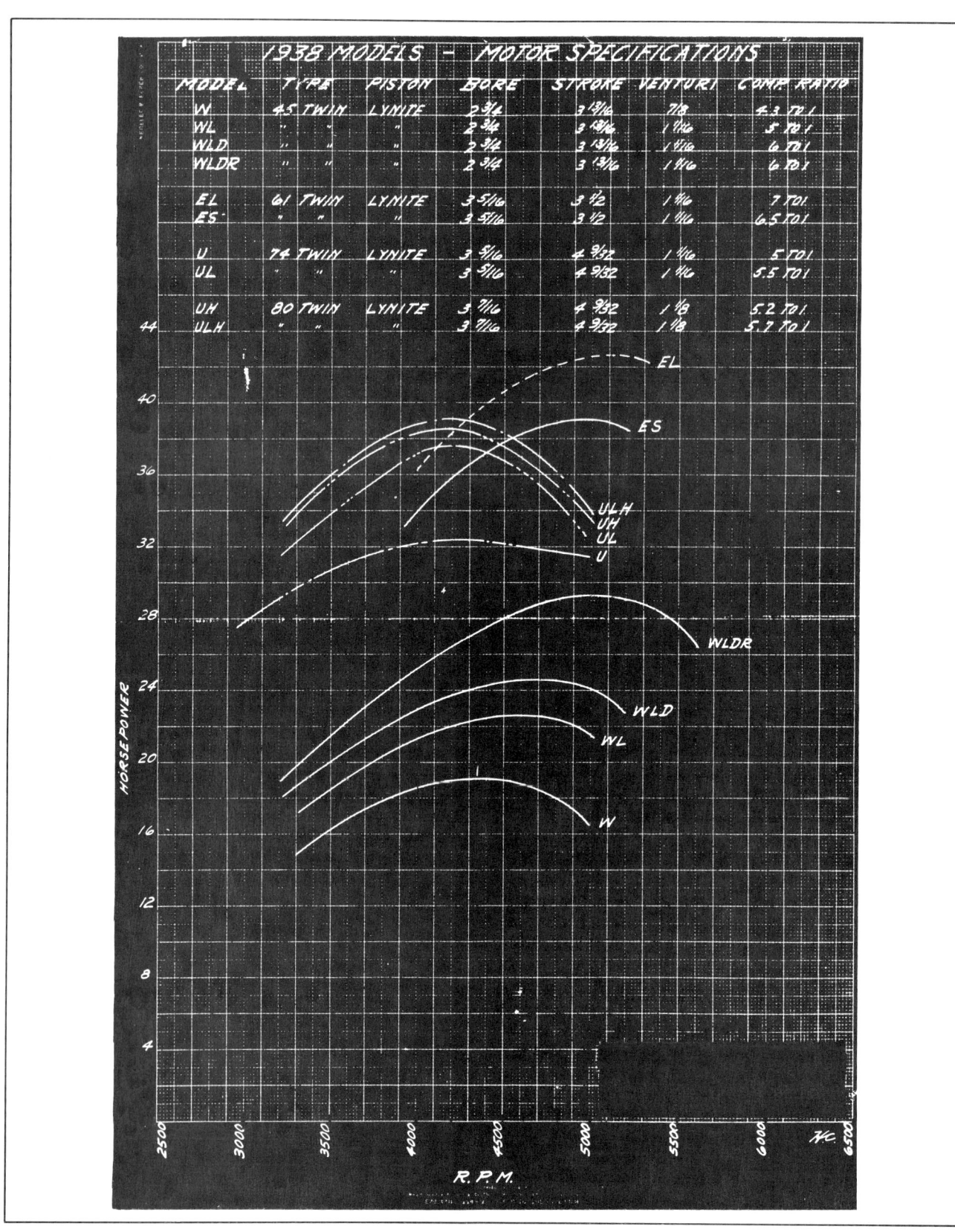

The 1938 factory horsepower curves. For the 61 OHV, Model 61EL maximum rpm and horsepower were up six percent from 1936 levels. Compared to 61 OHV models, the Eighty side-valve models produced less peak power but more mid-range power. This chart was approved December 23, 1938, by William S. Harley. Harley-Davidson

by installing a sheet-metal cover assembly over each valve. Each valve cover assembly consisted of upper and lower sheet-metal stampings and assorted gaskets, screws and spacers. The lower of the two main stampings had a conical section that tapered into a short cylindrical section, which in turn had a holed floor. The valve guide was inserted through this hole to hold the lower stamping to the cylinder head. The upper stamping was then fastened to the lower stamping with several screws that bordered the rectangular mating surfaces of the stampings. The oil tank vent line was enlarged from a ¼ in. to a ⅜ in. diameter. The valve guide oil return lines were enlarged to reduce the tendency to clog with carbon and to promote better oil return during cold weather.

Because of full enclosure, it was no longer necessary for oil to be piped to the intake valve guides through drilled passages in the cylinder heads. Instead, oil was now pumped through both the intake and exhaust rocker arms via a drilled passage in each arm. Exiting the rocker arms, the oil bathed the head of each valve stem, then flowed over each stem into the applicable valve guide.

The new valve cover assemblies could be retrofitted to earlier 61 OHV models. Retrofitting required grinding the cylinder head mounting tabs and cooling fins.

The 61 OHV, Seventy-four and Eighty now had considerable design commonality, so a number of

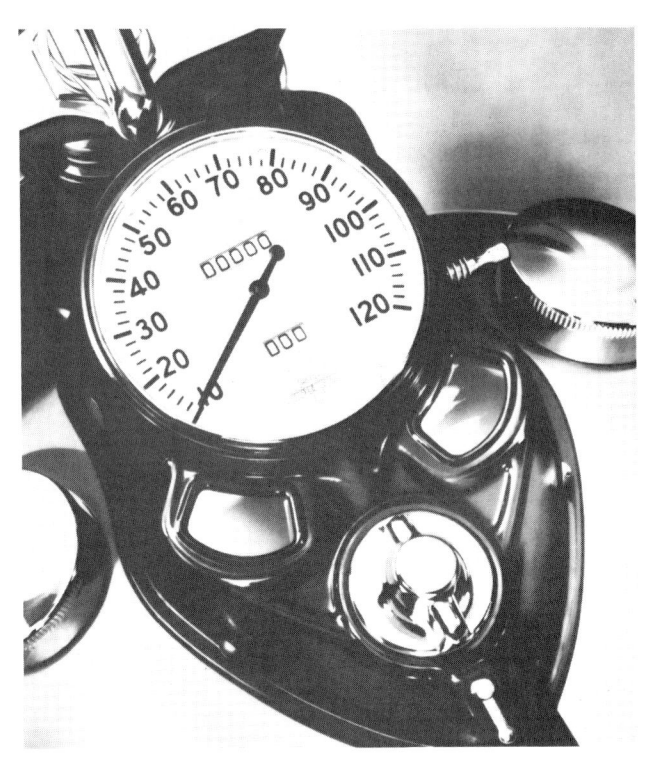

For 1938, warning lights replaced the ammeter and oil pressure indicator. Below the ignition switch is the speedometer light toggle switch, which was used on 1937 and 1938 models. Harley-Davidson

A new starter cover on the 1938 big twin transmission was heavier and no longer required provision for a gearbox support bracket. Changes in the 1938 big twin transmission included beveled lugs (dogs) on the fourth-gear shifter clutch for smoother shifting and additional third-gear shifter clutch clearance from the side of the lug for easier shifting. Harley-Davidson

The 1938 Forty-five featured several improvements to the clutch and transmission. The big twin style underslung clutch pedal was incorporated on the 1938 Forty-five. Harley-Davidson

A 1938 Seventy-four. Optional finishes were teak red with black and gold striping; hollywood green with gold and black striping; silver tan with sunshine blue striping; and police silver with black striping (for police use only). The instrument panel and oil tank were black. The oil tank remained black throughout the 1930s and 1940s. Harley-Davidson

changes were incorporated on all of these models. Hereafter, these models will be referred to collectively as the big twins.

Big twin frames were again strengthened. Upper and lower stays were 14 gauge instead of 16 gauge; the upper left stay was reinforced to the bend; the lower right stay received a longer reinforcement. The left rear axle clip that engages the brake side plate was reinforced. The heavier stays and stronger rear axle clip eliminated the brake chatter problem. The transmission mounting bracket and rear support were made of thicker gauge steel, and the upper frame strut tube was 1 in. instead of $\frac{7}{8}$ in. in diameter.

The rear brake shoes of big twins were interconnected through a two-piece arrangement of a cup bearing and an inner bushing. Higher handlebars were fitted and a self-aligning lower steering head cone was incorporated. The cone was ground with a spherical radius so that equal pressure would be put on all lower ball bearings. A new rear stand had flat-sided bracing combined with a main semi-tubular section. Larger oil vent pipes were fitted to all big twins.

Big twin clutches and transmissions were revamped. A longer and stronger clutch releasing finger (also called a release lever stud) was fitted. A ten-ball clutch thrust bearing replaced the eight-ball bearing. A new clutch pushrod with a larger end engaged the thrust bearing.

The big twin transmission was given a new starter cover, and the communicating hole between the starter cover and gearbox was raised to reduce ingestion of foreign particles. The fourth-gear lugs (dogs) on the shifter clutch were beveled to make shifting smoother. The third-gear shifter clutch was given more clearance from the side of the lug for easier shifting.

The Forty-five clutch and transmission were also upgraded. In the clutch, an eight-ball thrust bearing replaced the six-ball thrust bearing in the clutch pushrod assembly. To actuate the clutch, a new big-twin-style rock-under foot pedal was featured.

In the Forty-five transmission, a big-twin-style slotted drum shifter cam was incorporated, and a new housing was designed to accommodate this change. The new shifter cam had longer slots with more

A 1938 Seventy-four. The oil takeoff line was moved to the rear of the tank on all big twins, and fittings were changed from swedge style to compression type. All 1938 models were delivered with either the standard or deluxe accessory group.

The front fender light, Safety Guard, steering damper, trip odometer and Jiffy Stand were mandatory "accessories" of the standard accessory group. Harley-Davidson

A 1938 61 OHV. Unlike the side-valve big twins, the overhead-valve motor left little unused room under the tanks, and the result was better looking in the opinion of most riders. All big twin frames were again strengthened in 1938. The air nipple was no longer required on the front rocker housing as of 1938. Harley-Davidson

rounded corners than the earlier shifter cam. The slotted drum moved farther between gears, which smoothed the shifting action. A positive-locking device was added. Mainshaft second-gear strength was increased seventy-five percent, and second- and high-gear shifter clutches were made of better steel. All shifter clutches featured wider lugs.

A larger and more effective muffler was fitted to the Servi-Car. The Servi-Car also got an enclosed rear chain and a jaw-type clamp on the towbar.

On all side-valve models, an oil bath was provided for the rear exhaust cam gear. This gear then picked up the oil and distributed it over the remaining timing gears. To lessen oil seepage from the valve covers, there were new synthetic seals between the upper and lower covers. Special rubberized asbestos gaskets were installed for a better seal between the upper covers and valve guides. Extra-thick vellumoid paper washers were incorporated to improve sealing between the lower covers and tappet guides.

All models received Zerk-Alemite grease fittings compatible with service station equipment, so riders no longer needed the special grease guns used for the old button-style grease fittings. New horn and light wiring was claimed to prevent wire chaffing. Timing gears were shaved to eliminate high spots and to make the gear pitch more truly round, so the timing gears would fit closer together and mesh better.

The 1938 big twin oil tank was a one-year-only configuration. The 1938 tank consisted of an embossed tank top with the supply (takeoff) line moved from the unpopular drain plug location to the rear of the tank, as in the late 1936 oil tanks. The different twist for 1938 concerned the oil lines, which were the compression type instead of the banjo type. This change necessitated new part numbers for the oil tanks that mated with the new pressure lines.

For all models, the instrument panel display was new. A red warning light replaced the ammeter, and a green warning light replaced the oil pressure flag. The speedometer dial was calibrated in 2 mph increments instead of 5 mph increments (except for the Servi-Car).

Other restyling touches on all models included the traditional alterations to tank trim. Accent striping was changed to a single stripe running across the tank middle. On the fenders, the accent striping was moved from the fender crown to the valance. The front fender was graced with a chrome-plated auxiliary light (part of a mandatory accessory package). Some unspecified chrome parts were eliminated.

All 1938 models were delivered with either the standard or deluxe accessory group, so minimum accessories included the standard accessory group of front Safety Guards, front fender light, steering damper, stoplight, trip odometer and Jiffy stand. The deluxe accessory group included all standard accessory group

166

items plus four-ply tires, Ride Control, colored shift knob, air cleaner, deluxe saddlebags and a chrome-plated special package. The latter provided chrome plating of the headlight, handlebars, instrument panel, wheel rings, parking lights, fender strips and license plate frame. Not included in the solo groups was a new spotlight set. There were also standard and deluxe accessory groups for the sidecar, Servi-Car and Package Truck.

In January 1938 deliberations over the Forty-five overhead-valve model, William H. Davidson sided with William S. Harley, favoring reconfiguration of the Forty-five side-valve into an overhead-valve model. Citing the cost advantages of sharing forks, frames, tanks and transmissions, William H. Davidson's statement drew agreement from Arthur Davidson. So Walter Davidson's proposal for an entirely new Forty-five overhead-valve motor was dropped, and the engineering department began work on the development of a Forty-five overhead-valve derived from the existing side-valve design. However, no decision was reached on the transmission.

As usual, there were changes incorporated during the course of the production run. The 1938 big twin clutch assembly was changed to include new clutch springs, new spring disk and a new lined steel disk, all in combination with various old-style parts that were retained. This change was effective with all 61 OHV

A 1938 61 OHV police model. Among Harley-Davidson's claimed advantages for police use were a gear-driven waterproof electrical system, positive mechanically timed breather system, individual cam for each valve, strongest frame, constant-mesh transmission, dry-plate clutch unaffected by oil temperature, rock-under clutch pedal, easily read speedometer, electric speedometer control, enclosed starter gears and readily accessible Jiffy Stand. Harley-Davidson

models, Seventy-fours and Eighties shipped after February 1. The intent of the new clutch combination was to handle the severe stress placed on police and commercial clutches.

Also during February, new clutch pushrods were phased into 1938 model production of 61 OHV models, Seventy-fours and Eighties. The Seventy-fours and Eighties shipped after February 18 and the 61 OHV models shipped after February 25 had this change. Then, from March 8 on, all big twins were given new clutch pushrod bearings featuring twenty-five balls instead of ten balls. The new clutch pushrods and pushrod bearings were midseason replacements for the new early 1938 parts. These changes were needed because, in the early 1938 setup, the pushrods usually welded themselves to the adjusting screw.

Speaking of pictures! One of American motorcycling's famous "facts" is the New York City Police Department's exclusive use of Indian motorcycles until Indian's collapse in 1953. But here we see a 1938 Harley-Davidson exhibited as NYPD equipment. Of interest are the right-hand gearshift and the left-hand throttle, first offered in 1935. You can even bet the color is Indian red! Did Harley-Davidson make only this one example of an NYPD motorcycle? Was the motorcycle given or loaned for publicity purposes? Or is Indian exclusivity hereby debunked? Harley-Davidson

During February and March, the engineering department continued working on the Forty-five overhead-valve, and the general specifications on the motorcycle were worked out. However, continual engine problems resulted in a decision to cancel plans for a specific launch date for the Forty-five overhead-valve so that testing and problem solving could be accomplished at a measured pace. Management wanted to ensure the model would not be introduced until fully developed. Wooden patterns for the Forty-five overhead-valve cylinder heads were completed by April and were being studied for possible improvements.

Also under consideration was the use of 10 or 14 mm spark plugs in lieu of the standard 18 mm plugs on all models. This idea could save costs on the some 100,000 spark plugs purchased annually. Furthermore, the smaller plugs were considered advantageous because they permitted more room on the cylinder heads for better cooling.

From April through June, the engineering department concentrated on shedding pounds from the Forty-five overhead-valve. William S. Harley still believed that the Forty-five overhead-valve could be built for about the same cost as the Seventy-four side-valve.

On the sporting scene, Class C stock competition was now the dominant form of racing and hillclimbing. Harley-Davidson lagged Indian in Class C competition from 1934 through 1938, with the redskins winning most of the prestigious events, like the Savannah and Daytona Beach 200 mile road races and the Langhorne 100 mile dirt track titles. However, continuing factory attention was given to the 45 ci, 750 cc WLDR, and this model would soon prove the equal of the Indian Sport Scout in the most fiercely fought national championship events.

Meanwhile, a few riders of the old Two Cam F-heads were beating riders of the 61 OHVs. As well as causing embarrassment for Harley-Davidson, the Two Cam riders had in effect outflanked the idea of Class C competition, namely that riders should race or hillclimb the motorcycles they could buy at the shop on the corner. Two Cam expertise and Two Cam parts were now shared by a relatively few owners. So, for reasons that served both the interests of Harley-Davidson and the Class C concept, the AMA rules were rewritten at the end of the 1938 season. Effective with the 1939 season, F-head motors larger than 61 ci were barred from Class C competition. Eventually, the ruling was further restricted to eliminate all F-head eligibility regardless of piston placement.

During this period, development of a 74 ci overhead-valve twin began in response to police requests for a more powerful overhead-valve model. The management anticipated that the new Model 74 OHV would be ready in time for the 1940 season, but that the Forty-five overhead-valve model would be delayed until mid 1940. The side-valve Seventy-four and Eighty remained popular, but the future belonged to the overhead-valve models, thanks to the 61 OHV and the new image it gave the company.

Harley-Davidson began military planning in November. William S. Harley suggested to the board that the company go after military business in view of the government's increased defense spending. A month later, Harley traveled to Washington, D. C., to investigate the complaint that 100 Harley-Davidsons were out of commission at Fort Knox, Kentucky. From the capitol, Harley went to nearby Camp Holabird in Baltimore to attend a motorcycle reliability conference called by the Quartermaster Corps. During the conference, both Harley-Davidson and Indian received orders for 2,000 motorcycles. Military business would soon occupy much of the management's time.

Chapter 6

1939–1941

Good times and war planning

1939

In the Forty-five transmission for 1939, needle roller bearings replaced the former bronze bushing in the kickstarter side of the countershaft gear. A new washer and a redesigned bushing increased oil flow into the clutch gear bearing. The second- and high-gear shifter clutches were increased in section and the heat treating changed to increase impact strength. On the starter side of the countershaft was a newly designed seal of synthetic rubber.

In the Forty-five motor, new valve springs were advertised as having longer life. The crankcase main bearings were now lapped straight through both cases

A 1939 UL Eighty motor. The 1939 Seventy-four and Eighty valve spring covers were changed to a two-piece style. The two-piece covers were quickly detachable with a special tool. The front inlet tappet is clearly visible. The spiral on the rear inlet cam gear drives the circuit breaker. Harley-Davidson

The new instrument panel for 1939 eventually became known as the cat's eye panel. Harley-Davidson

at the same time to improve accuracy. New pistons had ring grooves ⅛ in. lower. Three compression rings were continued on the front piston, but on the rear piston the lower of the three rings was now an oil control ring.

Three Forty-five running gear changes were made. These were a new lower mounted Ride Control, new steering damper lever and new lighter foot brake lever that was stamped instead of cast.

The Servi-Car featured a permanently attached tubular steel towbar in response to dealer criticism and unfavorable comparison to the Indian three-wheeler. The new towbar setup eliminated the chores of the operator having to unload and reload the towbar from the box and also saved box storage capacity. Larger bodies were fitted to the Models G and GA Servi-Cars. Ribbing on the G model cover was changed to run parallel to the line of travel and present a more attractive appearance. Snubbing was improved by using a check strap and snubber spring on each side of the body to lessen side sway. Double taillights were incorporated. Streamlined handrails were available on the G model Servi-Car. On the G and GA Servi-Cars, a stainless steel strip was added where the rear apron joined the body.

A number of changes were made to the 1939 big twin clutch. The late 1938 twenty-five-ball clutch push-rod bearing, which had replaced the former ten-ball layout, now achieved official recognition as a new fea-

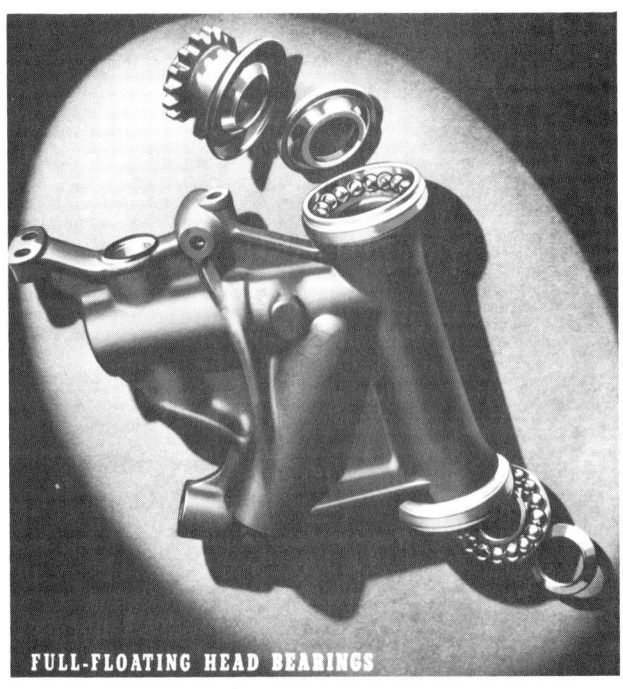

Rugged frame forgings were a hallmark of Harley-Davidsons. For 1939, all models were fitted with the self-aligning upper and lower head cones shown here. Lower head cones came out a year earlier on the 61 OHV, Seventy-four side-valve and Eighty side-valve. Harley-Davidson

A 1939 61 OHV. Available finishes were airway blue with white panel; black with ivory panel; teak red with black panel; and police silver with stripe (police use only). Stainless steel strips replaced fender striping. Fender strips were an accessory item on 1938 models. The taillight was restyled for 1939. Harley-Davidson

171

ture of 1939 models. The clutch release lever and finger were new. An oil deflector on the transmission main drive gear deflected oil away from the clutch and toward the chain. Fiber disks were now riveted to steel disks, which were splined to carry load to the clutch key ring. Spring tension was increased to reduce slippage and burning. Space was added between the key ring and fiber disks to prevent dust from packing into the clutch key ring slots and interfering with disk operation.

The big twin transmission was modified to incorporate a sliding-gear assembly. The idea was to give a better feel to the shifting because some riders objected to the clunking of shifter clutches in the purely constant-mesh layout. On the four-speed, the sliding-gear assembly shifted into second gear. Neutral on the four-speed was between second and third gears. As well as the traditional three-speed-and-reverse, the company offered the big twins with a new three-speed option. In these transmissions, the sliding-gear assembly was for engaging low gear. This was the only year for the combined sliding-gear-and-constant-mesh transmission and the odd neutral location on the four-speed.

Big twin transmission gear shifter fingers were now fitted with rollers. The depth of the high-speed notch on the transmission shifter gate was reduced by half to make it easier to shift out of high gear.

The big twin front fork on all solo models was equipped with a lighter cushion spring with more action. The big twin front Safety Guard was provided with more ground clearance at the lower outside corners.

The big twins were treated to the sixth and final configuration of the oil tank. The early 1936 61 OHV oil tank had a plain top, which gave way to the mid 1936 and later embossed top. Configurations two through five for 1936 through 1938 involved changes in the plumbing. For tank reinforcement on the 1939 and later tanks, the factory eliminated the embossed top. The 1939 and later oil tank was reinforced by a seamed top with a wall or fence about ¼ in. high around all edges.

Police Servi-Cars usually weren't fitted with tow bars. The 1939 commercial Servi-Cars featured a new permanently attached steel towbar in response to dealers' criticisms and unfavorable comparisons to the Indian three-wheeler. Larger bodies were available on some models. Harley-Davidson

Plumbing was the same as in 1938, with male compression fittings and the supply (takeoff) line exiting from the back of the tank.

On the Seventy-four and Eighty, steel-strutted horizontally slotted pistons were fitted. These pistons had been introduced as a running change in late 1938, but were advertised as a 1939 advancement. On early 1939 motors, two compression rings and a lower oil control ring were used on the rear piston, whereas the front piston used three compression rings and no oil control ring. Dealers sometimes fitted an oil control ring to the front piston of slow-running motors or during rebuilds when requested by the owners. During the 1939 model production run, the factory changed its policy and installed an oil control ring in both pistons.

A 1939 61 OHV. Deluxe accessory group items included front fender light, Ride Control, steering damper, Safety Guard, deluxe gearshift knob, deluxe saddle in two-tone russet rhino-grained leather, saddlebags and chrome-plate special. The chrome-plate special included the headlight, handlebars, instrument panel, license plate holder and wheel rings. The latter consisted of circular chrome strips about 6 in. wide, which gave the appearance of chrome rims, except with a little more dash. Harley-Davidson

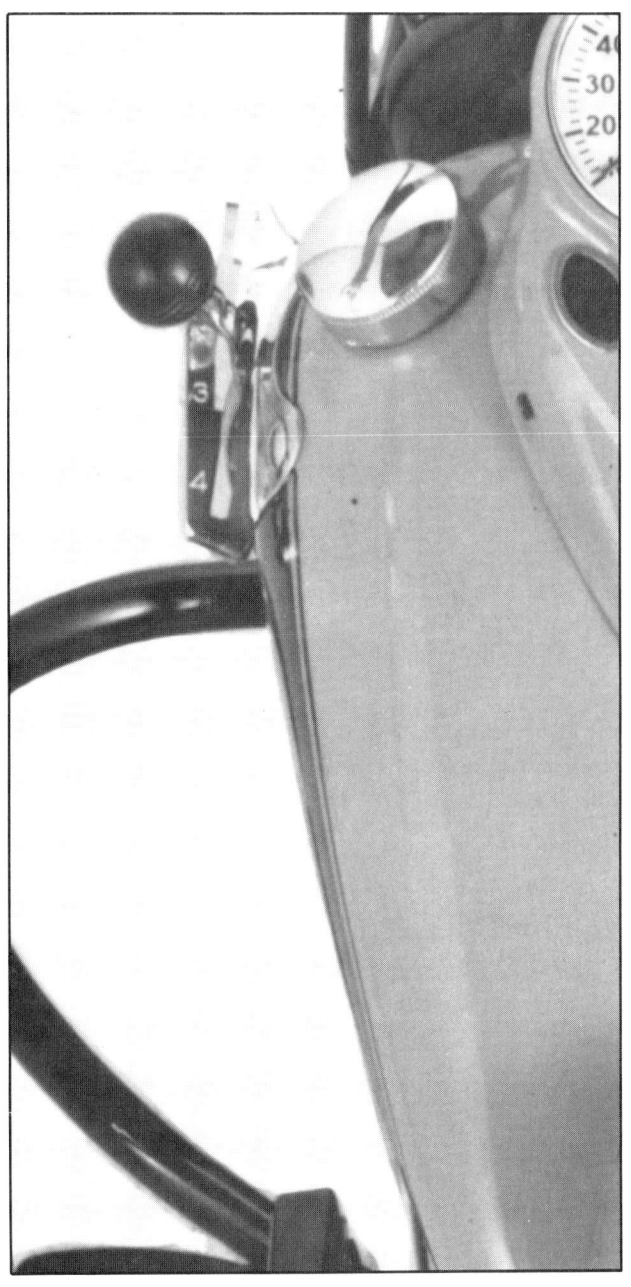

For 1939 only, neutral on the four-speed transmission was placed between second and third gears. Harley-Davidson

173

As on the Forty-five, the oil control (scraper) ring was of the new center oil channel style.

The crankcase baffle system was changed on the 1939 Seventy-fours and Eighties. Prior to 1939, the big side-valve models featured identical full baffles under each cylinder. In the 1939 Seventy-fours and Eighties, there were no baffles under the rear cylinder. Removal of the rear cylinder baffles reduced the air compressor effect in the crankcase, so power was increased.

But to keep proper lubrication with the new baffle setup, the connecting rod arrangement on the Seventy-fours and Eighties had to be reversed, so for 1939 the forked rod was for the rear piston and the standard rod was for the front piston. Additionally, half of the slot on the lower boss of the forked rod was closed off. With the new rod layout, less oil tended to be thrown into the rear cylinder bore by the spinning crankpin and rods, which was the desired effect. A final touch in the lubrication system was the addition of a perforated screen in the oil scavenge passage to prevent foreign matter from entering the breather valve.

The Seventy-four and Eighty intake manifolds were lengthened ¾ in., and a ⅛ in. asbestos-insulated gasket was placed between the carburetor and manifold. These changes were made to keep heat from building up in the mixture so that vapor lock would be avoided and low-speed running would be rid of occasional loping. On the Eighty, to better dissipate cylinder heat, the barrels were made thinner.

The Seventy-four and Eighty valve spring covers now featured only two telescoping pieces instead of three. The bottom piece of each cover was no longer screwed onto the tappet guide, nor were the two pieces screwed together in the middle of the cover assembly. Instead, a cover spring pushed downward from a shoulder in the top (female) telescoping piece against a tabbed washer, which then compressed a spacer against a shoulder or lip on the lower edge of the bottom (male)

Finishing of 1939 side-valve cylinders. More man-hours were required to finish one Harley-Davidson cylinder than the Chrysler Corporation required to finish an entire six-cylinder block. Harley-Davidson

telescoping piece and forced the bottom piece against the tappet guide. The cover spring pushed upward from the tabbed washer edges to compress the top telescoping piece against the cylinder barrel valve chamber. A third piece, termed a keeper, was wedged between the tabbed washers and shoulder on the lower piece. For valve adjustment, a special tool was provided to lift and rotate the tabbed washer into locking notches in the top piece. The keeper could then be removed and the lower piece telescoped into the upper piece to gain access to the tappet.

Detail engine changes were featured in the 61 OHV. A one-piece pinion gearshaft was introduced for better alignment of gears. The oil pump drive gear and pinion gears were now spline-fitted, the same as on other models. New pistons had more stock behind the third ring groove. Front pistons had three compression rings; rear pistons had two compression rings and one oil control ring. Parker-Kalon self-tapping screws were used on the rocker arm covers.

On the 61 OHV, a perforated cylindrical screen on the breather valve was introduced to prevent ingestion

Assembly of 1939 motors. Worker A in foreground cleans side-valve big twin timing case covers, then inserts bushings in each cover. Next, he places each cover on the fixture by the hammer, then drives in the dowel pins, which secure each bushing to the cover. Timing case covers then move out of camera range to be mated to crankcases, and all bushings are line bored. Behind worker A is a rack of side-valve big twin crankcases. The cylindrical covers from two electrical timers are used as dust covers for the cylinder bores. Worker B, staring out the window, assembles timing gears into gearcase—hope he did it right! Behind B is a rack of Forty-five crankcases, again with timing covers used as dust covers for the cylinder bores. To the left of B, six workers C through H complete lower end assemblies. To the left of D is a completed motor lower end that consists of the crankcase with flywheels and rods installed. Behind D on the rack is another completed lower end. Workers I and J in extreme right rear are doing something the camera didn't capture, perhaps truing flywheels. Behind I and J is a rack full of assembled flywheels and rods. Workers in the background of the center tables perform initial finishing operations on crankcases and timing cases. Nearer the camera, workers on middle tables install cylinders, pistons and cylinder heads. Most archive photos were made from 8x10 negatives. Note the small bottle on the left end of the workbench in the foreground; in the original archive photo, you can read the sales pitch and directions, totaling fifty-eight words! Harley-Davidson

Storage of 1939 61 OHV motors. Large inventories like these are expensive. On this score, Indian was more efficient because they didn't build up large stocks of finished motors. But times change—Harley-Davidson is now well respected for its MAN (materials-as-needed) system that avoids such large idle stock. Harley-Davidson

of foreign matter by the breather valve. Inlet and exhaust valve springs were changed to prevent the possibility of bottoming out. On late 1939 61 OHV models, pressure in the oil bypass valve spring was reduced to a range of 4 to 6 psi in order to increase the amount of oil bypassed and reduce the amount consumed.

Radio-equipped police two- and three-wheelers were fitted with an automatic current and voltage regulator. Most radio speaker units—those shipped after October 1, 1938—were now of the dynamic type instead of magnetic, which improved performance and reliability. The outward appearance of the speakers was unchanged. A new style of high-tension shielding permitted the use of standard ignition cable, and a new method was used to make contact with the spark plugs. Detail improvements were made to the Sterling rear wheel siren.

The sidecar wheel carrier was changed to permit installation of a spare wheel fitted with the optional chrome-plated wheel rings. A rubber floor mat replaced the linoleum mat. The brake crossover shaft lever was changed to a stamping.

Block test of 1939 61 OHV. The high-compression EL with a 7:1 compression ratio produced 42½ hp at 5100 rpm. The ES with a 6.5:1 compression ratio produced 39 hp at 5000 rpm. Harley-Davidson

Assembly of 1939 transmissions. The nearest three workers on the right are assembling big twin transmissions, and the next two workers are assembling Forty-five transmissions. Near the camera are five stacks of Forty-five gearboxes. Nine big twin transmissions have been completed and placed on the top right side of the storage rack. On the left side of the storage rack top are eighteen completed Forty-five transmissions. Harley-Davidson

On all models, the front wheel brake cable was fitted with an extra-large pushball cup for better lubrication. The brake cable was now of continuous design. A drain plug was provided at the bottom of the carburetor bowl, and a smaller gasoline strainer was fitted. The steering damper pressure disk was redesigned to simplify installation. Spark plug electrodes were now cemented clear to the end, and the electrodes were flattened across the spark gap. The ignition cable was covered with neoprene, an oil- and water-resistant synthetic rubber. The new stoplight switch was smaller and of Harley-Davidson manufacture. Self-aligning upper head cones were added, making all models now equipped with both upper and lower self-aligning cones.

The annual styling touches included a new instrument panel painted to match the main tank color instead of black in every instance. The new panel had "cat's eye" warning lights. The paint scheme included a tank panel of contrasting color and a black oil tank on the big twins; the big twin oil tank would remain black throughout the 1930s and 1940s. Stainless steel fender strips replaced pinstriping. Saddles were of two-tone russet rhino-grained horsehide. The taillight was restyled.

In February 1939, two test riders on prototype Forty-five and Seventy-four overheads returned from San Antonio, Texas, after having completed 5,000 miles of road tests. Favorable reports were submitted on both models. Only one significant problem eventually emerged in testing the Seventy-four overhead. The crankcases proved too weak for the extra power, and would crack just below the cylinders. This was cured by redesigning to include thicker crankcase walls.

Brazing 1939 big twin frames. Harley-Davidson

177

Painting 1939 fenders. Harley-Davidson

The need for these new crankcases on the Seventy-four overhead related to two other factors: the need to use the same crankcases on both the 61 OHV and the new 74 OHV in order to save costs, and the need to phase in the new crankcases smoothly so as not to discard any of the earlier style 61 OHV crankcases. In the end, the crankcase problem prevented the company from staying on schedule for a 1940 debut of the 74 OHV.

Meanwhile, new board member William J. Harley was in New York City attending a sportsmens show, calling on dealers and interviewing riders of small motorcycles, mostly of German manufacture, in an effort to scope the sales potential for a lightweight model. Another second-generation board member, Gordon Davidson, told fellow directors he believed a lightweight was needed that would sell for about $100 less than the Forty-five side-valve.

The Toronto motorcycle show was attended in March by Walter Davidson, engineer Christy Spexarth and William J. Harley. Except for a BSA 250 cc, all of

Assembly of 1939 tanks. This process was still as labor intensive as in the 1913 scene depicted in chapter one. Harley-Davidson

The 1939 final assembly line. Note the unfinished motorcycle in the right foreground. The light-colored frame and fork are special-order items. The 1939 sales catalogs and The Enthusiast *didn't mention the availability of special-order finishes.*

Long-time competition rider and dealer Armando Magri says any discontinued standard color was available in later years by special order. Harley-Davidson

A 1939 61 OHV being tested on the vibration station. The sixth and final oil tank configuration appeared on the 1939 big twins. The change, visible here, consisted of a raised edge or wall around the tank periphery. Harley-Davidson

179

Testers make final adjustments to controls and carburetion of 1939 models. Harley-Davidson

Crating a 1939 police model. Harley-Davidson

the displayed motorcycles were big machines, with 500 cc being the most popular size. Particular attention was given to the BSA 250 cc, which they considered fairly good but poorly finished in order to save costs. The trio got the impression that hand clutches were unreliable on all English motorcycles. The lack of apparent Canadian interest in lightweight motorcycles added new discouragement to thoughts of a Harley-Davidson lightweight.

The final nail in the lightweight coffin was hammered home by lightweight advocate Gordon Davidson. He concluded a five-state survey of Indian 30.50 ci side-valve twin sales that revealed the Indian company sold only ten percent as many Junior Scouts in 1938 as they sold in 1937.

The WLD Special was first offered during the spring. Some factory documentation termed this the WLDD. The Special featured new aluminum cylinder heads with 51½ percent more cooling surface; these weighed 8 lb., 2 oz. less per pair than the iron heads.

The WLD Special term replaced the name WLDR to highlight that the Special (or WLDD) had the new aluminum heads while the previous WLDRs had iron heads. Naturally, the factory enjoyed immediate and steady sales of aluminum heads to riders who wished to update their WLDRs. Soon, the term WLDR was reinstated to denote updated cylinders with $1^{7}/_{16}$ in. intake ports instead of $1^{5}/_{16}$ in. ports. Later parts books referred to all of the 1939 racers as WLDR models, with both types of cylinders listed.

After nearly two years of discussion, in April the Forty-five overhead-valve was canceled as a 1940 model. After working out the cost, the projected Forty-five overhead-valve would have been as expensive to build as the Seventy-four side-valve. Although Chief Engineer William S. Harley had been saying that all along, apparently the board at last decided that without any cost savings on the Forty-five overhead-valve, it would not be a marketable proposition.

Instead of working on the Forty-five overhead-valve, the engineering department would be concentrating on the new 74 OHV. Other development attention would be given to aluminum cylinder heads for the Seventy-four and Eighty side-valve models; consideration was being given to offering the Eighty only with aluminum heads.

Road tested in 1939, this prototype overhead-valve version of the Forty-five was built in late 1938 by combining new cylinders and heads with a modified crankcase from the production side-valve version. This idea originated with William S. Harley in June 1937. Restoration by Carman Brown. Focal Point

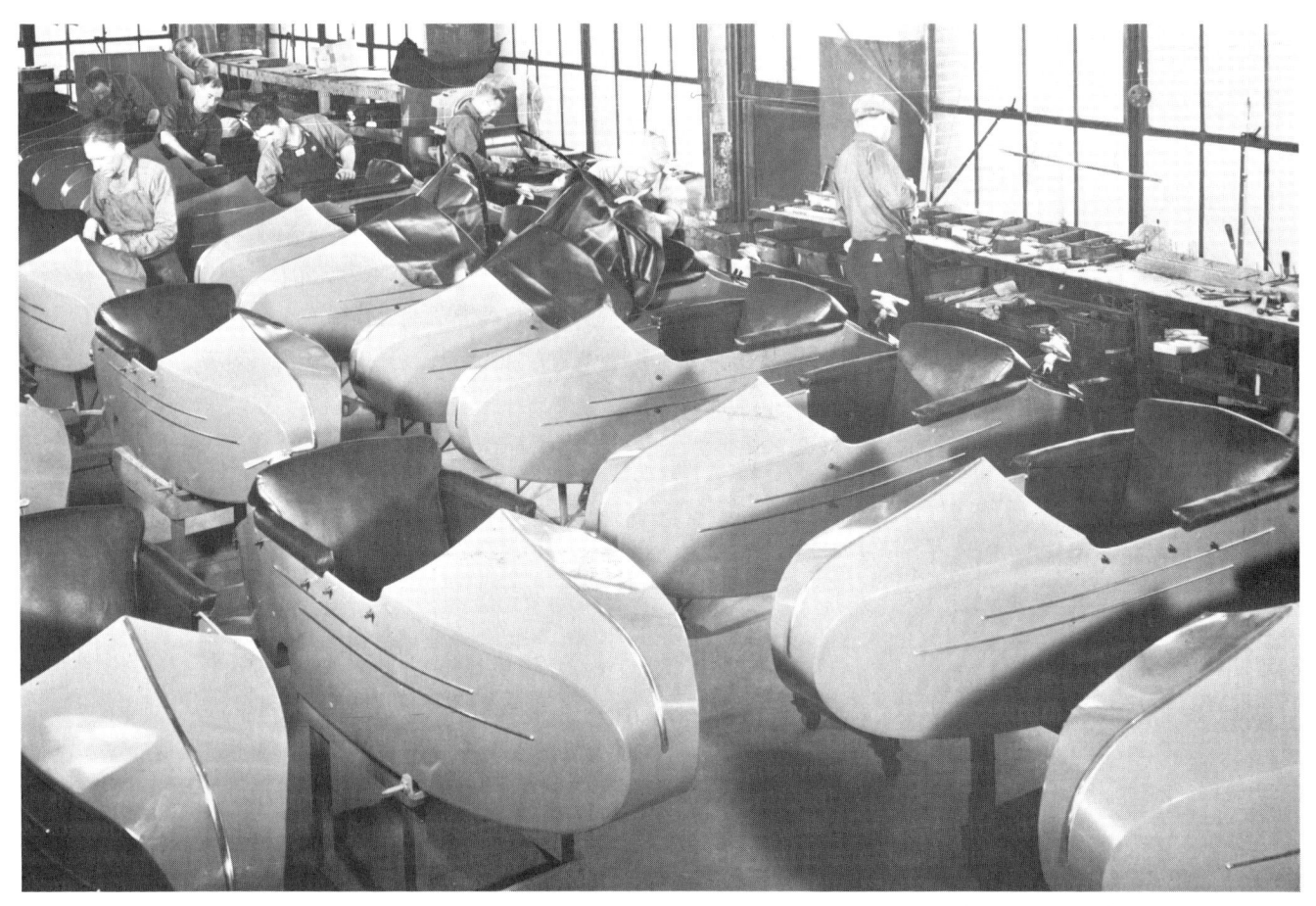

The 1939 Harley-Davidson sidecar shop. The 1936–1946 sidecar bodies were built by the Abresh Body Shop in Milwaukee. The Harley-Davidson factory took care of the rest of sidecar building. Harley-Davidson

181

The original Forty-five overhead concept model was built in August 1937 by combining overhead-valve hillclimber cylinders with the standard side-valve base. For production, full valve enclosure was a design requirement from day one, so the Knucklehead layout was abandoned to eliminate "tacked on" enclosures. Focal Point

Shown here are three of the four bolts that secured the cylinder head to the cylinder. The "north-south-east-west" head bolt pattern is like the 61 OHV. Forty-five overhead-valve hillclimber motors had the four head bolts at the "corners" instead, directly above the cylinder base bolts. Focal Point

Initial plans called for the proposed Forty-five OHV to debut in the 1939 lineup, but this was soon slipped until 1940. Only three Forty-five overheads were built, one of which was ridden round-trip from Milwaukee to San Antonio in February 1939. On the same trip was a prototype Seventy-four overhead, also intended to appear in the 1940 range. Continuing slow development would probably have pushed the Forty-five overhead debut into the 1941 lineup, the same as the Seventy-four overhead. Therefore, the 1941 styling is appropriate. Congratulations to owner Carman Brown for finding and restoring this historical motorcycle! Focal Point

The first Model WLA Army motorcycle was finished in August 1939 and shipped to the Mechanized Calvary Board at Fort Knox, Kentucky. Unusual features include an exhaust cutout, civilian white handgrips and glossy paint. Tall-finned aluminum cylinder heads debuted on the mid 1939 civilian WLD Special. Harley-Davidson

Late in the 1939 model 61 OHV production run around March, redesigned rocker arm shafts and rocker arms were introduced. Effective with motor 39EL1903 and above, this change was for the purpose of simplifying maintenance by incorporating a fixed oiling system. No longer would repairmen have to accurately align rocker shafts during the course of top end maintenance, since regardless of the installation geometry, the precalibrated amount of oil would be supplied. The holes in the rocker arm fingers were relocated to improve lubrication. The switch to the 1940 model 61 OHV production run began in mid-summer and included these changes, which were advertised as 1940 model improvements.

World War II

In May, Fort Knox complained about the performance of Harley-Davidson Seventy-four side-valve sidecar rigs. William S. Harley discussed the situation with Army officers and recommended the Army purchase one or two 61 OHV rigs for test purposes.

Two experimental Harley-Davidson Forty-fives were completed in August and shipped to the Mechanized Calvary Board at Fort Knox. These were the first prototype Model WLA Harley-Davidsons and were distinguished from previous military models by the absence of fender valances and the addition of a skid plate. The paint was high-gloss olive, and a few bits and pieces were chrome plated or polished. Handle grips were white rubber, the same as on civilian models. Forks were the same I-beam cross-section components used on the 1939 civilian Forty-fives.

At about this time at Fort Benning, Georgia, a tricycle built by the Delco Corporation underwent tests alongside an Indian tricycle. The Indian tricycle had been in testing for about a year, and results were sufficient to induce Delco to prepare their entry in the competition. The Delco trike consisted of a BMW-style front end and a Bantam automobile rear axle and differential. Although Harley-Davidson didn't compete in these tests, the favorable results would later affect the company.

World War II began on September 1 with Germany's invasion of Poland. Shortly thereafter, Fort Knox began an extensive testing program on two-wheeled motorcycles provided by Harley-Davidson, Indian and Delco. The two Harley-Davidson WLA prototypes were tested. Most of the testing at Fort Knox was done at extremely slow speeds. Riders were instructed to ride as slow as possible, and at periodic intervals, inspectors would test engine heat by placing their hands on the cylinders and cylinder heads. As for top speed, all models were capable of achieving the required 65 mph.

The telescopic forks of the BMW-like Delco were judged superior to the Harley-Davidson and Indian forks, and the Delco shaft drive was preferred to the

Harley-Davidson and Indian chain drive. The Delco motorcycle also drew praise for its extra ground clearance and lighter weight. The Harley-Davidsons and Indians were considered too heavy for some of the rough going.

The Indian left-hand throttle was preferred so that scouts could more easily pass messages to convoy vehicles. There was no preference on other controls, beyond the fact that they should be standardized among all Army motorcycles.

The Delco and Indian motorcycles sometimes failed while fording streams. Harley-Davidson showed up best in these tests. Harley handlebars were favored over Delco and Indian bars. In mud runs, the Delco and Indian models had sometimes suffered locked-up front wheels due to insufficient fender clearance, but the Harley-Davidsons were fine on this score. However, both of the test Harleys had trouble with the front chains and clutch due to water getting into the front chainguard.

Considerable Harley-Davidson attention was soon focused on a proposed Army shaft-drive tricycle. In October, the company received an invitation to bid on fifty trikes, but declined. Later that month, Walter Davidson and William S. Harley attended a conference at Camp Holabird, Maryland, along with representatives of Indian and Delco. In side discussions, Army officers convinced Davidson and Harley to submit a bid on the shaft-drive tricycles, and this bid was forwarded to the Army in November. The specifications included a Bantam automobile rear axle, as had been used on the Delco model exhibited during the conference. The Harley-Davidson bid was $3,248 per motorcycle. William S. Harley also asked the Army to consider development of a tricycle using dual ⅝ in. chain drive, but this request fell on deaf ears.

Meanwhile, William S. Harley arranged the purchase of a BMW from a source in Holland. In November, engineering work began on the BMW, which had commercial as well as military possibilities.

In December, William S. Harley and William H. Davidson as well as Indian and Delco representatives attended a motorcycle development conference at Camp Holabird. The Army stated they needed more two- and three-wheeled motorcycles. Regarding the latter, they had minimal interest in sidecar rigs but were interested in tricycles. Attendees were briefed on the results of the recent field tests at Fort Benning and Fort Knox.

The Air Corps testing officer voiced his opinion that much of the trouble with military motorcycles resulted from the riders tinkering with the carburetor adjustments. Harley responded that Harley-Davidson could supply motorcycles with a fixed-jet carburetor like those furnished to the California Highway Patrol. The Army revealed they had received a one-million-dollar appropriation for development of a forty-pound motorcycle radio. Consequently, they stressed the need for a stronger luggage rack.

In subsequent discussions, Harley pointed out that the Delco test model was nothing more than a BMW, and therefore the Army shouldn't award a large development contract for a design that had already been proven. He revealed that Harley-Davidson already had its own BMW for studies. Harley added that Harley-Davidson could enclose the rear chain drive on the Forty-five to produce a tricycle that would satisfy all of the Army's objections to conventional chain drive.

Harley-Davidson management was excited about the prospects for huge military contracts. The Jeep had yet to be invented, so Army reliance on motorcycles in the current war of mobility could be expected to greatly exceed the trench warfare needs of World War I.

Competition with Indian

Total sales for the 1939 business year were 10,352 units, which included 7,695 two-wheeled motorcycles plus three-wheelers and sidecars. Unit sales represented approximately sixty percent of 1929 sales. Nevertheless, Harley-Davidson was doing better than Indian, because for the past several years Harley-Davidson had been outselling Indian by about a 3:2 ratio.

In 1939 the Indian Motorcycle Company provided a table to Indian dealers comparing resale values between Indians and Harley-Davidsons. Several points were revealed.

Indian Sport Scout popularity was shown by the 45 ci Indian having a consistently higher average resale than the Harley-Davidson Forty-five. Across all five model years, the Indian Sport Scout average resale price was ten percent higher than the Harley-Davidson Forty-five.

The 1936 and 1937 Indian Fours were sales disasters. These were the cluttered upside-down models, so named for the reversal of valve gear arrangement so that exhaust valves were overhead and inlet valves were on the side. Note that in 1939, 1936 Fours had a lower average resale price than the 1936 Sport Scout, and 1937 Fours and Sport Scouts were dead even in average resale price. Indian Four popularity enjoyed a revival in 1938, but one-year-old 1938 models had a lower aver-

---

Harley-Davidson and Indian
resale comparisons 1934-1938

Model	1934	1935	1936	1937	1938
Indian Four	$167	$183	$205	$267	$330
Indian Chief	155	182	231	278	310
Indian Sport Scout	157	177	210	267	285
Harley-Davidson 45	145	162	195	230	264
Harley-Davidson 61			275	315	347
Harley-Davidson 74	187	200	247	280	322
Harley-Davidson 80			265	327	360

Note: This table is an extract from an Indian Motocycle Company table provided to Indian dealers in 1939. Prices shown represent the averages for each model based on sales data gathered throughout Washington, Oregon, California, Nevada, Utah, Arizona and Idaho.

age resale price than the 1938 Harley-Davidson Sixty-ones and Eighties.

Harley-Davidson's bread-and-butter 74 ci side-valve twin stood up well in resale competition with the Indian Four and Indian Chief. Over the entire five-year model span depicted, Harley-Davidson Seventy-four resale prices averaged seven percent higher than Indian Fours and Indian Chiefs.

Harley-Davidson Sixty-one and Eighty popularity is apparent. The average resale price for 1938 Harley-Davidson Sixty-ones was five percent higher than for the 1938 Indian Fours, while the 1938 Harley-Davidson Eighty bettered the 1938 Indian Four average by nine percent.

In summary, in the 1930s Indian enjoyed its traditional strength in the 45 ci field. However, most Americans favored the larger models where Harley-Davidson had gained the upper hand. Considering the terrible launching problems of the 1930 74 ci side-valve twins, this was quite a comeback for Milwaukee.

1940

Three changes on the 1940 Forty-five were consistent with Seventy-four and Eighty evolution. Front forks were now tubular instead of I-beam. The setup for rings, rods and baffles was now like the big side-valve twins. Shifting of the Forty-five was made faster by the use of a ball shift lock with adjustable spring load instead of a pin lock. Positions on the tank-side shifter guide were placed farther apart to allow for extra shifting motion, which further reduced shifting effort.

The gear shifter fingers on the Forty-five and Servi-Car were fitted with rollers. A longer transmission drum lever with a corresponding change to the drum took some of the effort out of shifting. The clutch release lever diameter was increased from $9/16$ to $3/4$ in. to minimize deflection. Six flat springs were inserted in

The 1940 Model WLD featured deep-finned aluminum cylinder heads. Tubular forks were a new feature on the Forty-five. Optional 1940 finishes were clipper blue with white stripe; flight red with black stripe; squadron gray with bittersweet stripe; black with flight red stripe; and police silver with black stripe (police use only). Harley-Davidson

Ribbed timing case covers were featured on the 1940 61 OHV. These were superceded by a running change to the 1941 style. Harley-Davidson

The 1940 WLD replaced the mid 1939 WLD Special. The 1940 WLD continued the deep-finned aluminum cylinder heads, 1¼ in. manifold and 1 1/16 in. venturi carburetor of its predecessor.

The 1940 WLDR racers had highly polished combustion chambers plus new cylinders and redesigned valve gear. The new cylinders had 1 9/16 in. intake ports. The valve heads were also closer to the bores due to the new valve gear. Earlier racers and all roadster Forty-fives, when viewed from the front, had valves parallel to the bores. The new racers, when viewed from the front, had valves tilted inward. The tilted valves rode on cam followers or shoes that were angled on the top side in order to thrust straight against the valves. Thus, although outfitted with full road gear, the 1940 WLDRs had evolved into pure racers.

On the Servi-Car, the axle housing was strengthened by adding more metal on both sides in the area around the chain opening, increasing resistance to whipping and slapping in case of chain failure. The rear chainguard clearance was increased ¾ in. to eliminate noise from the chain striking the guard. A turnbuckle device was provided to simplify brake adjustment. The rear wheel brake drums were changed from stampings to nickel-iron castings. The battery box bracket was changed to permit mounting the battery out of the way the clutch key ring to eliminate grabbing, chatter and rattle. The Forty-five sidecar chassis was given a hinged rubber-mounted front connection.

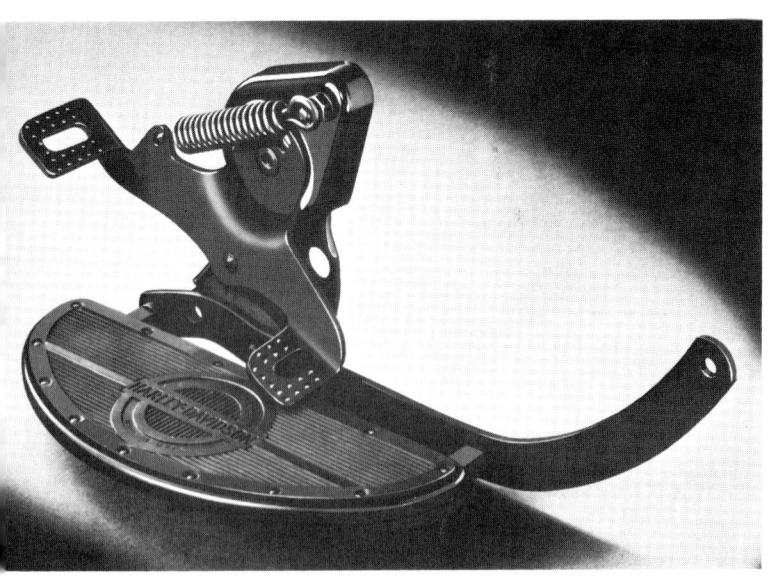

Streamlined D-shaped footboards replaced the rectangular style. The clutch bracket was elongated so the clutch operating rod would pass over the top of the front chainguard. Harley-Davidson

The 61 OHV, the Seventy-four side-valve and the Eighty side-valve were collectively referred to as the big twins. The upper part is a pre 1940 big twin crankpin of 1⅛ in. diameter and with a step up from the tapered ends to the middle section. The lower part is a 1940 big twin crankpin of 1¼ in. diameter and with no step up. Pre 1940 crankpins were supported by forty-two rollers; 1940 and later crankpins were supported by fifty-four rollers. Troy Ross

186

A 1940 61 OHV. The 5.00x16 tires were offered on all 1940 models. The new-model Dealer Bulletin said only 5.00x16 tires would be provided, but this policy was dropped. Big tires made rigid-frame Harley-Davidson com- *fort about as good as the new spring-frame Indians. Some riders overimproved the ride by underinflating the tires, which could cause a fall when the low frame grounded in a turn. Harley-Davidson*

of the clutch throw-out lever. A new type of reinforced towbar jaw clamp with a ratchet lock was featured. The towbar was widened to accommodate the new wider tubular front forks. The safety cable was snapped and secured through a hole in the upper towbar bracket.

Deep-finned aluminum cylinder heads were standard on the Eighty and optional on the Seventy-four. These silicon-aluminum heads had 41½ percent more cooling area than the former cast-iron heads and weighed 10 lb., 4 oz. less per set. The aluminum heads had cast-in brass spark plug inserts.

Several new features were common to all big twins. The crankpin diameter was increased from 1⅛ to 1¼ in., and the number of rollers was increased from forty-two to fifty-four. After removing a circlip, the closed ends of the crankcase bushings could be removed. This permitted a straight-through lap of the bushings while installed in the crankcase. Crankpins, roller bearings and the crankcase bushings were given a mirror lap. Cooling ribs were cast into the timing case cover of the big twin motors.

The front stand was redesigned and was now common to all big twins. The clutch foot lever bracket was new.

The big twin front wheel brake drum was cast instead of stamped nickel-steel. The cast construction and an integral stiffening ring were devised to stop vibration and chatter. Elimination of brake drum flexing was claimed to permit easier braking effort with the use of a $9/32$ in. narrower brake shoe and no loss of effectiveness. Front forks were now heat treated for extra strength.

The big twin clutch was reworked. Four slotted spring keys were provided on each lined disk assembly. These spring keys fitted into keyways of the clutch ring to take up slack and prevent rattle. A keyed spring steel disk was incorporated, and although advertised as a 1940 improvement, it had been in use for "some months" during the 1939 model production run.

Big twin transmissions returned to full constant-mesh for all road models. For police and commercial use, however, a three-speed or three-speed-and-reverse was offered with a sliding gear for the low-gear position.

The 61 OHV featured a number of changes. Oil distribution improvements were similar to those of the side-valve models. A difference was that neither cylinder base of the 61 OHV now had baffles, whereas the side-valve models had a no-baffle rear cylinder coupled with a baffled front cylinder. The change in baffles necessitated a new part number the 61 OHV crankcases.

As with the side-valve models, the 61 OHV had two compression rings and a lower oil control ring on both cylinders. For the 61 OHV, a fixed oiling system and redesigned rocker arms were advertised as 1940 improvements although these were actually running changes made during the 1939 models' production run.

The 61 OHV Linkert carburetor diameter was increased from 1¼ to 1½ in. and the venturi from 1 1/16 to 1 5/16 in. The intake manifold diameter was increased from 1¾ to 1 9/16 in. and was changed from a modified Y-shape to a T-shape. Larger cylinder intake porting matched the new manifolds. Higher horsepower was claimed. A change to the relay base plate provided more clearance between the base plate and the chrome stack on the front exhaust pipe.

A number of new features were incorporated on all models. All crankpins, roller bearings and crankcase bushings were lapped to glass smoothness. Main bearings were given a straight-through lap.

An "instant" gas reserve valve was provided. A movable rod topped by a knurled knob was mounted in the left tank. With the knob pushed down against the tank, the main fuel supply could be turned on or off by twisting the knob counterclockwise or clockwise. The reserve fuel supply was selected by pulling the knob up, where it was held by the spring loading of a neoprene packing. The extended rod served as a reminder to the rider. To work with the new gas reserve valve, the big twins got interconnected right and left tanks; the Forty-five continued to use one fuel tank and one oil tank.

Optional 5.00x16 in. tires were offered on all models; in fact, the new-model dealer bulletin said 4.50x18 in. tires would no longer be furnished. New heat treating was used on all forks. The clutch foot lever bearing cover was redesigned and more securely mounted to prevent rattle. The brake shackle fork stud was lengthened and secured with a nut and special lock washer.

On all models, the high-tension spark cable was neoprene. Flange-type copper electrical connectors replaced the soldered twisted type. The stoplight became standard equipment throughout the line. Spark plugs were fitted with Harley-Davidson-Champion insulators. Zerk-Alemite grease fittings were changed to make lubrication more convenient. The flange on the drive side of the interchangeable wheel hubs was switched from a stamping to a carbon steel forging; this

Winter-equipped 1940 police Eighty. New legshield brackets and legshields worked with the new floorboards. Harley-Davidson

new wheel hub was standard on all models except the front wheel on the Forty-five and Servi-Car.

All models got regular saddles in smooth brown finish or deluxe saddles in black or brown. Black or brown buddy seats were fitted with a thick cushion of whipped latex (rubber), and valances were walrus-grained with three ruby ornaments. Buddy seats got extra padding on the front end.

Styling changes were across the board, except for the Speedlined toolbox used on the big twins but not on the Forty-five. Fuel tank transfers gave way to chrome nameplates. Streamlined D-shaped floorboard replaced the rectangular style. New legshield brackets and legshields were incorporated to work with the new floorboards.

Three solo accessory groups were offered instead of two. These were the utility solo group, the sport solo group and the deluxe solo group. The utility solo group included a front Safety Guard, steering damper, Jiffy stand and four-ply tires. The sport solo group consisted of the utility solo group plus air cleaner, trip odometer, fender light, colored shift ball, chrome wheel rims and chrome exhaust pipe covers. The chrome wheel rims and exhaust covers were part of the full chrome group obtainable as a set. The deluxe solo group included additional style strips for front and rear fender tops, a chevron for the front fender and the full chrome group. In addition to the chrome rims and exhaust covers, the chrome group included the following parts in chrome plating: handlebars, headlight, instrument panel, relay cover and license frame.

On radio-equipped police models, a vertical rod antenna replaced the former screen type. The 1939 running change to radio speaker units was made an

A 1940 police Eighty shows off impressive aluminum cylinder heads, which were standard on the Eighty and optional on the Seventy-four. New timing cover cooling ribs were standard on the Eighty and Seventy-four side-valve. A Speed-lined toolbox was used on the Eighty, Seventy-four and 61 OHV. Harley-Davidson

189

official 1940 feature. Speaker units were changed from the magnetic Utah type to the dynamic type. Detailed improvements were made to both the RCA and General Electric radios.

Army business is Harley business

Another visit to the Indian factory was made by William H. Davidson in January 1940. Since the previous summer, Indian had tripled its workforce, which now numbered between 750 and 850 employees, including forty-five in the office force. Indian was making sixty motorcycles per day and hoped to climb to seventy-five per day shortly. Davidson further learned that Indian was preparing to bid on a three-wheeled military shaft-drive model of its own design. Indian had won a number of orders for its 74 ci military V-twin from the Allies. Indian also hoped to sell its 30.50 ci military V-twin.

The late Red Wolverton, long-time dealer and confidant of Arthur Davidson, related the following story told to him by Arthur. At a meeting in Washington, D. C., government officials asked William S. Harley to build 30.50 ci military motorcycles.

"Bill Harley said, 'Well, we won't build a thirty-cubic-inch motor.' And they wondered why, and were really storming around there. One of them said, 'If you don't make that thirty-cubic-inch motor for us, you can consider yourself out of the motorcycle business.' And Bill Harley said, 'If we make that thirty-cubic-inch motorcycle, we'd be out of business anyway, because it just won't do the job and we're not going to make it.'"

Harley's stubbornness paid off. The Army later agreed with him, and Harley-Davidson's capture of most of the United States military business was partly because the Indian 30.50 twin was considered underpowered by testers.

At Harley-Davidson, extensive big twin testing with the new motor baffling and piston ring setup proved that oil pressure could be raised considerably without over-oiling problems. Effective with motors 40EL2306 and 40U2164, higher big twin oil pressure settings were achieved by installing a stronger regulator

A 1940 WLA. Forks were extended 2 3/8 in., for about 2 in. more ground clearance at the front of the motor. Harley-Davidson

(bypass) spring in the oil pump. In March, dealers were advised to fit the stronger regulator spring to earlier big twin motors having two oil control rings. This was emphasized for the 61 OHV because field reports were indicating excessive oil mileage in the opinion of the engineering staff.

The Army tricycle bid request was received in March, and Harley-Davidson responded with a bid based on an assumed production of fifteen to twenty pilot models. The company received an order for 745 Army 45 ci WLA motorcycles. The WLA models produced under this contract had the new tubular front forks introduced on civilian models. Additionally, the rigid and spring fork legs were extended 2⅜ in., to give about 2 in. more ground clearance under the engine—6 in. total. The 1940 WLA models were equipped with buddy seats, a cargo rack, saddlebags and the D-shaped floorboards used on civilian models. Harley-Davidson submitted a bid for an additional 185 Army motorcycles, including both WLA solos and 74 ci side-valve sidecar jobs.

Within a few weeks, the company was awarded a contract to build sixteen shaft-drive three-wheelers. The design featured the 61 ci overhead-valve V-twin motor of the popular 61 OHV. Much of the work would be simple; the main problems were expected to be in the shaft-drive components.

In April, engineer Christy Spexarth visited the Gleason company in Rochester, New York, to nail down a subcontract for the production of bevel gears. Spexarth then went to the Spicer plant in Toledo, Ohio, to arrange a subcontract for rear axles. The Spicer deal led to a side trip to the Thompson Products Company of Detroit as Spicer's product was built under a royalty arrangement with Thompson. Within a few days, all subcontracting complexities were resolved, and the

The first of sixteen overhead-valve tricycles was completed in June 1940 and underwent testing at Camp Holabird, Maryland. The last trikes were delivered in January 1941. These were the first Harley-Davidsons equipped with automatic ignition control. Harley-Davidson

The shaft-drive three-wheelers had a 69 ci motor with a 5:1 compression ratio. Success of the four-wheeled Jeep killed the trike project. Harley-Davidson

Harley-Davidson engineering staff began the process of integrating the factory and subcontracting operations in order to deliver on schedule.

While Spexarth was traveling in the East and Midwest on Army business, William S. Harley and William H. Davidson attended Army maneuvers near Alexandria, Louisiana. The Army criticized Harley-Davidson and Indian solo motorcycles for their heavy weight, which made slow-going difficult. Harley-Davidson was directed to deliver all future Army Harley-Davidsons without any chrome trim or polished parts. During the maneuvers, these shiny parts were taped over.

The standard wire-mesh air cleaners of Harleys and Indians were considered inadequate for severe dust conditions; Harley and Davidson promised the Army a cure for this problem. The Army stated that all motorcycles being tested were too noisy, were too difficult to handle in mud and heavy sand, ran too hot at slow speed and didn't have enough ground clearance

Only a handful of the more than 80,000 military Harley-Davidsons were finished with glossy paint. This 1940 Seventy-four side-valve Model UA was built for the Marine Corps and probably was used for shore patrol. The low-compression engine used cast-iron heads. Harley-Davidson

for cross-country riding. "In the main, however, Harley-Davidsons stood up very well compared to the competitive make," William H. Davidson told the board of directors.

Harley-Davidson's busy factory schedule steered it away from a sizeable military contract. Indian completed delivery of 5,000 motorcycles to the French government shortly before the Germans occupied France in June.

At the annual Atlantic City police convention in early summer, New England traveling representative Charles Cartwright received a telephone call from Walter Davidson. Walter said, "You know, Charles, I think there's something doing in Washington. I think there's going to be a war. I'd like you to go down there and stay three weeks, if necessary, and get the lay of the land." So Cartwright left for a three-week trip, not realizing that he would operate out of his Washington, D. C., office for the next five years.

Shortly after Cartwright arrived in Washington, he called on the Russian Amtorg Company regarding its possible purchase of military Harley-Davidsons. In early 1940, the Russians had bought some Indian motorcycles. Cartwright was surprised to find his old acquaintance Mr. Karsov now in charge of motorcycle purchases for the Soviet Union. Back in 1924, Cartwright had helped Karsov purchase Harley-Davidsons on credit—helped Karsov out of a jam, in other words. After Cartwright and Karsov hit it off again, the Russians switched to Harley-Davidsons.

In late June, the pilot shaft-drive trike was finished and ridden to Camp Holabird by George Schulteti of Department 21. Schulteti and Army personnel put the Harley three-wheeler through several tests, witnessed

A few civilian carryovers were on military models, such as the sidecar fender running light and the trim strip in the middle of the sidecar body. Harley-Davidson

by Cartwright. Indian trucked down a competitive tricycle, but only for Army inspection as the Indian three-wheeler wasn't yet ready for testing.

The Harley-Davidson trike immediately went into vigorous testing. The results were disappointing. Vibration was so bad, especially at high speed, that the gas line was replaced four times. The motor leaked oil excessively, and the brakes had to be continually adjusted. High-gear power was inadequate, and the motor stalled when trying to negotiate heavy mud. The tricycle was tail-heavy and tended to lift the front end off the ground. However, testers acknowledged that some of the handling peculiarities were inevitable in the tricycle configuration, rather than evidence of any Harley-Davidson shortcoming. Schulteti, Cartwright and Capt. Mosely prepared test reports that were reviewed by the board of directors on July 14.

In August, the Army trike was returned to the factory and disassembled. The motor was swapped for a 69 ci variant built up by modifying a prototype 74 ci OHV motor to obtain a 5:1 compression ratio.

Examination revealed the frame was broken, so the rear end was strengthened and replaced. An oil-bath air cleaner was fitted to the safety bar, and a few other minor changes were made. Testing got under way in order to have the machine ready for return to the Army by August 30 at the latest. The order for the remaining three-wheelers was being held up pending approval of the pilot model.

The improved tricycle was delivered on schedule, and the Army approved the design for continued production. Manufacturing of the remaining fifteen units began at once.

On September 3, William S. Harley attended a meeting at Camp Holabird on the subject of shaft-drive solo motorcycles. The upshot of the meeting was that Harley-Davidson was asked to bid on three different types of solo shaft-drives. These were a standard V-twin with shaft drive, a BMW type and a modified BMW type with 5 in. tires and 8 in. ground clearance.

During this meeting, the Army also expressed its opinions on the performance of the test motorcycles previously submitted by Harley-Davidson, Indian and Delco. The motors of each competing brand had been torn down for inspection following several thousand miles of testing, and the cylinder bores were inspected for scuffs and scratches. Harley-Davidson was rated best, Delco second and Indian third.

The first of a long line of 74 OHV models appeared in the 1941 lineup. The deluxe air cleaner was 1 in. larger than previously. A little cheating here, as the motorcycle has a 1940 motor number. However, the photo was processed in March 1941. Strange! The crankcase exhaust air passage was visible over its entire length because the new timing case cover was redesigned to work with thicker crankcase walls without encroaching on footboard and brake pedal clearances. Harley-Davidson

194

The next day, Harley attended a Pentagon meeting to explain the Harley-Davidson bidding position: the company was not submitting a bid for the BMW variant. Harley stressed that this configuration would have poor handling, and that 8 in. ground clearance was excessive; skillful riders could maneuver their way around most high obstacles and with a skid plate could handle many obstacles by plowing across. Frank Long, the Indian engineering representative, endorsed Harley's position.

Long stated that the Indian firm had been working on its own design of a solo shaft-drive motorcycle for the past year. The engine had originally been built for a nonmotorcycle application for the Navy and Air Corps. Harley-Davidson and Indian advised the Army that it was impossible to provide specialized motorcycles within two years. The Army stated that it would buy considerable quantities of standard motorcycles.

After further deliberation in Milwaukee, William S. Harley's formal response to the Army request for bids included only the basic BMW type, which drew flak from the Army because it still wanted bids on all three options. Walter Davidson and William H. Davidson believed the company should bid on only one type, but William S. Harley and his son William J. felt bids for all three types should be submitted. This matter was not resolved at the September board meeting and continued to be discussed in other company forums for several days.

Harley-Davidson business for the 1940 business year was up twenty-three percent over the previous year. Pending additional military orders included 2,056 motorcycles and 156 sidecars for South Africa and 659 motorcycles for the US Army. Current motorcycle production was up from 10,855 in the 1940 business year to a projected 16,200 for the 1941 business year—about seventy percent of the 1929 boom level. The rise in defense spending put extra money into the pockets of the company's best customers, young industrial workers. Conversely, dealers were worried about a possible military draft, which would make debt collection difficult.

1941
Debut of the 74 OHV

The highlight of the 1941 announcement was the new 74 OHV. The 74 OHV was brought out primarily in response to police requests for additional power. In keeping with the company's conservative approach, only a few 74 OHVs were built in order to test customer reaction. The larger capacity was achieved by increasing the 61 OHV bore from $3\frac{5}{16}$ to $3\frac{7}{16}$ in. and the stroke from $3\frac{1}{2}$ to $3\frac{31}{32}$ in. Pistons on the 74 OHV featured a milled relief on the lower skirt edge, so the rods wouldn't hit the pistons. Piston choices provided a 6.6:1

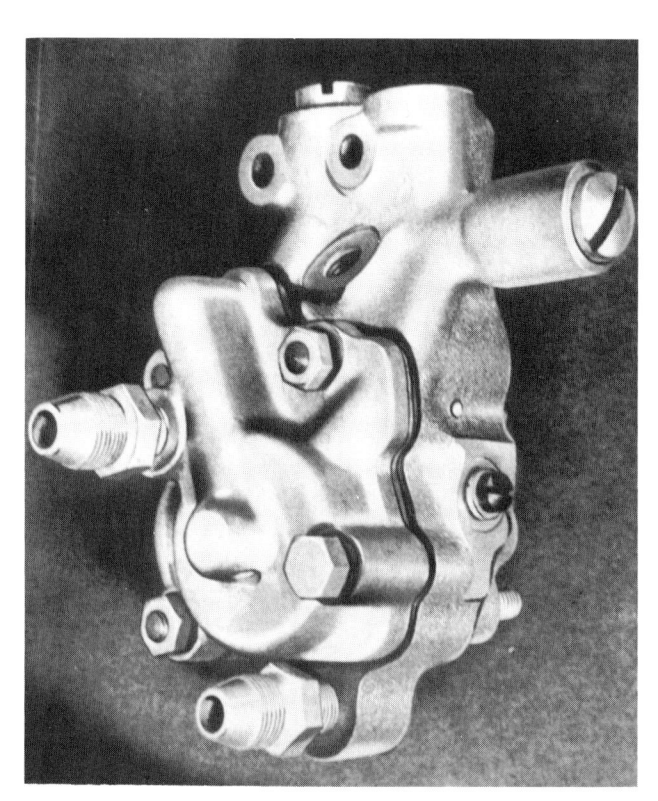

The 1941 overhead-valve model oil pump was changed from a gear type to a vane type. A centrifugal bypass valve was featured. Harley-Davidson

Some early 1941 74 OHVs suffered cracked crankcases, so in midyear the crankcase was thickened and given longer reinforcing ribs on the left side. Harley-Davidson

compression ratio for the F model and a 7:1 compression ratio for the FL model. The company provided only one power rating for both models: 48 hp at 5000 rpm.

The 1941 74 OHV used the 1 5/16 in. venturi carburetor introduced on the 1940 61 OHV. On the 1941 61 OHV the carburetor venturi was 1 1/8 in., a running change introduced on late-1940 models.

Each of the 74 OHV flywheels weighed 4 lb. more than the previous years' 61 OHV flywheels and were 8 1/2 in. in diameter compared to earlier 61 OHV flywheels with a 7 3/4 in. diameter. The 74 OHV flywheels were also used in the new 61 OHV, though of course the 61 OHV flywheels were drilled for a shorter stroke. Connecting rods of both models were identical.

The 74 OHV and the 61 OHV used the same crankcase design. The 1941 overhead models' crankcases had thicker walls to provide the extra strength needed by the 74 OHV. To maintain necessary clearance on the right side for the brake pedal and footboard, the timing case cover was redesigned. Prior to 1941, the crankcase exhaust air passage was cast into the middle of the timing case cover, and only about an inch of the exhaust air passage, the bottom rear portion near the scavenge pump, was discernible with the timing cover installed. For 1941, the timing case cover was "brought in," which had the effect of making the exhaust air passage protrude over its entire length from the upper middle of the cover to the lower rear of the cover.

Problems with the new 74 OHV were mostly minor. There were, however, a few instances of cracked left crankcases despite the thicker crankcase walls

A 1941 WLD. Optional finishes for 1941 were skyway blue, cruiser green, flight red, brilliant black, and police silver (police use only). Harley-Davidson

The 1941 Forty-five oil pump. The vane-type pump layout on side-valve models dated from 1937, but the centrifugally controlled bypass valve was new for 1941. Harley-Davidson

Winter-equipped Forty-five with iron cylinder heads. The taillight housing on 1940 models was black instead of color-matched to the fender. Harley-Davidson

designed into the 1941 overheads. This problem was cured by a midyear running change which increased the length of the left case reinforcing ribs.

On the Forty-five, the valve spring free length was increased from $2^3/_{16}$ to $2^{19}/_{32}$ in. The installed length was $5/_{16}$ in. longer than previously. The objective was to prolong valve spring life. New upper valve spring covers were required.

The compression ratio on the WL models with cast-iron cylinder heads was reduced from 5:1 to 4.75:1, and the Servi-Car compression ratio was increased from 4.5:1 to 4.75:1. Production and spares stocking was simplified by making all Forty-five cast-iron heads identical.

A number of changes to the Forty-five and Servi-Car concerned the clutch and its operation. The clutch release lever was strengthened and straightened. A stranded steel cable connected the release lever and clutch pedal; the cable ran in a stainless steel tube that acted as a guide. A larger clutch pushrod bearing with improved shielding was designed to keep out dirt.

On the Forty-five and Servi-Car, the clutch was equipped with two fiber disks and one spring disk—six frictional surfaces including a backer friction disk and a frictional surface on one side of the spring disk. The fiber disks were riveted to the steel disks, which followed big twin practice. The operating spring load was decreased from about 500 lb. to about 300 lb. A larger clutch hub was incorporated with two staggered rows of thirty-six steel balls, each $7/_{32}$ in. in diameter and each individually retained. The hub was fitted to the mainshaft by splines instead of a taper and key. The new clutch and clutch-operating features smoothed the clutch action.

The Forty-five and Servi-Car transmission gears were strengthened and increased in diameter. Gears were made slightly farther apart for easier adjustment. The dog clutches were heavier and their diameters increased. Easier shifting was achieved by redesign of the transmission cam and shifter lever gear—the ratio of the shifter lever was increased and the track of the shifter cam lengthened. These were the last major changes to the Forty-five transmission, which had been modified frequently.

The gearbox was $7/_{16}$ in. wider to accommodate the increased spacing between the gears. The gearbox was mounted to the frame with three studs instead of two. The transmission oil filler plug was lengthened and relocated for improved access.

The Forty-five front inner chainguard was changed to a one-piece construction. The outer chainguard was changed to work with the new clutch and provide a better seal between the outer and inner guards. The rear end of the chainguard was clamped to the frame instead of the transmission.

Extension of the Forty-five rear chain line by $7/_{16}$ in. made it possible to use a wider rear brake drum and shoes. The top of the brake lever arm was offset to

Left closeup of 1941 civilian Forty-five Model WLD. Clutch cover has been removed for pushrod adjustment via the center screw and locknut. Harley-Davidson

retain the original brake rod lineup with the wider drum. Braking area was increased forty-four percent in order to increase brake lining life. On the Forty-five front brake, heavier-gauge metal and a slight change in

Until 1941, the Forty-five clutch was a descendant of the Peashooter clutches. For 1941, the Forty-five clutch received the same layout as the new big twin clutch. Harley-Davidson

the shape of the front brake shell provided greater structural strength.

A streamlined toolbox was now fitted to the Forty-fives. The rear Safety Guard accessory was redesigned to prevent fouling of the leg during starting. Stronger kickstarter springs were fitted. The WLDR, now termed a regular road model, pulled 5500 rpm and had a claimed 7 hp margin over the WLD. Joining the WLDR in the stable were the new WRTT and WR, which were the first Harley-Davidsons outfitted purely as Class C racers. With the WRTT, Class C riders no longer had to remove lighting equipment and the front fender for TT racing (predecessor of the motocross). The WR came without brakes, so riders didn't have to remove these for flat track racing.

The 1941 WLDR, WRTT and WR had a 1¼ in. crankpin and connecting rod assembly, special intake and exhaust cam gears, a 1½ in. carburetor, twenty-five percent stronger valve springs, and polished intake ports, manifold and combustion chamber. Additionally, the WRTT and WR had lighter flat tappets in lieu of roller tappets.

On the Servi-Car, the big twin front wheel, front brake shell and brake mechanism were featured. The

The 1941 big twin clutch was substantially different from earlier units. Instead of thirty tabs in the hub, there were six keys. These keys drove the three steel discs. The ten driving pins drove the fiber discs. Harley-Davidson

New "airplane-style" speedometer dial for 1941, with large silver numerals over black background and white pointer. In front of the left filler cap is the gas reserve valve, introduced on the 1940 models. Harley-Davidson

A 1941 74 OHV and two happy occupants. Advertising hammered away at the fun of riding two-up. Militaristic apparel was at the height of its popularity, but remained popular until the 1950s. Harley-Davidson

front axle was strengthened, and the frame was redesigned to accommodate the larger gearbox of the all constant-mesh transmission. The axle tube was now welded instead of riveted. Other improvements included a new recoil strap guide, replaceable guide and special oil control oxide-coated piston rings.

The 61 OHV featured the heavier flywheels of the 74 OHV. Additionally, the 61 OHV T-shaped intake manifold length was increased ½ in. to reduce a vapor lock tendency. The venturi on the 61 OHV carburetor was increased from 1 11/16 to 1 1/8 in.

The big twin clutch was considerably reworked again. Three steel disks, three friction disks and one spring disk were used. The spring disk had a fiber facing on one side, so there was a total of seven friction surfaces instead of five. Frictional area was up from 73 to 121 sq. in., a sixty-five percent increase. To overcome sticking and grabbing, the milled splines were replaced by ten driving pins on the clutch hub. Six hardened-steel keys were riveted to the key ring. The driving pins drove the friction disks, and the steel disks were driven by the keys. Looseness and rattle in the clutch plates were prevented by two spring-loaded balls on each steel disk. The clutch hub was larger, with thirty-six ball bearings arranged in two staggered rows, each ball 7/32 in. in diameter and individually retained—the same improvement made on the Forty-five and Servi-Car. The clutch foot lever assembly was improved with a longer foot lever bearing and a one-piece release lever.

A popular form of racing in the 1930s was the so-called TT race, named for the Isle of Man Tourist Trophy (TT) event. American TTs were supposed to be miniature versions of the Isle of Man race and had to include at least one right turn and one jump. Such courses were easier to lay out and maintain than the deceptively simple looking flat track courses, which required careful banking and surfacing. The popularity of TT races spurred Harley-Davidson toward building the ready-to-race Model WRTT. Riders are Ed Kretz (38) on an Indian Sport Scout and Sam Arena (79) on a Harley-Davidson Forty-five. The course was at Lodi, California. Hap Jones

The 1941 WRTT was the first Harley-Davidson built solely for Class C racing. The WRTT was used in road races or TT (motocross) events; the companion WR without brakes was used for flat track racing. Harley-Davidson

199

A quieter muffler was fitted to the big twins. The new muffler contained no steel wool packing, which disintegrated, burned and blew out on earlier mufflers.

On police models, the radio carrier was redesigned and relocated 3¾ in. lower and 2⅜ in. farther forward to lower the center of gravity and improve handling. A ring tip was provided to the vertical rod radio antenna as a safety feature. Detail improvements were made to the current and voltage regulator. A three-point shockproof mounting was also provided.

On all 1941 models, a centrifugally controlled bypass valve regulated the flow of oil to the motor according to engine speed. At higher speeds, more oil flowed to the motor bearings and cylinders, and at lower speeds, more oil was diverted to the motor gearcase. Similar oil regulation was already accomplished with the spring-and-ball regulator valve, but the new centrifugal setup was more reliable and accurate. The spring-and-ball regulator valve was retained.

Gearshifter levers on all models were cyanide hardened to prevent wear and cutting at the shifter gate. A longer brake handlever of cast aluminum was fitted to improve leverage. The brake handlever mounting bracket geometry was changed to eliminate cable binding. Piston rings were now oxide-coated to reduce scuffing and the formation of ridges in the cylinder walls.

On all models the reserve fuel capacity was increased to 1 gallon. Batteries were grounded to the frame instead of to an oil line. A heavier clamping ring on the horn prevented deflection when mounted on the motorcycle and helped the horn work effectively over all speed ranges.

A more attractive windshield was available for all models. The new windshield had stainless steel edges

Closeup of a typical Harley-Davidson military Forty-five motor. Its output was 23½ hp at 4600 rpm and its compression ratio was 5:1. By comparison, the civilian Model WLD produced 24½ hp at 4600 rpm with a 6:1 compression ratio. Harley-Davidson

for support instead of rubber-covered steel tubes and was made of Plastacele instead of pyralin to combat discoloring under the sun. The new shield was twice as thick as the earlier one.

Two styling changes applied to all models. A chrome band was added to the tanks, and an airplane-style speedometer was fitted. The new speedometer had large silver numerals and a white pointer with triangular sides.

In January 1941, deliveries were completed on the contract for sixteen overhead-valve tricycles. The Army's request for shaft-drive solo bids arrived late, and Harley-Davidson's response was due within thirty days.

Shaft-drive XA

On February 17, Walter Davidson, William S. Harley and William H. Davidson went to Washington, D. C., to negotiate on shaft-drive motorcycles. The bids submitted were all on the basic BMW copy, henceforth called the XA.

XA bid prices

Quantity	Unit price
1,000	$870.35
1,500	$731.01
3,000	$569.61

The Army selected the option for 1,000 XAs. All deliveries were to be completed by July 1942.

The XA was a copy of the BMW 45 ci, 750 cc side-valve military model. The bore-to-stroke ratio was "square," equal at 3 $1/16$ in. Valves were actuated from a single camshaft mounted along the top side of the crankcase.

A two-throw crankshaft was featured. Thus, the motion of each set of pistons and connecting rods was

Early 1941 WLA featured a new round oil bath air cleaner and an extended front end as used on the 1940 WLA series. The buddy seat was advocated by Col. Benson of the Mechanized Board at Fort Knox, but relatively few Forty-fives used the civilian buddy seat. The luggage rack is the tubular civilian type introduced in the teens. Harley-Davidson

Specifications
Year and model	1941 XA
Engine	Horizontally opposed twin
Bore and stroke	3¹¹⁄₁₆x3¹¹⁄₁₆ in.
Displacement	45.038 ci, 738 cc
Compression ratio	5.7:1
Horsepower	23 bhp at 4600 rpm
Clutch	Dry, single disk
Gearbox	Four speed, constant-mesh foot shift, auxiliary handlever for locating neutral
Gear ratios	Low: 14.19:1; second: 8.55:1; third: 5.82:1; high: 4.7:1
Shift	Left foot
Wheelbase	58¾ in.
Ground clearance	7 in. (under skid plate)
Wheels	18 in.
Suspension	Front: leading-link; rear: plunger
Weight	538 lb. (standard equipment)
Seat height	30.5 in. (estimated)
Fuel consumption	35 mpg

the opposite of the other set, so that nearly perfect mechanical balance was achieved.

Because the cylinders were well exposed to the air stream, the average operating oil temperature was 250 to 350 degrees Fahrenheit. In contrast, the WLA average oil temperature was typically 350 to 450 degrees Fahrenheit. XA cooling was further enhanced by the double-decker cylinder head cooling fins. The Army was pleased that XA models typically ran 10,000 to 15,000 miles before extensive engine overhaul was required, which was attributed to the lower operating temperatures.

Connecting rods were two-piece, with automotive-style removable big end caps. Connecting rod lower end bearings were rollers; crankshaft bearings were caged balls; camshaft bearings were bronze bushes.

A 1941 WLC. The big twin front wheel and brake were used instead of the standard Forty-five components. This made front and rear wheels interchangeable. The front brake drum wasn't integral with the hub; it was attached with lug screws.

Big twin fork rockers and fender braces were used. The toolbox on the front fender was unique to the 1941 WLC. The solo seat was moved forward on 1941 WLCs and WLAs. Harley-Davidson

Ignition timing was automatically governed by centrifugal flyweights.

XA lubrication was wet-sump, all of the engine oil being carried in the crankcase. Oil was circulated by a gear-type pump in the bottom of the crankcase, the pump being driven by a worm gear on the end of the camshaft. From the pump, oil traveled through four channels. The first two channels fed oil to the front and rear crankshaft bearings. Surprisingly, oil was not pressure-fed to the connecting rod big ends. Instead, oil draining from the front and rear crankshaft bearings was caught by two oil-slinging rings, which threw the oil to the connecting rod big ends. The third oil channel carried oil to the crankcase pinion gear, which slung oil to the other gears in the case. The fourth oil channel took oil to the left cylinder wall. Viewed from the front, the XA crankshaft turned clockwise, so the right cylinder got plenty of oil sling from the crankshaft and rods, but the left cylinder needed the dedicated oil channel to receive adequate lubrication. Crankcase ventilation was by a timed rotary breather operating from the camshaft drive gear. The breather was mounted in the backside of the timing case cover.

With a contract for 1,000 shaft-drive solo motorcycles ready for signature by mid-April, a hangup developed over the ownership of the tooling to build the XA. Considerable tax savings could be realized by letting the title to the XA tooling pass to the government, but at the same time, Harley-Davidson wanted to apply accelerated depreciation techniques and use the tooling for commercial purposes.

The upshot was that Harley-Davidson signed the original contract, but applied for a certificate of necessity and a certificate of government protection. The effects of these procedures were twofold. First, the company could write off the cost of the tooling over a five-year period or at the end of the war, whichever occurred first. Second, Harley-Davidson could use the tooling for commercial purposes, but only after the expiration of a six-year period, during which the government would have first priority on the use of the tooling.

Material shortages

During 1941, standard 45 ci V-twin production remained the top military motorcycle priority. WLA models for 1941 were equipped with a cylindrical oil-bath air cleaner mounted on the left side, and this air cleaner was retrofitted to earlier WLAs. The buddy seat was continued. The taillight was changed to the civilian unit used from 1934 through 1938, with an overhead bracket that supported a single blackout light. The Army cargo rack had a rear section cutout, so that when the rear fender was swung upward during a tire change, the bulky lights would pass through the cutout. Other 1941 WLA details, such as the teardrop toolbox and new clutch release arm, followed 1941 civilian Forty-five practice.

Although the United States wasn't yet in the war, Canada had been in the war since the outset in September 1939. Accordingly, in 1941 substantial numbers

Typical 1941 XA, basically a copy of a BMW. The throttle was on the left and the handclutch on the right, according to Army specifications for the shaft-drive competition program that pitted the Harley-Davidson XA against the Indian 841. Shifting was by the left foot. The lever on the transmission case was an auxiliary shifter on BMWs, but on the XA with left-hand throttle, the lever was usable only for locating neutral. Harley-Davidson

A 1941 XA. During 1941, the luggage rack of channeled steel replaced the tubular style. The new luggage rack fit in with a program to develop a 40 lb. motorcycle radio, which was considered too heavy for the old-style rack. Harley-Davidson

of the Model WLC were contracted for Canadian armed forces but were designated as 1942 WLCs. The WLCs differed from the WLAs in several respects. Most WLCs did not have a cargo rack on the rear fender like the WLAs. The WLC had the Harley big twin front wheel and brake, the latter affixed by lug screws rather than being integral with the hub. Big twin fork rockers and fender braces were used. Unlike the WLA, on the WLC the front and rear wheels were interchangeable. An auxiliary hand clutch was mounted to the right handlebar. Other WLC points included a toolbox mounted to the front fender, Canadian-style blackout lights, a rear chain oiler and a front wheel stand.

The company had ordered new frame heads for WLAs back in January. Delivery had been promised by May 1. Although the United States was still officially neutral on the war in Europe, the American government and industrial base were already preparing the nation for eventual war against Germany. By June, Harley-Davidson found it increasingly difficult to obtain materials for orders other than defense. Despite a defense priority for the January steel order for frame heads, steel delivery to the drop forgers didn't happen until September.

There was enough aluminum on hand to make 1,000 overheads, 1,000 Seventy-four side-valves except gearcase covers, 250 Servi-Cars and 250 non-defense Forty-fives. At the suggestion of Arthur Davidson, the directors decided someone should be sent to the company's major aluminum supplier in Manitowoc, Wisconsin, to expedite their existing orders before the situation got worse and to check on other materials with the purpose of getting as much on order as possible. In addition, William J. Harley was assigned the task of checking with the Aluminum Company of Minneapolis as a possible additional source of aluminum castings. The materials situation was so bad that William S. Harley recommended domestic orders be parceled out to

A 1941 XA. This was Harley-Davidson's first footshift. Oil in the air cleaner was to be changed at least as often as the engine oil was changed, and more frequently under dusty conditions. Harley-Davidson

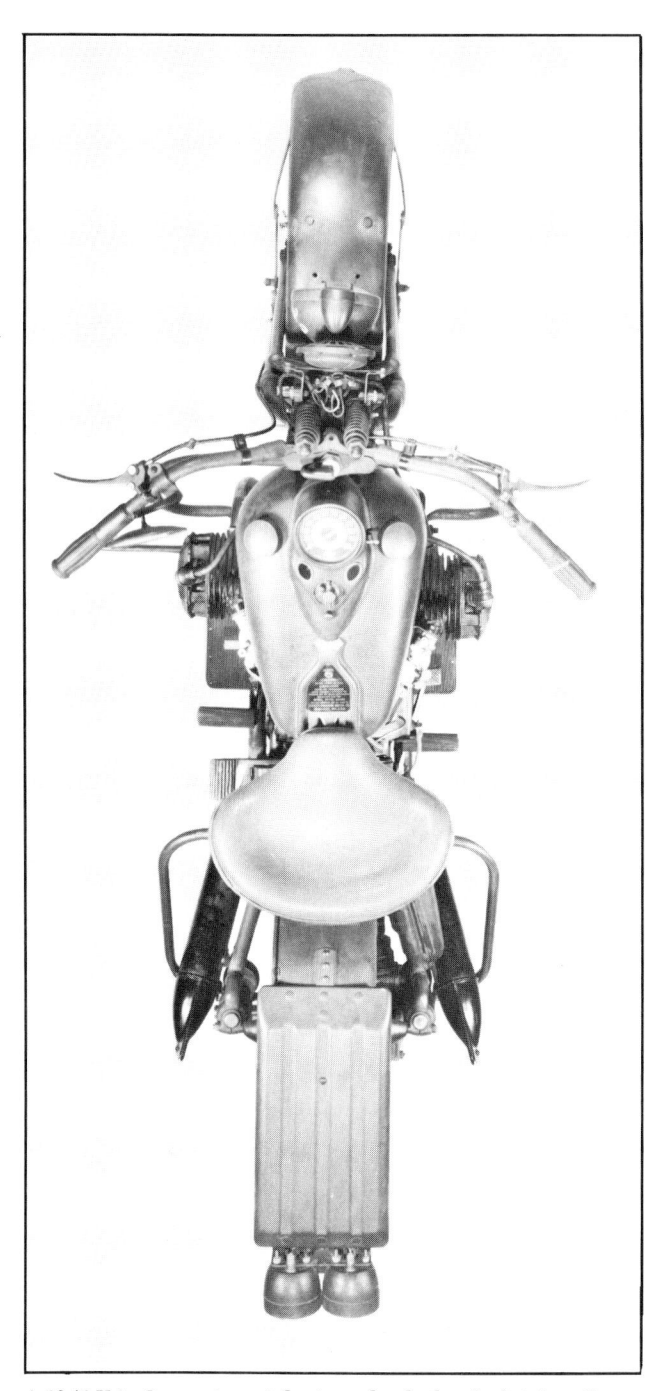

A 1941 XA. Operation of the front brake by the left handlever is clearly shown. Dual taillights were introduced on 1941 WLAs as well as on XAs. Harley-Davidson

dealers slowly in order to stretch them as far as possible and therefore keep them alive. The board of directors approved Walter Davidson's suggested twenty-percent cut in the commercial motorcycle production schedule for 1942 models. This eliminated 2,000 motorcycles from the civilian market. The board discussed rationing spare parts and motorcycles, but no decision was reached.

The company mailed the annual new-season bulletin, dated September 8, but the theme was uncertainty instead of the customary optimism. The opening paragraphs dramatically described the buildup in military production and the consequent difficulties in producing civilian goods. Next, the bulletin commented on materials shortages:

"The general public seems to be under the impression that aluminum is the only vital defense material on which the country is short. That is not the case. The shortage of steel is equally great, and there is not enough to go around on practically every item entering into the building of motorcycles—right down to cork and Neoprene.

"We hope to be able to produce a VERY LIMITED number of Harley-Davidsons between now and the first of the year. Just what this number will total is difficult to say, and when deliveries can be made is also impossible to state in general terms. So few motorcycles will be available, we can accept your order at this time for only ONE MACHINE. You may rest assured the factory is doing everything in its power to improve the situation and obtain materials for other than defense needs. No definite promises can be made now as to the success of these efforts."

On the outlook for new sales aids, the bulletin noted, "Yes, there will be a new catalog folder.... We will not be able to furnish this folder in unlimited quantities. It was only by the greatest good fortune we were able to secure paper for part of our usual run."

A bulletin header read, "Many Promotional Activities Must Be Passed Up!" and was followed by, "With the delivery situation what it is we can't pursue our usual promotion plans. There would be little benefit in

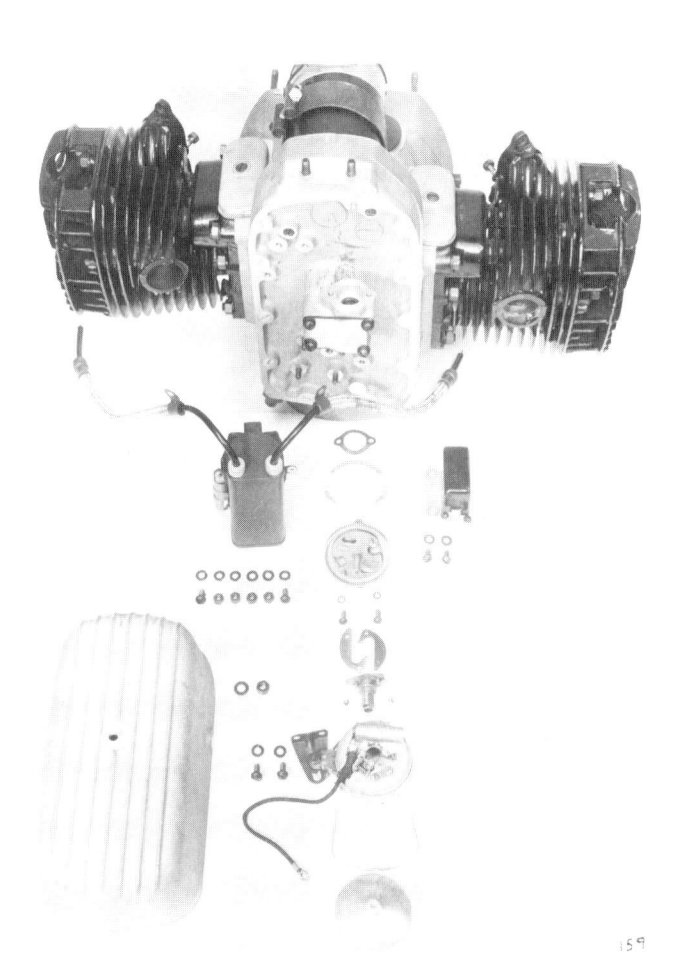

The XA motor used double-decker cooling fins, which may have been the inspiration for the cylinder heads on the postwar Model K V-twin. The XA engine was wet sump. Large sump and horizontal cylinders helped keep the oil temperature between 250 and 350 degrees Fahrenheit, compared to the regular Forty-five range of 350 to 450 degrees Fahrenheit. The interval between major overhauls was 10,000 to 15,000 miles, which was considered good. Harley-Davidson

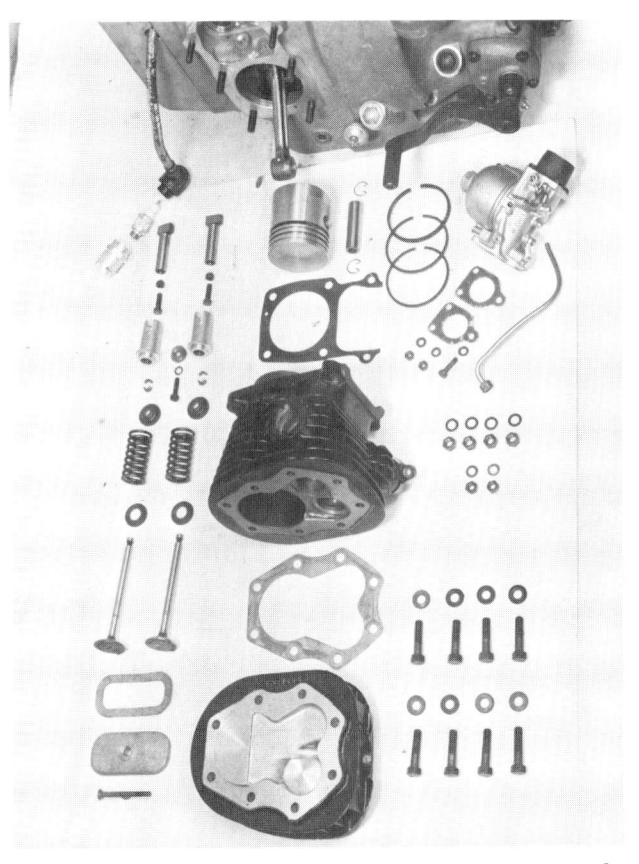

The cylinder head squish pattern was extreme—note the peculiar shaping above the inlet valve. Harley-Davidson

205

having an Open House Party this fall. We will not get out the usual Announcement Streamer, although we will of course, get out competition posters as we register important victories from time to time."

The September 8 bulletin concluded under the header, "You Have The Facts—Now You Must Chart Your Course!" after which appeared, "Each dealer should take the time to carefully analyze his business and to put into effect the changes that today's problems are imposing. The main thing is to keep solvent until better days are with us again."

Work on the XAs was in progress in the tool room. By November, four pilot models were completed and tests were encouraging. On December 1, management projected completion of fifty XAs in January 1942, 450 in February and 500 in March, so that the contract would be completed four months ahead of schedule.

Meanwhile, the Army was quite pleased with the development of lightweight scout cars. The competition between the Bantam, Willys and Ford four-wheel-drive lightweights had determined a winner, Willys, but the production contract was split between Willys and Ford. The outcome was the famous Jeep, whose success greatly diminished the military's need for both two- and three-wheeled motorcycles. The most immediate effect of the Jeep was the death of the tricycle projects that Harley-Davidson and Indian had supported. There was no specific and dramatic cancellation date for the tricycles—Harley-Davidson's hope for them just withered away as the months passed and the Army failed to award a tricycle production contract.

On December 7, the Japanese attack on Pearl Harbor brought the United States into World War II as a combatant, but the American industrial base had long been at war. Harley-Davidson activities were typical of the industrial situation throughout the nation. Four days after Pearl Harbor, the pilot Model XA left Milwaukee, steered by a factory test rider toward Camp Holabird for testing. And four days after that, William S. Harley and William H. Davidson left Milwaukee to be at Camp Holabird by the time the XA arrived.

One comment from the new-season bulletin for 1942 seems to speak out across the decades as a summary of the Harley-Davidson spirit: "We have all had days of trial in the past and we have come out on top. We will do so again."

Many WLCs were fitted with English-style passenger seats. WLCs were fitted with a front stand; WLAs weren't. Harley-Davidson

Chapter 7

1942–1945

The war years

1942

Few 1942 model civilian Harley-Davidsons were built. The Eighty and the Forty-five WLDR were discontinued in the autumn of 1941, and the WR racer was canceled in December. The 1942 new-model dealer bulletin, issued September 8, 1941, illustrated the Servi-Car, the Package Truck and a police-equipped 61 OHV, but no pleasure models.

The deluxe solo accessory group was expanded to include chrome fender tips, pedal rubbers, chrome mirror, chrome parking lamps and chrome front Safety Guards. Tires were strictly 5.00x16 in., except for special orders. The former deluxe saddle with whipped latex filling was now provided as standard issue. The taillight was waterproofed by a new rubber seal.

Other changes to solo models, if any, were minor and were made during the course of the year to facilitate wartime production. The Servi-Car was available with a 7 cu. ft. body only, the 4.4 cu. ft. body having been discontinued. The new body was slightly smaller than the former GD Servi-Car body. Two plunger-type shock absorbers replaced the former check straps.

In January, the factory notified dealers that government restrictions on the use of synthetic rubber prevented supplying dealers with seals for the overhead-valve rocker arm enclosures. Dealers were advised to reuse seals as much as possible during repair jobs on the overhead-valve big twins.

Patriotic duty

In January 1942, the company won a contract for 31,393 motorcycles to be completed by December 31, 1943. This Army contract and subsequent prototypes provided most of the company's wartime business. The profit margin was only six percent before taxes, but Harley-Davidson had no alternative.

The pilot XA performed well in testing at Camp Holabird from December 1941 through February 1942. After 6,100 miles of rigorous testing, the XA had burned out a valve, broken the gear housing and broken the propeller shaft cushion flange. The propeller shaft flange was of no concern, since it was made from manganese-bronze only on this prototype because a production forging couldn't be obtained quick enough to incorporate in the test model. The XA problems were typical of experimental models in Army testing programs.

The Army decided not to make a decision on massive production of the XA until all 1,000 of the produc-

This 1942 WLA was shipped to China in late 1941 and was among the last with the high-mounted headlight. Motor number is 42WLA2580. Forks are standard length instead of the earlier extended variety. Front fender lights on WLAs were changed to blackout style. The oil bath air cleaner was smaller than on early 1941 WLAs. Harley-Davidson

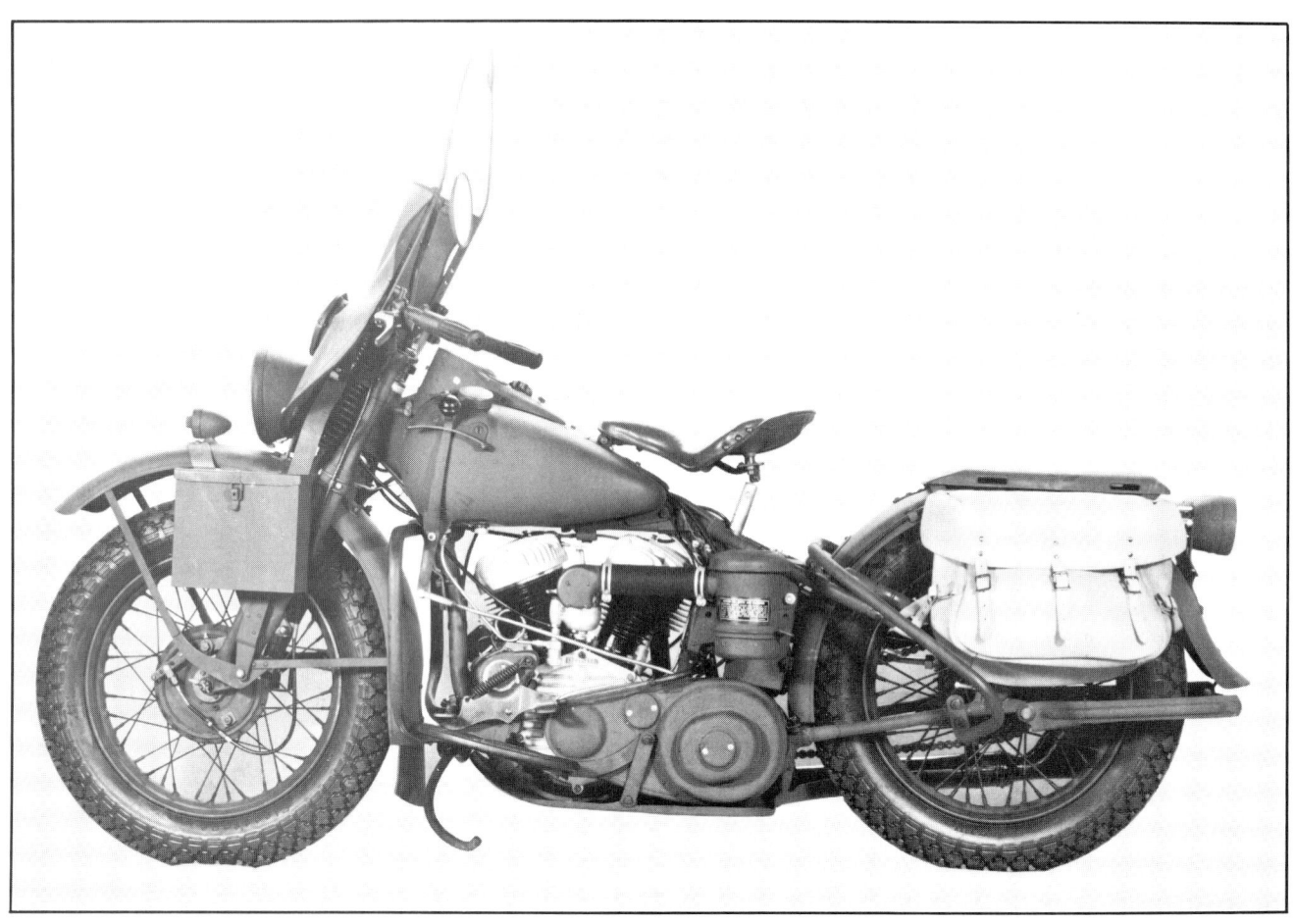

This 1942 WLA photo was processed Christmas Eve 1941. The headlight was moved to a lower perch to lessen the likelihood of damage in a fall. The air cleaner is different from the WLA shipped to China; air cleaners were probably bought from a number of sources. Most WLAs were built to this configuration, and few of the 1940 and 1941 models were shipped overseas. Motor number is 42WLA7103. Harley-Davidson

Few 1942 civilian models were built, but this was apparently one of them. Several motorcycles with a two-color finish were pictured in wartime issues of The Harley-Davidson Enthusiast. *Harley-Davidson*

tion versions had been tested. The XA was competing head to head against the shaft-drive Indian Model 841, a transverse V-twin along the lines of today's Moto Guzzis.

On February 7, death claimed the second of the four cofounders, Walter Davidson, Sr. Harley-Davidson's ultimate advantage over Indian was management continuity, never so well demonstrated as in this instance. On the motion of cofounder William S. Harley, the board of directors elected the second generation's William H. Davidson to the position of company president. Either Bill Harley, Sr. or Arthur Davidson might have laid claim to the title, but the title was less important to these pragmatists than planning for an orderly transition of company affairs into a new generation of leaders.

On February 9, the war reached the production lines. All civilian vehicle production was halted.

In March, the company signed a Navy contract to deliver 1,622 motorcycles and sidecars to South Africa.

Specifications

Year and model	1942 Model WLA
Engine	Side-valve 45 degree V-twin
Bore and stroke	2¾x3¹³⁄₁₆ in.
Displacement	45.12 ci
Horsepower	23 bhp at 4600 rpm
Torque	28 lb-ft at 3000 rpm
Compression ratio	5.0:1
Gearbox	Three speed, hand actuated, constant mesh
Gear ratios	Low: 11.71:1; second: 7.45:1; high: 4.74:1
Wheelbase	57½ in.
Wheels and tires	Standard: 4.00x18 in.; desert, 5.50x16 in.
Suspension	Front: leading-link; rear: rigid
Weight	576 lb. (with gas, oil and accessories)
Seat height	32 in.
Ground clearance	4 in. (amidship)
Fuel consumption	37 mpg
Top speed	65 mph
Maximum grade ability	30 percent
Fuel capacity	3⅜ gal.
Approximate cruising range	125 miles

This jumping XA was equipped with 5.50x16 desert tires. Testing occurred in mid 1942, and large low-pressure tires worked well in the sand. Harley-Davidson

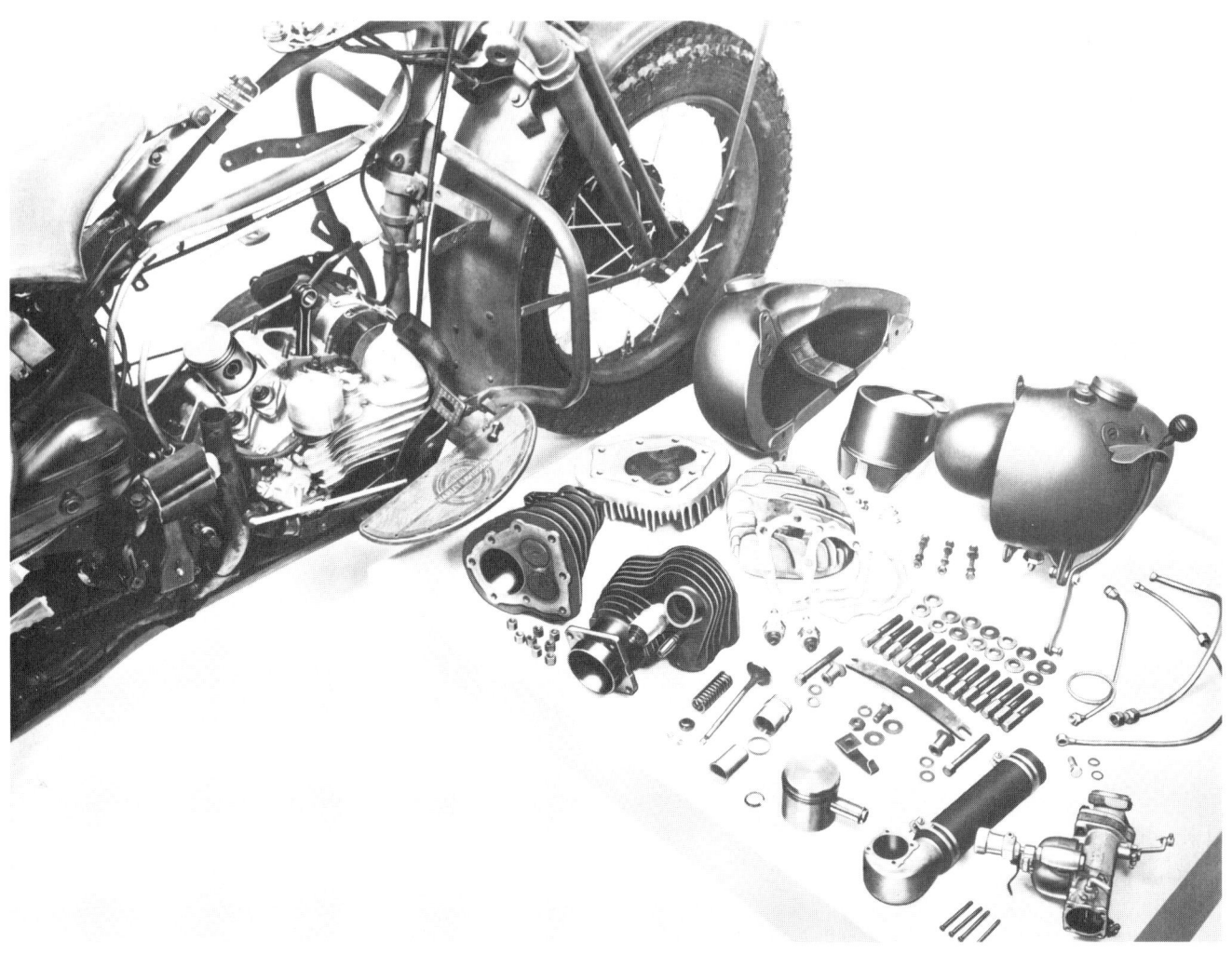

Maintainability was stressed by the US military forces, and detailed service manuals and rider's handbooks were produced. Note the left tank: 1937 and later Forty-fives used this type with expanded center section to increase fuel capacity. Right tank was for oil only. Harley-Davidson

209

There was concern that material shortages might keep the company from fulfilling military contracts. Tin and rubber were scarce, so the Army Quartermaster Department requested that all unnecessary rubber be eliminated from motorcycles and sidecars ordered by the War Department. Rubber was used for gaskets, kickstarter pedals, handlebar grips, packing in saddles and so on, and there was some question about the feasibility of substituting other materials in its place. William S. Harley began investigating the use of alternate materials.

On May 3, the national speed limit was set at 40 mph in order to save fuel. On May 17, gasoline supplies in seventeen eastern states were cut fifty percent. The speed limit was later lowered to 35 mph.

Initial Harley-Davidson deliveries on major motorcycle contracts began in May. During May, the Army asked Harley-Davidson to design a 61 ci side-valve opposed twin.

In June, the company completed an evaluation of the New Orleans-built Servi-Cycle, a one-speed belt-drive two-stroke. Sales manager Arthur Davidson opposed building such a machine because he considered it underpowered and not up to Harley-Davidson quality standards. The Servi-Cycle concept was dropped.

By the latter part of June, the production rate reached 750 motorcycles per week, which included Army, Navy and Canadian military contracts. Raw material shortages caused the rate to drop to 675 motorcycles per week in August. So far, weekly military production for 1942 was averaging out at about three times the 1941 peacetime rate for almost exclusively civilian production.

Most WLA models from mid-June on were built to 1942 specifications. The longer fork and rear frame sections of the 1941 model, which provided a 6 in. ground clearance, were abandoned in favor of the standard components, which provided only a 4 in. clearance. Most 1940 and 1941 WLAs were eventually retrofitted to the standard-length fork. The seat was moved forward in order to work well with the new wider and lower handlebars. The M88 carburetor with a smaller venturi and a fixed high-speed jet was phased into production. The headlight was moved from its civilian perch above the handlebars to a fender mount-

A 1943 WLC. The 1942 and 1943 WLCs and WLAs were fitted with a box-shaped oil bath air cleaner. Harley-Davidson

ing in order to reduce damage during falls. This change necessitated a new horn face because the winged horn face couldn't be mounted level, so the 1931-1935 sunburst horn face was used.

The 1942 WLAs had several changes to prevent damage caused by vibration or crashing. Heavier frame castings and thicker handlebar tubes were installed to preclude the cracking and bending experienced on earlier machines. The toolbox mounting bracket was larger and had three mounting points instead of two. The earlier tubular cargo rack was replaced by a stronger rack of channeled construction. The round oil-bath air cleaner was replaced by a rectangular oil-bath filter and a new mounting bracket.

The wording of the data plate on the gas tank was the same, but the format was changed to emphasize lubrication requirements. Wheels were 18 in. except for desert prototypes, which were provided with 16 in. wheels. Many accessories were available, including an ammunition box, gun scabbard, blackout driving lamp, windshield, mirrors, leg shields, engine breather for water crossings, tire pump, rear chain oiler, saddlebags, red lights and siren.

XA solo deliveries were completed in mid 1942. The company then undertook the design and development of a special sidecar outfit with a driven sidecar wheel. This 800 lb. rig was to be powered by an overhead-valve version of the XA engine. The special sidecar outfit was an unsolicited program, so Harley-Davidson was spending its own money for this experiment.

On September 12, 1942, the Army ordered production to drop to a level of 345 motorcycles per week for its contract. This remained the Army production rate for the next fourteen months, but other contracts kept total production averaging about 475 motorcycles per week for most of the war. Wartime production was therefore more than twice as intensive as 1941 production.

In October, progress stepped forward. Due to the War emergency, Harley-Davidson decided to permit married women to work in the office.

A 1943 WLC. The front brake cable on all WLCs was routed from above the brake, rather than from below as on WLAs. Front and rear axles were changed to include handholds, so axles could be pulled out instead of knocked out. The blackout light on the front fender is smaller than on earlier models.

The headlight mounting was moved to the low position. A shortage of rubber due to Japanese conquests forced the use of plastic olive drab handgrips. A simple tube-style starter pedal replaced the bicycle-style pedal. Harley-Davidson

In the closing months of 1942, the first of several wartime non-motorcycle contracts was initiated. The company contracted with the Canadian Department of Munitions and Supply to deliver a dual-engine combination featuring two 74 ci overhead-valve motors. The host vehicle had an undisclosed purpose.

While waiting for the final Army decision on the shaft-drive bid, Harley-Davidson was able to pursue use of the XA engine in various non-motorcycle applications. Management's first success in this effort was a contract negotiated in late 1942. Harley-Davidson agreed to supply Allis-Chalmers with two XA snow sled engines, each with three-speed-and-reverse transmissions and transfer cases.

As the war continued, Japanese conquests placed most of the world's natural rubber in enemy hands. The resulting rubber crisis became a national issue on December 1, when nationwide gasoline rationing was declared in order to save rubber and, to a lesser extent, save fuel.

1943
Snow sleds, generators and military motorcycles

On February 4, 1943, the dual-motor overhead-valve powerplant was shipped to Canada. Testing soon revealed the powerplant didn't function satisfactorily in the intended environment, and no further business was forthcoming.

For reasons unknown, the 1942 WLA did not become the 1943 WLA, but continued with 42 WLA order numbers until the end of the war. By careful examination, however, it's possible to determine the year of manufacture. The factory mated each crankcase half during the assembly process by placing an identical assembly serial number on each half. These assembly numbers, which began with the manufacturing year and a hyphen, can be found near the generator.

In early 1943, management became concerned about the results of the competitive testing of the Harley-Davidson XA and the Indian Model 841 transverse V-twin shaft-drive. In mid-February, William S. Harley and William H. Davidson went to Detroit to find out whether the test reports had been received.

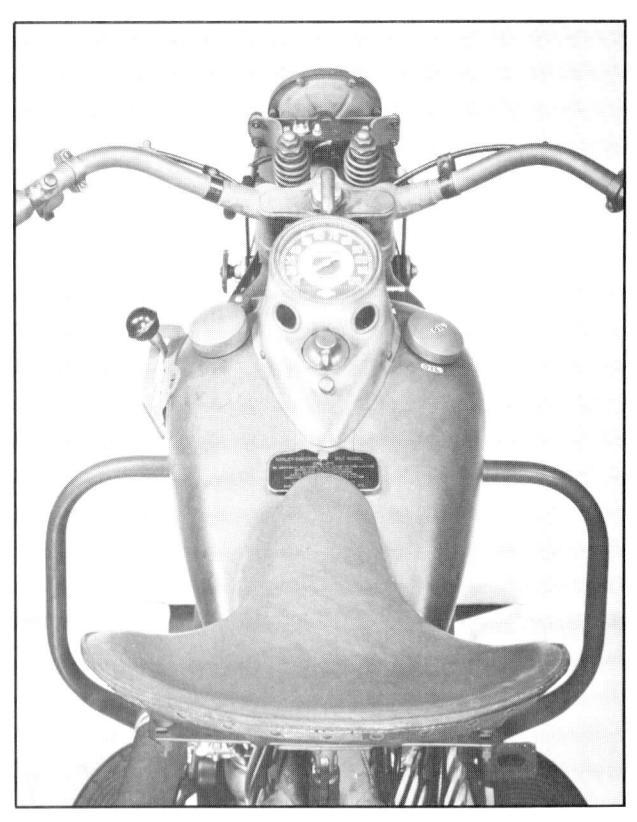

Rider's view of 1943 WLC. The rear of the shift gate was bent down to lessen chances of rider injury. The 120 mph speedometer was a little imaginative, as top speed was about 65 mph. Data plate provided lubrication instructions and cautioned that no additional equipment was to be added to the motorcycle. Harley-Davidson

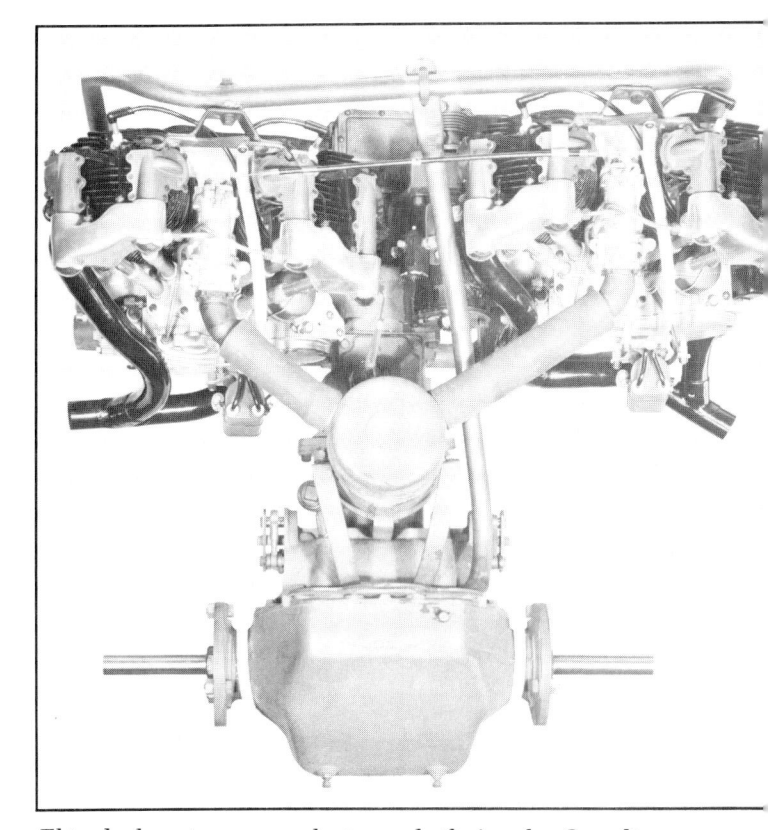

This dual-engine powerplant was built for the Canadian Department of Munitions and Supply and may have been intended for a remotely controlled mine sweeper. The outfit was begun in 1942 and shipped in February 1943. The prototype design didn't satisfy the Canadians, and no further business resulted. Harley-Davidson

Initial planning for this XA sidecar rig called for an overhead-valve version of the XA motor, but this example is powered by the conventional XA side-valve motor. A single hydraulic shock absorber was fitted on the right side of the fork. Harley-Davidson

This special XA featured a driven sidecar wheel. The shift knob to the right of the rider's seat is to shift the sidecar wheel into or out of gear. Harley-Davidson spent its own money to develop this prototype with the hope that the company could win a production contract after demonstrating the rig to the Army. The German Army used many such rigs, but American brass weren't interested because of the Jeep. Harley-Davidson

213

On May 12, 1943, Harley-Davidson received the first of its three awards for military production. President William H. Davidson receives the banner from Col. C. J. Otjen. Harley-Davidson

They were disappointed when informed by Col. VanDusen that the reports hadn't arrived, but encouraged by another remark. The colonel told them that both Harley-Davidson and Indian would be given orders for 25,000 shaft-drive motorcycles, and that all shaft-drive machines would be either the XA or the 841, whichever was the winning design. In response, William S. Harley told the Colonel that Harley-Davidson would be able to start production in ten months if the XA were chosen, but that an additional six months would be required to prepare for production of the Indian Model 841. Col. VanDusen said he didn't believe the Army could afford that much delay, but further discussion on this issue was deferred pending receipt of the test results.

During March 1943, the XA appeared to be the winner. The only significant problem was the use of excessive aluminum in the XA, according to Army authorities. A total of 65 lb. of aluminum was used in the XA, compared to 45 lb. in the WLA.

Superintendent George Nortman evaluated the production requirements and reached the following conclusion. Five months were required to assemble the necessary material, and another six months were needed to get the first mass-production XA on the assembly line. Additional machinery was essential, but this wasn't a problem because the machinery situation had eased off considerably in the past few months. The estimated unit cost on the proposed order for 25,000 XA motorcycles was about $50 more than the standard WLA, or roughly $430 per XA.

In April, Harley-Davidson shipped the four snow-sled XA motors to Allis-Chalmers. Meanwhile, Harley-Davidson had obtained two additional XA motor contracts. The company was to deliver four blower-cooled

Harley-Davidson's first telescopic forks were used on this 1943 XA. Harley-Davidson

49 ci XA motors with three-speed-and-reverse transmission to Willys-Overland. These were for a 1,000 lb. miniature Jeep called the WAC (Willys Air Cooled). Harley-Davidson contracted with the Detroit Wax Paper Company for delivery of a blower-cooled 45 ci overhead-valve version of the XA motor to be used to power a generator. Later, this contract was modified to add delivery of a blower-cooled 49 ci overhead-valve XA motor. These Model XOD generator sets were for the Signal Corps and the Air Corps.

The Army-Navy E (for excellence) Award was presented to Harley-Davidson on May 12, 1943. The colonel presenting the award called the Harley-Davidson workers "soldiers of the production line."

On July 3, the Chicago District Office of the Army Ordnance Department notified Harley-Davidson that the XA was dropped from all Army plans, and that the WLA 45 ci twin would be the standard Army motorcycle. The company filed a claim with the government for maximum amortization of the tool cost and other expenses incurred in the development of the XA. Also

To boost morale, wartime motorcycling magazines depicted movie stars with motorcycles. From left to right, Clark Gable, Ward Bond and Victor Fleming, director of "Gone With the Wind." Gable once remarked that he practiced some of his lines for the immortal movie while riding his Harley-Davidson. Harley-Davidson

A 1943 WLC. Beginning in mid 1943, WLC and WLA crankcases were painted olive drab. Cylinders and aluminum heads were painted black. Footboards were no longer covered with rubber mats that included the Harley-Davidson name. This saved rubber and also brought Harley-Davidson in compliance with government regulations forbidding brand names on military equipment. The simple metal footboards had a ribbed pattern to increase traction. Harley-Davidson

215

The 1943 Willys-Overland WAC was powered by a 49 ci overhead-valve version of the XA motor. Four such motors were delivered—one in September 1943, one in October 1943 and two in early 1944. Harley-Davidson

canceled was the two-wheel-drive sidecar outfit powered by the overhead-valve XA engine.

Although the XA motorcycle was dead, both sidevalve and overhead-valve versions of the XA engine continued to figure in military plans. On August 17, the 45 ci overhead-valve XA motor was shipped to Detroit Wax Paper for testing as a generator set. Overhead-valve XA motors of 49 ci displacement, with transmissions, were shipped to Willys-Overland on September 1 and October 21. At about this time, a contract was obtained with the Tank Automotive Center in Detroit to deliver two blower-cooled XA motors for a generator set to be used in a tank.

Because of rubber shortages, several changes were made during the 1943 production run of 45 ci V-twins. For a while, the company used olive drab plastic handlegrips on the 1943 WLC models. The bicycle-style kickstarter pedal with rubber cleats was replaced by a simple tube type, which was used on both the WLA and WLC. American and Canadian Forty-fives also featured metal floorboard pads instead of rubber pads. This change brought the company into compliance with military directives, because the rubber pads had the Harley-Davidson name embossed, and military policy was against exhibiting a brand name.

Tom Sifton relates how shortages were beginning to affect the quality of motorcycle manufacture and dealer repairs:

"Up to the war, the best metal for cylinders was nickel alloy. During the war, the War Materials Board wouldn't let Harley-Davidson use that, so they started substituting silicon alloy for nickel alloy. We started to wear out rings in six to eight hundred miles in police motorcycles, especially with cops who ran a lot at idling speed to keep their batteries up for their radio. That's when Harley-Davidson started to use chrome rings, with about twenty thousandths of chrome all the way around the outside. The chrome rings would go 20,000 miles with no trouble at all, and we could never get that kind of mileage before."

Police models were among the few non-military motorcycles the government allowed to be built. The few non-military motorcycles sold were permitted based on their ensured used by state and local governments, or, in a few instances, on their use as transportation to and from jobs in the defense industry. Substantial paper shuffling was necessary by both buyer and seller to execute one of these "essential" sales.

During 1943, the federal government permitted 137 police departments to purchase new Harley-Davidsons. Here's how the red tape worked. The police department placed its order with the local Harley-Davidson dealer. Additionally, the police chief, the mayor or the purchasing agent wrote a letter to the dealer explaining why the new motorcycles were needed. This letter had to include a listing of the mileage of used police motorcycles, which were to be traded in. The dealer then forwarded the customary dealer-to-factory order form, a copy of the police department's official purchase order and the letter of explanation to the factory. Upon receipt of all paperwork, Harley-Davidson then filed an application with the War Production Board. Upon approval by this board, the factory then notified the dealer of the expected date of shipment. Incidentally, the federal government allowed only 139 civilian passenger cars to be built in 1943 and another 610 in 1944. These were the only years in the history of the United States that motorcycle production exceeded passenger car production.

September 18, 1943, marked the passing of William S. Harley. Following in his engineering footsteps was his son, William J. Harley, who became chief of the engineering department. Of the four monumental figures who had started the Harley-Davidson Motor Company in April 1903, there was left only Arthur Davidson, who remained in charge of the sales effort. One can only imagine the feelings of Arthur Davidson, to be the last of four men who had chased their dreams, caught them, kept them, and passed them on to a new generation of Harleys and Davidsons.

Late in 1943, the Willys-Overland WAC arrived at the Army's Aberdeen, Maryland, proving grounds. Test reports were encouraging, and Harley-Davidson

One of two 1943 blower-cooled XA motor-powered generator sets built for the Tank Automotive Center in Detroit. The generator was to be used in a medium tank. The contract was awarded in late 1943, and this photo was processed March 13, 1944. Harley-Davidson

With the hood closed on the 1943 WAC, the left cylinder head is still visible under the left passenger seat. Harley-Davidson

217

agreed to work with Willys-Overland on production versions if the Army awarded a production contract. Work on uncompleted XA motor projects continued for the balance of 1943 and into early 1944.

Harley-Davidson was already planning their postwar motorcycle lineup. The top priority was given to developing a new Servi-Car using the XA engine. Another planned XA spinoff was a solo shaft-drive sports motorcycle using an overhead-valve XA motor and having performance equal to the 61 OHV.

In November, the War Department canceled orders for 1,105 motorcycles and associated spare parts. This action was mitigated by a large production backlog. However, 11,331 more motorcycles were canceled in February 1944, which forced the company to cut the workweek to forty hours and lay off more than 500 workers.

With the loss of so much military motorcycle business and the yet insignificant level of authorized civilian motorcycle production, Harley-Davidson tried to find additional production for the factory in the form of subcontract work. Many other companies still faced heavy wartime production schedules and could use Harley-Davidson capabilities to good advantage.

1944

During 1944, gasoline rationing was cut to 2 gal. per week, but enterprising riders and dealers found ways to get around rationing. Some rigged their motorcycles to run on kerosene. Cleaning solvent for parts could be made to run a motorcycle, even if poorly. "We cleaned a lot of parts!" chuckled Indian dealer Ed Kretz in recalling those days. Unexpectedly, synthetic rubber motorcycle tires lasted for 30,000 miles or more. Unfortunately, these tires were so hard that they had little traction—they skidded as though they were made out of wood, recalled one wartime rider.

There was even a way to have a race meet, despite the federal government's prohibition on racing. A few southern California motorcycle racers were employed in the defense industry and/or were married, and therefore hadn't been drafted. The racing bug finally got to them, and they organized a so-called TT—a miniature road-race. This was simple enough; they just held it

Mid 1944 prototype XOD generator set powered by an overhead-valve version of the XA motor. Successful Air Force testing resulted in a May 1945 order for 2,397 sets, which was increased in late June to 4,975 sets. Two atomic bombs in August ended the war, and none of the 4,975 generator sets were completed. Harley-Davidson

across the Mexican border! All low key, of course, to avoid bad publicity.

In April 1944, only five weeks after the big motorcycle cutback, a major subcontract was obtained for the production of 9,609 two-speed power-takeoff transmissions. These were for use on Heil winches designed for installation in General Motors military trucks.

During this same period, other subcontracting work was obtained from Allis-Chalmers Manufacturing Company, Massey-Harris Company, Boeing Aircraft Company and numerous other firms. Harley-Davidson was now well into the swing of subcontract work, with projected business exceeding $1,000,000. Eventually, more than 13,000 truck winches were produced as well as thousands of Navy electrical switch box covers and hundreds of pieces for various subcontracts, including shell parts and B-29 aircraft fittings.

Even with the contract cancellations, WLA production remained the mainstay of Harley-Davidson business. The 1944 WLA motorcycles differed in several respects from the 1942 and 1943 models. The front fender was now just a simple curved strip without a beaded edge and tip. The crankcases were painted olive drab and the cylinder heads and barrels were painted black. Ignition switches were keyless. Radio noise-suppression equipment was installed and the instrument panel marked with an S to indicate this feature. The carburetor air intake elbow was changed from a casting to a stamped component. After serial number 42WLA60000, an enlarged data plate without the lubrication emphasis was applied.

In June, the order for truck winch transmissions was increased by an additional 3,505 units. In mid-July 1944 came a surprising order from the Ordnance Department for 5,000 more motorcycles and the requisite spare parts. Within two weeks, an additional bid was requested for 3,480 military motorcycles and applicable parts. Then, on July 27, the War Production Board increased the allotment of essential civilian motorcycles by 450 units. These developments completely changed the subcontracting picture, so that the company abandoned subcontracting indefinitely except for those situations in which it was already committed.

The 1944 WLA had a front fender built as a simple stamping without a beaded edge or decorative front tip. The S on the instrument panel denoted full radio noise-suppression equipment. The ignition switch was keyless. The clutch release arm was wider. Harley-Davidson

The allotment of essential civilian motorcycles was increased by another 600 units on September 8. Incidentally, all 1944 civilian models were finished in either silver or gray with black frames and forks. Confusing signals were sent by the government during October. On the 11th, the Army Air Force awarded Harley-Davidson an urgent developmental contract for a specially designed engine generator unit to be used in ground testing bombers. With the resulting development funding, the company began its design, which was based on an overhead-valve variant of the XA motor, termed the XOD. Only one week later, the War Production Board authorized Harley-Davidson to produce 6,000 additional civilian motorcycles.

1945
Poised for postwar success

In May 1945, the Army Air Force awarded Harley-Davidson a contract for delivery of 2,397 XOD generator sets for use in bombers. In late June, the quantity was upped to 4,975 units. Average unit price was $646.88

Immediately after the victory over Japan in August, the unfinished portions of all military contracts were canceled; none of the 4,975 generator sets were completed. On October 11, two months after victory, came a surprising contract for development of an improved XOD generator. This project was also can-

Your basic military motorcycle. Black surfaces radiate heat better than light-colored surfaces, so aluminum heads were painted black. The 1944 WLA had a stamped sheet-metal carburetor air intake elbow instead of the cast-alloy elbow used since 1941. Harley-Davidson

celed. The generator sets were the last military spinoffs of the XA motorcycle development.

From 1940 through 1945, Harley-Davidson produced more than 88,000 motorcycles for the allied forces. Army-Navy contract management officials presented the company with two followup Star awards in the latter half of the war, so when the war ended, the two-starred Harley-Davidson factory banner given to the company symbolized three thank yous from the government.

From a motorcycling perspective, the war left Harley-Davidson a winner and Indian a loser. Harley-Davidson had been busy for most of the war doing what it did best, building motorcycles, while Indian struggled to stay alive by doing a variety of subcontracting work. During the war years, Harley-Davidson invested a total of $1,263,904 in tooling and other factory improvements. As soon as the war was over, the company aggressively pursued opportunities to purchase additional equipment from government surplus stocks. The management understood that a postwar sales boom was on the way.

WLA and WLC production proved to be a postwar blessing to the company. In the immediate postwar period, thousands of surplus Forty-fives were sold by Harley-Davidson dealerships, while others were sold by auto dealers but serviced by Harley-Davidson shops. As well as helping the dealers, these war surplus bikes brought into the sport many riders who might otherwise have been left out.

A proposed XA-derived sports motorcycle and an XA-powered Servi-Car were on the company agenda as 1945 drew to a close. These projects remained at the paper stage. A more urgent need was to get existing V-twin designs into production as soon as possible and in numbers as great as possible to fill the pent-up recreation demands of a war-weary generation.

Looking to the future

Back in 1930, Indian had Harley-Davidson on the ropes. Harley-Davidson's climb back from the depths of 1930 to sales predominance by the late 1930s was almost as dramatic as their earliest years of explosive growth. The climb back would not have been possible without the network of outstanding dealers, among whom were men like Tom Sifton and Red Wolverton, giants in the history of American motorcycling.

The Harley-Davidson dealer network had survived the war because it was built around the core of dealers who had earlier weathered the Great Depression. These dealers had toughness, tenacity and shrewdness befitting the founding four and the second generation that was now in charge in Milwaukee. In the dealerships and among those inside the big, red brick building in Milwaukee, there was justifiable pride. But this was no time to rest on laurels. There were motorcycles to be built and motorcycles to be sold, and Harley-Davidson was ready. The Milwaukee brand was—and ever remains—a tough outfit.

The XA-derivative Servi-Car, called the Model K, was discussed a lot in company meetings and remained on the new-model plan at the close of 1945. Harley-Davidson

First styling exercise for postwar civilian telescopic forks. The black air cleaner was standard fare during the war due to a shortage of chromium. This photo was processed November 28, 1945. Harley-Davidson

Index

Abresh Body Shop, 181
Ace Four, 71, 72
Allis-Chalmers, 214, 219
AMC (AJS-Matchless) engines, 140
American Motorcycle Association, 57
Amtorg Corporation, 193
Arena, Sam, 199
Aurora company, 17
Auto-Lite generator, 160
Automatic inlet valves, 8, 14

Bendix, 55
Berling magneto, 36
BMW motorcycles, 183, 184, 194, 195, 201, 203
Boeing Aircraft Company, 219
Bond, Ward, 215
Bosch magnetos, 32
Brough-Superior motorcycles, 74, 82, 105, 140–141
Brown, Carman, 181, 182
BSA motorcycles, 130, 160, 178, 180
Budelier, Rich, 132
Burgess mufflers, 101, 108, 109

Cameron, John, 31, 36, 37, 38, 56, 67, 68
Cartwright, Charles, 57, 193, 194
Child, A. R., 114
Class A racing, 121
Class C racing, 121, 127, 150, 152, 169, 199
Cleveland motorcycles, 71, 72, 76
Clymer, Floyd, 31
Connelly, Bill, 151
Corbin wheel hubs, 20
Courtesy Car Company, 105, 111
Crankcase baffles, 9, 14, 81, 174
Cyclone motorcycles, 77

Dauria, Fred, 151
Davidson, Allan, 85
Davidson, Arthur, 8, 9, 10, 76, 104, 105, 111, 112, 113, 120, 121, 124, 136, 151, 152, 160, 167, 190, 208, 210, 217
Davidson, Gordon, 85, 97, 161, 178
Davidson, Walter, 6, 10–11, 12, 48, 54, 55, 57, 66, 85, 86, 97, 105, 106, 111, 112, 120, 151, 153, 160, 167, 178, 195, 201, 205, 208
Davidson, William A., 10, 111, 120, 136
Davidson, William C., 8
Davidson, William H., 102, 113, 130, 134, 135, 151, 152, 153, 160, 161, 167, 184, 190, 192, 195, 201, 206, 208, 212, 214

Davis, Jim, 59
Daytona Beach, 160, 169
Delco Corporation, 183–184, 194
DeLong, Everett, 76
Detroit Wax Paper Company, 215, 216
Dixie magnetos, 31
Dixon, Freddy, 36
DuPont, E. Paul, 119

Eclipse company, 20, 55, 61, 76
Electric lighting, 13
Enthusiast magazine, 63, 72, 73, 74, 79, 96, 103, 104, 108, 111, 118, 179
Excelsior Keystone frame, 35
Excelsior motorcycles, 26, 27, 35, 43, 77

F-head theory and motorcycles, 7–28, 21, 29–77, 80
Feilbach motorcycles, 77
Fenwick, Red, 150
Finishes, 9, 14, 15, 17, 19, 21, 32–34, 37, 46, 49, 53, 54, 55, 63, 72–73, 74–75, 79, 85, 89, 97, 101, 102, 103–104, 108, 111, 113, 118–119, 120, 123, 126, 131, 132, 150, 152, 154, 164, 171, 177, 185, 192, 196, 215
Finishes, Summer Color Special, 123
Fleming, Victor, 215
Franklin, Charles B., 55

Gable, Clark, 215
General Motors, 219
Gleason company, 191
Goulding company, 117, 134
Goulding Litecar, 85
Great Depression, 86, 87, 107, 121, 221

Ham, Fred, 160
Harley, William J., 161, 178, 195, 204, 217
Harley, William S., 8, 12, 13, 31, 54, 55, 60, 66, 76, 82, 104, 105, 107, 121, 124, 136, 150, 160, 161, 162, 167, 169, 181, 183, 184, 190, 192, 195, 201, 206, 208, 210, 212, 214, 217
Harley-Davidson factory, 9, 12, 43, 105, 174–176, 178–179
Harley-Davidson generators, 64
Harley-Davidson Motor Company, 8, 77, 169, 206, 221
Harley-Davidson models
  21, 128
  21.35, 59, 61
  30.50, 90, 109, 128
  45 OHV, 160, 170–171, 177, 181, 182, 184, 185, 196, 197, 199

45 side-valve, 78, 81–82, 83–85, 94, 109, 127, 133, 147, 148, 153, 157, 164
61 F-head, 43, 46, 47, 49, 50, 53, 55, 69, 70
61 OHV, 105, 114, 120, 133, 135, 136–137, 138, 147, 153, 154–155, 156, 158, 161, 165, 166, 167, 168, 169, 171, 173, 175–176, 179, 182, 184, 185, 186, 187, 190, 207, 218
61 OHV, Japanese, 114, 120
74 F-head, 37, 42, 43–46, 47, 49, 51, 53, 66, 69, 70, 76, 91
74 OHV, 169, 177, 178, 181, 194, 195–197
74 side-valve, 85–86, 99, 109, 127, 132, 148, 149, 150, 154, 156, 158, 164, 165, 168, 170, 174, 181, 184, 185, 186
80 side-valve, 127, 148, 149, 153, 154, 156, 157, 158, 166, 168, 170, 174, 181, 184, 185, 186
D Series, 109
F Series, 21
J Series, 93
R Series, 109
U Series, 155
V Series, 86–87, 89, 93, 100, 118, 122
W Series, 155

Model 10A, 21
Model 10G, 21
Model 11E, 25
Model 11H, 25
Model 11J, 23, 25
Model 16-R, 31
Model 16-S, 31
Model 16-T, 31
Model 8E, 16
Model 9A, 18
Model 9B, 18
Model 9C, 18
Model 9G, 18
Model A, 61, 61
Model AA, 61, 66
Model B, 61, 62, 107, 109
Model BA, 60, 61, 62
Model BB, 61, 66
Model BE, 18
Model C, 96, 97, 100
Model CB, 118, 128
Model CD, 48, 49
Model D, 81, 84, 94, 95
Model DCA, 51
Model DCB, 51
Model DL, 81, 84, 94, 95

223

Model DLD, 94, 95, 109
Model DS, 85, 94, 95
Model EH, 21
Model EL, 162
Model F, 196
Model FDCA, 58
Model FDCB, 58
Model FL, 196
Model G Servi-Car, 171
Model GA Servi-Car, 171
Model GD Servi-car, 207
Model JD, 75
Model JDCA, 58
Model JDCB, 58
Model JDH, 67, 89, 90, 118
Model JDL, 69, 89
Model JH, 67
Model JL, 69
Model K, 205, 221
Model R, 109
Model RL, 109, 147
Model RLD, 109, 122, 147
Model RLDR, 127, 155
Model RS, 109
Model UA, 192
Model UL, 155, 170
Model V, 85, 86, 87, 88, 92, 100
Model VC, 100, 103, 116, 122
Model VCR, 100, 103, 116
Model VDDS, 127
Model VL, 85, 86, 87, 88, 89, 90, 93, 100, 108, 118, 155
Model VLD, 118, 123
Model VLDD, 127
Model VLDJ, 127
Model VLE, 118
Model VLM, 86, 87, 88, 93
Model VM, 86, 87, 88, 100
Model VMG, 100, 103
Model VS, 86, 100, 103
Model WL, 197
Model WLA, 183, 190, 191, 201, 203, 204, 207, 208, 209, 210
Model WLC, 202, 204, 206, 210, 211, 212, 215, 216, 221
Model WLC, 211, 214, 215, 216, 219, 220, 221
Model WLD Special (WLDD), 155, 183, 186
Model WLD, 185, 186, 196, 197, 198, 200
Model WLDR, 155, 160, 169, 180, 181, 186, 198, 207
Model WR, 198, 199, 207
Model WRTT, 198, 199
Model XA, 201-203, 205, 206, 207, 209, 211, 212, 213, 214, 215
Chicago racers, 26
Cycle Tow, 99
Eight-valve racers, 31, 36, 37, 38, 48, 53, 66
Four-valve racers, 31, 48, 53
Package Truck, 123, 207
Peashooter, 61
Servi-Car, 99, 105, 118, 123, 126, 127, 149, 156, 166, 171, 172, 185, 186, 189, 197, 198, 199, 204, 207, 218, 221
Silent Gray Fellow, 10, 14, 15, 21
Special Sport Solo, 67, 68, 69
Sport, 38, 39-40, 43, 48, 49, 52, 53
Two Cam racer, 36, 37-38, 51, 53, 56, 57, 66-69, 75, 76, 92, 152
Two-port 30.50 racer, 127
Harley-Davidson motors
A motor, 21, 24, 46
B motor, 46

Chicago motor, 25, 26, 54
DCA motor, 51, 52
E motor, 40, 46, 51, 52
F motor, 21
Liberty motor 34, 35
M motor, 23
XA motor, 216, 217, 218, 220
XOD motor, 218, 220-221
Harley-Davidson power-takeoff transmission, 219
Harley-Davidson production, 18
Harley-Davidson production, 204, 221
Harley-Davidson prototypes
30.50 OHV, 97-99, 124, 130, 136
45 side-valve, 98
45 twin, 107
65 twin, 104
69 OHV three-wheeler, 191, 192, 193
Industrial motor, 114
Snow sled, 212-215
Tractor, 115
V-four, 82-83
XOD generator, 212, 215
Harley-Davidson radios, 110, 112, 153
Hartley, Peter, 55
Henderson motorcycles, 105, 160
High-flo mufflers, 123, 124
Hillclimb racing, 95, 96, 99, 121
Hoecker, Bill, 82
Hosley, Joe, 135

Indian motorcycles, 27, 31, 33, 34, 35, 43, 55, 64, 75, 77, 78, 80, 83-84, 119, 120, 121, 122, 134-135, 152, 160, 168, 169, 183-184, 190, 192, 194, 195, 206, 218, 221
Indian models
Ace, 72
Chief, 78, 184, 185
Dispatch-Tow, 152, 172
Eight-valve racer, 55
Four, 71, 72, 184, 185
Model 841, 208, 214
Overhead-valve racer, 78
Scout, 52, 63, 78, 150
Series 101 Scout, 77, 83-84
Sport Scout, 150, 152-153, 160, 161, 169, 184, 199

Jack Pine Enduro, 102, 153
Janke, Irving, 31
JAP motors, 105, 140, 141
Jeep, 206, 213, 215
John Brown Motolamp, 101, 106
Jones, Maldwyn, 60, 66

Kieckbusch, Ed, 136
Kretz, Ed, 150, 199, 218

Linkert carburetors, 117, 122, 134, 135, 188
Long, Frank, 195
Ludlow, Fred, 150

Magri, Armando, 179
Massey-Harris Company, 219
Mathewson, Harold, 153
Mechanical inlet valves, 18
Merkel motorcycles, 77
Military motorcycles, Canada, 201, 204, 210, 216
Military motorcycles, US, 33, 115, 184, 190, 192, 193, 194, 195, 201, 203, 206, 207, 209, 210, 212, 216, 218, 220

Moto Guzzi motorcycles, 208
Motorcycles exported to South Africa, 195, 208
Motorcycles exported to Soviet Union, 57, 193
Motorcyclist magazine, 150, 158

Nortman, George, 105, 136, 150, 214
Nortman, Robert P., 161
Norton motorcycles, 55, 56

O'Donovan, D. R., 56
Ollerman, Frank, 12
Ottaway, William, 31, 55
Overhead-valve engines, 31

Petrali, Joe, 96, 112, 120, 159, 160
Police motorcycles, Canada, 136
Police motorcycles, US, 97, 101, 105, 110, 111, 125, 126, 134, 153, 167, 168, 172, 176, 180, 188, 193, 216
Pope motorcycles, 77

Reiber, Herb, 112
Remy Electric Corporation, 23, 35
Ricardo cylinder heads, 66, 75, 92
Ricardo racing cylinders, 75
Ricardo, Harry, 31, 56, 61, 69, 76
Riccy chip, 68, 76, 92
Robinson, Dot, 134
Robinson, Earl, 134
Ryan, Joe, 86, 89, 105

Sachs motorcycles, 160

Sankyo, 114
Schebler carburetors, 13, 32, 53, 58, 60, 66, 101, 117, 122
Schulteti, George, 193, 194
Schwinn, 105
Sears & Roebuck, 113
Servi-Cycle, 210
Shop Dope, 72, 73, 104, 140
Side-valve theory and motorcycles, 55-57, 61-62, 78-116
Sidecars, 24, 28, 45, 46, 57, 65, 85, 89, 117, 123, 134, 176, 181, 186, 195, 213
Sifton fix, 107
Sifton, Tom, 82, 85, 86, 87, 90, 105, 107, 121-122, 150, 216, 221
Smith, E. C., 57
Spark plugs, 71
Spexarth, Christy, 178, 191
Spicer company, 191
Straight-bore cylinders, 125-127, 130
Sucher, Harry, 105

T-slot pistons, 70, 127, 130
Tank Automotive Center, 216, 217
Tapered pistons, 8-9, 22
Thompson Products Company, 191
Thor motorcycles, 17, 20, 31
TT racing, 152, 199, 218

USA motorcycle, 34, 35

Walker, Otto, 26
Willys-Overland, 206, 216, 217
Wire control, 12
Wolverton, Charles "Red," 87, 97, 121, 156, 190, 221
World War I, 33, 34-35, 77
World War II, 43, 87, 183, 207-221

Zenith carburetors, 53, 58, 60, 63